T0302927

What are people saying about

Spirituality Rekindled

This is a surprising and awe-inspiring book. It is at once an erudite introduction to the wisdom of the Qur'an; a compelling call to rational spirituality; a profound musing on the modern condition; and much more. Written with estimable elegance, passion, and reason, this book will be of great interest to anyone interested in religion, spirituality, Islam, and indeed, human happiness and well-being in the modern condition. The author has chosen to write in fields of knowledge saturated with redundant and very often tiresome scholarship, but what he produced is highly original and exciting. I hope this book gets the wide readership it deserves.
Professor Khaled Abou El Fadl is the Distinguished Professor of Islamic Law at UCLA School of Law and the author of *The Search for Beauty in Islam: The Conference of the Books*.

I have read many chapters in *Spirituality Rekindled* by Professor Sabah and found many things there to be a roadmap to spiritual enlightenment and freedom. Throughout the book Professor Sabah distills essential spiritual wisdom, explaining with clarity and precision what it means for men and women to live as spiritual beings enveloped and showered by The Creator of All's Love.

Spirituality Rekindled is a thought-provoking journey for the mind, and a delightful guide for the heart, offering every soul an infinity of worlds to explore.
Sheikh Muhammad bin Yahya al-Ninowy, MD, PhD, Founding Director of Madina Institute and Madina Seminary

Life is commonly difficult and wearisome, and its hardness robs most people of peace of mind and calmness of soul. Nassir Hussni Sabah provides a stunningly beautiful and engaging explanation of where and how to find meaning, acceptance and contentment, and his comprehensive but manageable roadmap, if followed, will undoubtedly lead to greater personal fulfilment and success.
Professor Joel Hayward, scholar, writer, and poet, author of *Pain and Passing: Islamic Poems of Grief and Healing*, *Warfare in the Qur'an* and *The Leadership of Muhammad*

Dr. Sabah elucidates a grounding for human spirituality beyond any religion or atheism. Based on the power for interior transformation grounded in the holy words of the Quran, *Spirituality Rekindled* provides a doorway into a synthesis of science and the divine realities of our existence which is both traditional and freshly alive for our own days. I am happy to recommend this book and wish it wide circulation.
Jonathan Montaldo, internationally recognized writer and editor, author of *Bridges to Contemplative Living with Thomas Merton*

This beautifully crafted book will fascinate Muslims and non-Muslims alike because of its unique mix of meticulous scientific research and deep spiritual wisdom.
Imam Jamal Rahman, author of *Spiritual Gems of Islam*

Professor Sabah, an eminent scientist, shows in this book how science and spirituality are compatible. We need to better understand both science and religion if we are to understand our world. This book also helps us to better understand ourselves through using the Qur'an to deepen our spirituality.

Amir Hussain, Chair and Professor of Theological Studies, Loyola Marymount University, Los Angeles, author of *World Religions: Eastern Traditions* and *World Religions: Western Traditions*

This book is for everyone who is seeking happiness, serenity, satisfaction, and peace. Dr. Sabah uses miraculous numerical and scientific revelations to show that the Quran is of divine origin and has reached us in its original form. I wish for those who are unhappy or facing problems to read this book and to continue reading the whole Quran in order to fully benefit from its wisdom and guidance.
Dr. Ali Hajj, Professor of Electrical and Computer Engineering, American University of Beirut

Nassir Hussni Sabah approaches faith in God with the clarity and incisiveness of his scientific training, so can guide contemporary seekers to the inherent richness of a life of faith.
David B. Burrell, C.S.C., Hesburgh Professor Emeritus of Philosophy and Theology, University of Notre Dame

In a time of persistent pandemics, states being torn apart, lawlessness, and utter confusion, *Spirituality Rekindled* is much needed as a reminder of what anchors believers. This text provides an introduction for some not initiated to the scope of Islamic studies. The themes are not new but are redressed here for the 21st century. It offers the mechanics of an application of The Qur'ān to daily problems especially in times of crises.
Dr. Aminah Al-Deen, Professor Emerita, Islamic World Studies and Department of Religion, DePaul University

Spirituality Rekindled

The Quest for Serenity and Self-Fulfillment

Spirituality Rekindled

The Quest for Serenity and Self-Fulfillment

Nassir H. Sabah

Winchester, UK
Washington, USA

JOHN HUNT PUBLISHING

First published by O-Books, 2023
O-Books is an imprint of John Hunt Publishing Ltd., 3 East St., Alresford,
Hampshire SO24 9EE, UK
office@jhpbooks.com
www.johnhuntpublishing.com
www.o-books.com

For distributor details and how to order please visit the 'Ordering' section on our website.

ISBN: 978 1 80341 145 3
978 1 80341 146 0 (ebook)
Library of Congress Control Number: 2021924769

A CIP catalogue record for this book is available from the British Library.

Design: Matthew Greenfield

UK: Printed and bound by CPI Group (UK) Ltd, Croydon, CR0 4YY
Printed in North America by CPI GPS partners

Contents

Previous Titles

Sabah, Nassir H. (2008) *Electric Circuits and Signals*, Boca Raton FL, CRC Press, 896 pp. ISBN 9781420045895.

Sabah, Nassir H. (2010) *Electronics: Basic, Analog, and Digital with PSpice*, Boca Raton FL, CRC Press, 764 pp. ISBN 9781420087079.

Sabah, Nassir H. (2017) *Circuit Analysis with PSpice: A Simplified Approach*, Boca Raton FL, CRC Press, 837 pp. ISBN 9781498796040.

Sabah, Nassir H. (2021) *Neuromuscular Fundamentals: How Our Musculature is Controlled*, Boca Raton FL, CRC Press, 574 pp. ISBN 9780367456924.

To those who seek liberation from the cage of worldly concerns to the heights of serenity and self-fulfillment.

Preface

This book is about the attainment of ultimate serenity and self-fulfillment through a rational (that is, reason-based) spirituality. Spirituality in this context is to be understood as the quality of being that is predicated on a sense of connection to the supernatural, that is, to something greater than ourselves that is beyond explanation by natural laws. As such, spirituality is ingrained in the human psyche but is suppressed in the vast majority of people by prevailing cultural and societal norms including the misguided perception of it being somehow superstitious and unscientific. To rekindle spirituality, it must first be recognized and accepted as quintessentially human. Second, scientific thinking should be reconciled with spirituality, which requires scrutiny of the realities of present-day science on the one hand, and on the other hand, an objective, incontestable evidence for the supernatural as being very real (that is, not imaginary or alleged) but encompassing and transcending present-day science.

The linchpin of this spirituality is therefore the existence of the supernatural, identified herein as The Divine Being and referred to in this context as The Almighty. Several kinds of argument have been presented over the years for the existence of The Divine Being. The arguments ranged from the philosophical, to the theological, to those based on special considerations such as a universal morality. The evidence that is presented in this book for the existence of The Almighty is more concrete and incontrovertible, derived from the Quran, the Holy Book of Islam, because as far as the author is aware, the Quran provides the best evidence for the existence of The Almighty. For the purpose of the spirituality advocated in this book, the

Quran is to be regarded by non-Muslims as a stand-alone text that should be appraised on its own merits without prejudice or bias. In this assessment, it may come as a complete surprise to many that the Quran cannot possibly be of human origin. The argument for this non-human origin is based on: (i) numerous, unmistakable references to physical phenomena that were well beyond observation or explanation in the 7th century CE when the Quran was revealed and which have since been confirmed by science; 14 of these revelations are presented in Chapter 4 together with their essential scientific background, plus another miraculous, non-science-related revelation; and (ii) an intricate web of numerical relations involving letters, verses, and chapters of the Quran, and which could not possibly be all coincidental or of human origin. Twelve sets of such relations, out of many more, are given in Chapter 4, with additional relations continuing to be discovered. On top of these manifestations of miraculousness, the Quran touches authoritatively on many diverse topics – such as cosmology, geology, oceanography, zoology, botany, physiology, psychology, ethics, legislation, and economics – and all in a captivating style that has proved linguistically and literarily inimitable and which makes the text easy to remember. In all intellectual honesty, denial of the Divine origin of the Quran faces the insurmountable challenge of seeking human-based explanations for all these characteristic features of the Quran.

The objective, incontrovertible, and reason-based evidence for the existence of The Almighty that is provided by the Quran constitutes a rational basis for the spirituality advocated in this book. Believing in the Existence of The Almighty and in His Revelations in the Quran, would imply believing in the Afterlife, as presented in the Quran, and in the Quranic view of the human condition and its spiritual ramifications, which constitute the mainspring for the advocated spirituality.

From a practical viewpoint, the advocated spirituality is the foundation for ever-fulfilling self-development, focusing principally on the spiritual, psychological, moral, and intellectual advancement of personality and character and driving toward a target state of sublime serenity, peace of mind, and self-fulfillment. The roadmap for this spirituality is detailed in Chapter 7 in terms of: foundational beliefs, engendered feelings and thoughts, formative attitudes, and the eventual outcome of all these in virtuous conduct. The test for this comprehensive self-development is the answer to the simple question: "Am I a better person today than I was yesterday?" It is argued that this self-development is a most worthy and humanistic endeavor that provides meaning to life and is the practical objective of the advocated spirituality.

The immensely beneficial impact of the advocated spirituality is discussed in terms of: (i) conquering negative feelings, such as envy and anger, (ii) alleviation of anxiety and stress, with their detrimental effects on health and well-being, (iii) fostering positive feelings and attitudes in promoting tolerance, understanding, and compassion toward all in contrast to ruthless competition, mindless materialism, and all forms of injustice, oppression, corruption, and exploitation, (iv) experiencing the joy of living without craving and greed, without excessive indulgence or anxiety about the ending of life's pleasures, and with a liberating awareness of what is really important in life and what is vain, superfluous, and illusory, and (v) an elating spirituality that is reflected in an intense feeling of closeness and connectedness to The Almighty. Moreover, when the advocated spirituality is embraced by a sufficient number of individuals in a given society, it will have a very significant salutary influence on interpersonal relations, transforming the very fabric of society.

It cannot be overemphasized that the spirituality advocated in this book goes beyond what is normally experienced by adherents to any particular religion. Even a great majority of practicing Muslims, though ipso facto *are supposed to believe in the Divine origin of the Quran, would not automatically be experiencing the advocated spirituality, for this is based on a deep understanding of the meaning and purpose of life. Non-Muslim believers in The Divine Being should be able to reap the immense benefits of the advocated spirituality while incorporating and accommodating it within their belief system as a highly personalized way of experiencing a close connectedness with The Almighty. Hopefully, many atheists and agnostics will be sufficiently convinced of the existence of The Almighty, or at least admit of this existence, for them to embrace the advocated spirituality and experience its immense benefits.*

The book is divided into 7 chapters, each chapter having a theme that is an element of the reasoning in support of the advocated spirituality. The theme of Chapter 1 is:

Spirituality is the most characteristic, innate human attribute.

The mental activities of humans are compared to those of animals to conclude that spirituality is unique to humans. The development of spirituality is briefly traced from animism in prehistoric times to the numinous experiences of the present. Compared to human-centered philosophies such as humanism and its variants, spirituality provides the motivation and vigilance for virtuous conduct, satisfaction of some deep psychological needs, and a profound meaning and purpose of life. It is the much needed antidote to the misery and stress that prevail in modern life.

The theme of Chapter 2 is:

Present-day science can only give a tunnel view of the world.

The limitations of present-day science are expounded to conclude that science, as valuable and praiseworthy as it is, does not address such fundamental questions as the meaning and purpose of our existence and cannot meaningfully serve as the mainspring of one's worldview and as a life guide. This is not repudiating or depreciating science but rather like using science as a springboard to what is beyond the scope and reach of present-day science. One must therefore boldly venture beyond science to the supernatural while remaining firmly anchored to within the bounds of evidence-based rationality, open-mindedness, and thoughtful contemplation. Science and spirituality are not incompatible.

The theme of Chapter 3 is:

The Quran exhorts to exerting one's intellect and is inimitable in its language and style.

The chapter provides some necessary background for Chapter 4 on relevant features of the Arabic language and discusses particular aspects of the revelation of the Quran, highlighting some of the distinguishing characteristics of the Quranic text, specifically its authenticity, its emphasis on rational thinking, and its linguistic and literary inimitability.

The theme of Chapter 4 is:

The Quran provides incontrovertible evidence for the Existence of The Almighty.

This chapter is concerned with the crucially important issue of the Existence of The Almighty based on the Quran and its revelations. The aforementioned 15 miraculous revelations are presented together with their relevant scientific background, and 12 sets of numerical relations are discussed in the wider context of the intricate web of numerical relations that seem to be imbedded in the Quranic text and their implications.

The theme of Chapter 5 is:

The Almighty is Transcendent, Omnipresent, Omnipotent, and All-Perfect.

Following the belief in the existence of The Almighty, one must know about Him in order to fully embrace the advocated spirituality. The Qualities and Attributes of The Almighty as revealed in the Quran are presented, with particular reference to The Most Exalted Names. The varied attitudes toward the indescribable Greatness, Majesty, and Glory of The Almighty are examined. The question that is sometimes posed as to why The Almighty, with all His Compassion and Mercy, allows suffering and evil in the world is addressed.

The theme of Chapter 6 is:

Death is not the end. It heralds the beginning of what has no end.

The different ways in which people face death and react to its imminence are reviewed, including the acclaimed classic *The Epic of Gilgamesh*. Near-death experiences are discussed, emphasizing their main features, interpretations, and implications for the mind-brain problem and the nature of consciousness. Rupert Sheldrake's morphic fields and David Bohm's implicate order are considered, not by way of endorsement, but as illustrations of unorthodox paradigms that seek to provide explanations for what has hitherto eluded satisfactory explanation. The Quranic views on the Afterlife, Heaven and Hell are presented.

The theme of Chapter 7 is:

Spirituality is the foundation for ever-fulfilling self-

development, which gives meaning and purpose to life.

The main thesis of the book is expounded, namely that, from a practical point of view, self-development – spiritually, psychologically, morally, and intellectually, driving toward a target state of sublime serenity and self-fulfillment – is what gives meaning to life, with the advocated spirituality providing the solid foundation for this continuing and ever-fulfilling self-development. A roadmap for this spirituality is presented in some detail in terms of beliefs, feelings, thoughts, attitudes, and conduct. The beneficial psychological impact of the advocated spirituality is emphasized, and its implications for self-development are discussed. Essentially, the chapter advances a *Manual for Living.*

"The gist of it" in terms of the Quranic view of the human condition and the role of spirituality and self-development is summarized simply, coherently, and succinctly as follows:

The Almighty has created humans for a purpose, which, out of His infinite Mercy and Love, is for them to have eternal bliss in Heaven. In His Omniscience and Wisdom, He created them with a wondrous conscious self having a free will that allows them to choose between the right path that leads to eternal bliss in Heaven and the wrong path that leads to suffering in Hell. The right path is that of submitting to His Will and Serving Him. Progress along this path is through self-development, spiritually, psychologically, morally, and intellectually, driving toward a target state of sublime serenity and self-fulfillment.

A profound and highly important tenet that emerges from the Quranic message, and which is implied in the preceding view of the human condition and emphasized in several places in this book, is:

Had The Almighty wished, He could have made all human beings believers and angel-like, living in perfect peace and harmony. But life would then have no meaning. Humans have to earn the reward of eternal bliss through their conduct in this life, which has therefore been made a trial for them.

It is seen that the spirituality advocated in this book has a solid rational foundation that makes it very credible, natural, and rewarding.

Acknowledgements

I would like to express my deep gratitude to my wife Gharid for her understanding and forbearance while I have been preoccupied with working on this book, to my daughter Maysa, my son Ziad, and my daughter-in-law Zeena for their keen interest, suggestions, and help throughout this project. I am very much indebted to my friend and colleague, Professor Maher Jarrar, Civilization Sequence Program and Department of Arabic and Near Eastern Languages, American University of Beirut, for his valuable critique of the manuscript, suggestions, and advice on Islamic thought, Arab history, and the intricacies of the Arabic language. I would also like to express my great appreciation of the help extended by my friend and colleague, Professor Leila Musfi, Department of Architecture and Design, American University of Beirut, concerning the figures of the book and my sincere thanks to graphic designers Luna Akil and Dana Al-Assir for their contributions in preparing these figures.

Conventions

Translation of Quranic Text

Translations of verses from the Quran rely on the following seven English translations:

- Asad, M. (1980) *The Message of the Quran*, Gibraltar, Dar al-Andalus Ltd.
- Khalidi, T. (2008) *The Qur'an*, London, Penguin Classics.
- Khattab, M. (2016) *The Clear Quran*, Bolingbrook IL, Book of Signs Foundation & Al-Furqaan Institute of Islamic Education.
- Maulana Muhammad Ali (1951) *The Holy Qur'an, Arabic Text, Translation and Commentary*, 4th edn, Lahore (Pakistan), Ahmadiyyah Anjuman Ishaʿat Islam.
- Nasr, S.H. (editor-in-chief) (2015) *The Study Quran: A New Translation and Commentary*, New York, HarperOne.
- Pickthall, M. (1930) *The Meaning of the Glorious Koran*, New York, A.A. Knopf.
- Yusuf Ali, A. (1983) *The Holy Qur'ān: Text, Translation and Commentary*, Brentwood MD, Amana Corp.

In general, no single translation is adopted in this book for any Quranic verse; rather, some combination of these translations is used that is deemed by the author to be the most appropriate.

The word Allāh when occurring in a Quranic verse is retained, and not translated as God, because Allāh is the proper name in Arabic for The Divine Being. Moreover, the word "God", as commonly used, has somewhat different connotations from the word Allāh as used in the Quran and discussed in Chapter 5. In other than Quranic verses, The Divine Being is referred to as The Almighty.

The Arabic word *Rabb* is retained, and not translated as "Lord", as explained in Chapter 5, Section "The Image of God".

Citation of Verses of the Quran

Verses of the Quran are cited in the format (number:number), where the number in parenthesis, before the colon, is the number of *sūrah*, or chapter, in the Quran, and the number after the colon is the number of *āyah*, or verse, in the *sūrah*. Quranic verses are in boldface.

A superscripted endnote number used in connection with a Quranic verse refers to the verse itself, or to the commentary on the verse (as would be clear from the context), in the Quranic translation of the verse in question. The page number in the reference is not relevant in this case, as the verse and its commentary can be readily located in any translation using the chapter number and the verse number. The page number is included where more than one verse is involved or when referring to the commentary of a verse other than the one in question.

Transliteration

Arabic words that have an established form in English are used as such and not transliterated, as in the word "Quran" and the proper name "Muhammad". Transliteration follows the convention and guidelines of the aforementioned translation of the Quran edited by Nasr, S.H., pp. xix-xxii. Arabic words that are not proper names are italicized.

Chapter 1

Why Spirituality?

Theme: Spirituality is the most characteristic, innate human attribute.

The Human State

Evidently, a human being has two discernible facets: body and mind. The body is the multitude of atoms and molecules that make up the 40 trillion cells or so of the human body (a trillion is a million million, or 10^{12}), organized as tissues, organs and various body systems. On the other hand, we will argue that activity of the mind that one is aware of can be considered to have four aspects: cognition, feelings, consciousness, and spirituality. Although distinguishable from one another, these mental activities overlap and interact within the same individual. For example, feelings can interfere with reasoning and judgement, which are part of cognition. Spirituality requires consciousness and cognition but goes beyond them. Cognition, feelings, and consciousness are briefly considered in what follows, before concentrating on spirituality in the rest of the chapter.

Cognition refers to the mental processes of acquiring knowledge and understanding. Knowledge may be acquired by perception through the senses using vision (by reading, for example, or watching television, or simply observing our surroundings) or hearing, as by listening to what others are saying. Knowledge can also be acquired deliberately and systematically through learning, as by schooling, studying, or through exploration and discovery. It can be expanded and elaborated by thought processes such as reasoning and deduction, abstraction, and generalization, as in the sciences, mathematics, and philosophy, which may involve some imagination and creativity. Cognition encompasses processes such as judgement and evaluation, decision-making, and problem-solving.

Feelings are subjective and, therefore, mental experiences. Feelings could be autonomic, in the form of physical sensations, such as pain or hunger, or could be expressions of emotions such as feelings of fear and anger. Emotions are physical, caused subconsciously by neurophysiological responses to an external or an internal stimulus.[1] If one encounters a bear in a forest, for example, there is an immediate and automatic emotional reaction that releases stress hormones that mobilize the body for action (the fight-or-flight response that, among other effects, increases the flow of oxygenated blood to skeletal muscles by dilating blood vessels in these muscles, making the heart beat faster and stronger, raising blood pressure, and increasing the breathing rate). These emotions are expressed as a feeling of fear. There is, however, a complex, two-way, long-term interaction between feelings and emotions, which is studied in psychology.[2] Moreover, one can learn to control one's emotions and feelings to varying extents depending on experience, judgement, psychological makeup, cultural background, and circumstances. Encountering a bear in a zoo, for example, does not evoke the same reactions as the encounter in the forest. More complex feelings, such as compassion and patriotism are part of the conscious self.

At its most basic level, consciousness is awareness of the environment and being able to respond to environmental stimuli. As such, consciousness is the substrate of mental activities that one is aware of in the normal state of being, for these mental activities cease when consciousness is lost.

But even with partial loss of consciousness, an autonomic feeling such as pain and the response to it can persist. At a higher level, the conscious self is at the essence of our human existence. As conscious beings we are aware of the world around us and of ourselves in this world as individuals having our own subjective worldview based on our own opinions, attitudes, and past experiences. We have our own ideas, beliefs, thoughts, desires and hopes as we plan for the future. We have volition to make decisions and free will to choose between alternatives based on our motivation and drive, value system, circumstances, past experiences, and judgement. Consciousness influences our feelings: no two people experience physical pain in the same way, nor perceive smells and colors in the same way. It is this conscious self that provides the unity of being and continuity in time that defines each human being as a unique individual.

Conscious individuals express themselves through language, as an effective means of human communication, and through creative work and thought as in art, literature, philosophy, scientific discoveries and technological innovations. The aggregates of these expressions and interactions together with their associated collective norms, beliefs, and behaviors produce cultures and civilizations.

An intriguing aspect of consciousness is its relation to quantum theory. According to the conventional interpretation of quantum theory, a conscious observer exercising free will is required to yield a particular result in any quantum experiment,[3] which defines what is eventually interpreted as "reality". Consciousness is further discussed in Chapter 2, Section "Nature of Science".

The fourth aspect of mind, which is of primary

concern in this book, is spirituality. So what do we mean by spirituality? As there is no generally-agreed-upon definition of spirituality, the definition adopted in this book is based on a widely-held view,[4] namely: *spirituality is the quality of being that is predicated on a sense of connection to the supernatural, that is, to something greater than ourselves that is beyond explanation by natural laws.*

Spirituality, in its various connotations, including the religious experience, or acceptance of the nonmaterial or supernatural, has been extensively studied and debated by philosophers, theologians, and psychologists for many years, and more recently by neuroscientists.[5] The majority of scientists, being materialists, consider spirituality, as commonly understood, to be superstitious and unscientific.

Human Development

From a biological viewpoint and according to the more recent classifications based on molecular techniques, humans belong to the family of the great apes together with chimpanzees, bonobos, gorillas, and orangutans. Within this family are divisions and subdivisions that place chimpanzees closest to humans followed by bonobos (sometimes referred to as pygmy chimpanzees because of their close relation to chimpanzees), then gorillas, with orangutans being the farthest from humans. The physical similarity between humans and chimpanzees is evidently striking though unflattering to humans (and maybe to chimpanzees as well). Even more striking is the similarity in the genetic material.[6] A major physical difference between humans and chimpanzees is in brain size and architecture.[7] The volume of the human brain is 1200-1400 cubic centimeters and its mass is 1.3-1.5 kilograms. The brain consumes roughly 20 watts of power. Although this may seem rather small, it represents in fact a whopping 20 percent or so of the total power consumption of the body at rest, despite the fact that the mass of the brain is only about 2 percent of body mass. The size of a chimpanzee brain is about one-third that of the human brain; but the crucial difference is in the cortex of the brain – the outer layer of brain tissue, approximately 2-4 millimeters thick, that is highly convoluted so as to pack a larger surface area in a given volume. The cortex is at the top of the hierarchical organization of the human nervous system; its frontal part, in particular, is associated with our higher mental functions. According to the most reliable estimates, the cortex of the human brain has about 16×10^9 nerve cells. Estimates of the number of neurons in the cortices of other animals are varied, depending on the method used for counting. The cortex of a chimpanzee brain is about as thick as that of a human brain but has less than half the number of nerve cells. In fact, the cortex of the human brain has the largest number of nerve cells compared to any other species.[8] In addition to their greater number, the nerve cells of the cortex of the human brain are more developed and varied, with more complex wiring, or interconnections.

It is generally believed that humans originated in Africa about 2.5 million years ago. They subsequently developed into a number of human species, both in Africa as well as in Europe and Asia as a result of migrations out of Africa. Examples of these early human species are *Homo erectus* and *Homo neanderthalensis* who inhabited mostly Europe and parts of Asia. Our own species, *Homo sapiens* (the wise humans), are believed to have originated in Africa some 200,000 years ago, and to have spread out since to all parts of the globe. All other human species subsequently became extinct, mostly through elimination by *Homo sapiens*, isolation, and eventual disappearance. There probably was some interbreeding as well. It should be noted that interbreeding that produces fertile and viable offspring is excluded by the conventional, although somewhat controversial, definition of a species. Thus, the offspring of a male donkey and a female horse is a sterile mule, as donkeys and horses belong to different species.

The following salient aspects of the development of *Homo sapiens* should be emphasized: First, the human brain grew in size over a span of some two million years, from the earliest human species to *Homo sapiens*, despite its energy demand. Some adaptations of the human body are believed to have taken place to cater for this demand, in addition to having to spend more time to procure food. Other high-energy consuming organs of the body were reduced in size, mainly muscle and intestines. Cooking helped in several ways. A wider range of foodstuff became available, and less energy was required for digestion, which allowed shorter, less energy-consuming intestines. The returns for the larger brains were meager for a long time, mainly some primitive tools such as pointed sticks and sharp stone. So what was the drive for larger brains? No one really knows. But it has been shown that the regulatory sequences of glucose-transporting genes of the brain, which cater for the higher energy demand of the brain, underwent mutations at a faster rate than can be accounted for by chance alone.[7]

Second, *Homo sapiens* are believed to have developed some new thinking and communication abilities between 70,000 and 30,000 years ago in what has been dubbed the Cognitive Revolution.[9] Its cause is assumed to be some chance mutation that affected the brain somehow, with dramatically far-reaching results. One was a highly-developed language that allowed effective communication and the transfer of a tremendous amount of detailed information. More important is imagination, that is, the ability to form mental images, thoughts, and sensations of things and entities that are not physically real. Imagination begot creativity, which led to finding new solutions to problems encountered. The products of imagination could also be shared with others through language, or some form of artistic expression, making use of the amazing and unsurpassed manual dexterity of humans, which was enabled by developments in the brain and the rest of the neuromuscular system. An early example of this imaginative artistic expression is the human-lion figurine found in the Stadel Cave in Germany in 1939, dated about 35,000 years ago. It is about 31 cm tall, depicting an upright human body having a lion head carved out of ivory with impressive detail, presumably using a flint-stone knife.

The triad of creative imagination, language, and manual dexterity was a formidable combination that propelled *Homo sapiens* to unprecedented accomplishments. Some very useful implements were invented such as: bows and arrows that made hunting more efficient, oil lamps for combatting darkness, fishhooks and harpoons for fishing, bone and ivory needles for stitching clothing together, and boats to venture into the open waters. *Homo sapiens* spread far and wide, reaching eastern Asia about 55,000 years ago, Australia about 45,000 years ago, and the Americas, probably at an earlier time. Through planning, cunning, social skills, productive labor, and creative thinking, *Homo sapiens* prevailed over all other human and animal species to become the undisputed masters of planet Earth.

It is truly astounding that a chance mutation of the brain would take *Homo sapiens* far, far beyond what is biologically needed for survival and continuation of the species at the detriment of other forms of life, whole ecosystems, and the environment. By the time of the Agricultural Revolution, about 12,000 years ago, nearly half of the planet's large terrestrial animals were driven to extinction by *Homo sapiens*. The slaughter has not only continued since, but has extended to marine life. Vast areas of forests and dense vegetation were deliberately burnt, to be replaced by open grasslands, which also destroyed whole ecosystems. Following the Industrial Revolution, the environment was ravaged for raw materials and sources of energy. The relentless pursuit of progress and affluence in terms of consumerism and material possessions has had devastating effects in terms of pollution and degradation of the environment. Today, we even face the potential risk of a nuclear holocaust that eradicates life on earth, including *Homo sapiens* themselves. Clearly, this is untenable from a purely biological standpoint. And all as a result of a chance mutation? We will return to this chance explanation toward the end of Chapter 2.

Manifestations of Spirituality

For much of their history until the Agricultural Revolution, humans existed as hunter-gatherers. They subsisted through foraging, that is, searching for and consuming food from sources in the wild. This is in contrast to relying on domesticated plants and animals, which began with the Agricultural Revolution. As hunter-gatherers, humans subsisted on vegetation, fruits, seeds, nuts, and whatever meat they could get. In the early days, the sources of meat were small animals that they could catch relatively easily, dead animals, or leftovers from large predators. Human hunting skills steadily improved over the years. Spears were invented around 500,000 years ago, which allowed hunting larger animals from a distance, but mainly by solitary hunters. A big step was in male hunters banding together to pursue large animals. There is evidence of group hunting as far back as 300,000 years ago. *Homo sapiens* later applied their mental, communication, and manual skills to make cooperative hunting of large animals more effective and rewarding.

Despite the length of the hunter-gatherer period in human history and the availability of many archaeological findings dated to this period, particularly its more recent part, little is known for certain about the spiritual beliefs of the hunter-gatherers. One can only build on what has been surmised from tomb relics, cave paintings, and other artistic artefacts and speculate in a manner that builds a plausible and coherent narrative about the spiritual beliefs of the hunter-gatherers.

The creative imagination of *Homo sapiens* is evident in several early belief systems, the most pervasive being animism.[10] The core belief of animism is that everything in nature, living and nonliving, as well as natural phenomena, has an animated character, that is, it has some sort of spirit or vital force that endows it with a will, desires, needs, feelings, and influence on human affairs. This applies to animals, plants, mountains, rivers, thunder, and other natural phenomena. Animism essentially blurs the distinction between what is physical or material and what is not. It opens up to the world of spirits, whether of the dead, of ancestors, or of benevolent or malicious beings. Intervention of these spirits may be required for good fortune or to ward off evil. Such intervention can be accomplished through a shaman – a person endowed with the ability to communicate with spirits. The intervention may require some rituals performed individually or communally.

One can think of a *Homo sapiens* huddled in a corner of his cave on a stormy night with the wind howling outside and the sound of pelting rain interrupted by loud claps of thunder. Flashes of lightning pierce through the darkness while casting ominous shadows around. Naturally, our *Homo sapiens* would feel some fear, as would the animals outside while they sought shelter to protect themselves from the storm as best as they could. But with his imagination, our *Homo sapiens* harbors something more: a sense of confronting something greater than himself and his fellow beings, forces of nature that they were powerless against. He imagined that these forces were guided and controlled by spirits that he could connect with, spirits he should appease to protect himself and his family sprawled beside him.

In *Homo sapiens'* imagination, hunting called for supportive intervention of invisible forces and spirits for the hunt to yield a plentiful supply of meat and to ward off accidents and physical injuries to the hunters. An elaborate set of rituals was practiced for these purposes including acts of worship, fasting, abiding by certain abstentions and taboos, performing ceremonial dances, and looking for portending signs and omens. Animals that hunt in groups or packs never engage in such activities. To them, the hunt is a largely innate and physical act based on the realities of the situation such as the location of the prey, the nature of the surroundings, the direction of the wind, and the right timing for the final push. By virtue of their cognitive powers, *Homo sapiens* learned to continually improve their hunting skills taking into account the relevant physical factors and using more effective hunting tools. But they had to contend, additionally, with the products of their imagination, which had no physical form but were, nevertheless, very real to them and governed their behavior before, during, and after the hunt.

Though animism in various forms was widespread among ancient hunter-gatherers, it remained localized to what was encountered within a few hundred or so square kilometers that defined the area over which a particular group of hunter-gatherers foraged during their entire lifetimes. Spirits and vital forces were associated with particular plants, animals, geographical features, or natural phenomena that the group of hunter-gatherers experienced or came in contact with. There was no universal spirit for all trees or all mountains, for example, as the group was primarily concerned with a particular mountain, or tree, or a collection of trees.

The imagination of *Homo sapiens* had to expand with the Agricultural Revolution as new needs arose whose fulfillment was beyond human abilities. There were crops that needed rain and to be kept free of pests and unseen blights, trees that should bear abundant fruit, and domesticated animals that should remain healthy, useful, and multiply in numbers. The spiritual beings that could cater for these needs were powerful, specialized gods, such as the rain god who can bring rain, the river god who can keep the river flowing and prevent its damaging floods, and the god of the wind and storms, whose wrath can be devastating. The rituals to appease these gods and gain their favor also became more demanding, involving: elaborate rites of worship and the intervention of a larger number of more organized clergy, animal and sometimes human sacrifices, stone monuments, and eventually temples for the gods.

In the wake of the Agricultural Revolution, as settlements grew into cities and societies became more complex, morphing into city states, nations, and dynasties, the creative imagination of *Homo sapiens* kept pace. New gods came into being who were more concerned with the new needs and aspirations. A god of war, properly appeased, would ensure victory over enemies. There were gods for the afterlife and the underworld, that is, the world of the dead. Befittingly, there were also goddesses for beauty, love, and fertility. Ancient civilizations, such as the Babylonian, Greek, or Egyptian civilizations, had hundreds of gods covering a wide range of human activity. A rich mythology arose about the imagined exploits of these gods, their often complex interrelationships, and their interactions with humans, sometimes leading to the birth of part-human and part-divine beings. Almost all the ancient polytheistic religions had a supreme god who ruled over the universe and other gods so as to maintain order, keep the lesser gods in check, and arbitrate their inevitable disputes.

The foregoing illustrates the intertwining of the existence of *Homo sapiens* with spirituality, as a sense of connection to something greater than the individual, something supernatural that was perceived through *Homo sapiens'* fertile, creative imagination. The appearance of what are today the most influential, organized religions – Judaism, Christianity, Islam, Buddhism, Hinduism, and Confucianism – placed spirituality on a firmer footing, at least for the true believers. The first three of these six religions are monotheistic, Islam vehemently so. The other three religions, together with a host of less influential religions in various parts of the world, either lacked the belief in a supreme, universal deity, or had no need for gods altogether. Nevertheless, they shared the belief in the existence of some natural order that translates into laws or codes of conduct that should be obeyed for salvation or enlightenment. In Hinduism, for example, a principle of natural order (*Rta*) governs the operation of the universe and everything in it. In Buddhism, *dharma* is cosmic law and order applied through the teaching of Buddha to guide human conduct. Confucianism also has standards of behavior in everyday life for being in harmony with the Law of Heaven.

In modern times, many adhere to an organized religion only nominally. In actual fact, these individuals may be atheists, agnostics, or believers in one of several ideologies or creeds that have sprung up, such as communism, nationalism, or humanism. Although these belief systems have no use for the supernatural, they do nonetheless invoke or imply some universal forces, absolute truths, or immutable natural laws that are superhuman, that is, transcend the individual and are not ordained by humans. Such belief systems can powerfully motivate and govern human behavior, even to the extent of dying for the cause. Communism, for example, involves a belief in absolute, historically inevitable, class struggles based on the control of the means of production; historically, societies have transformed from feudalism to capitalism and will ultimately be ruled by the working class. We will return to humanism later in this chapter.

Human Uniqueness

How about animals? Do they have the same mental activities as humans? It will be argued in this section that animals do have cognitive abilities, feelings, and consciousness to some degree but not spirituality in the sense used here.

It is well established that animals learn and have cognitive abilities,[11] which they must in order to survive, perform their daily activities, and adapt to changing circumstances. So we will not dwell too much on this aspect of animal behavior other than give some examples of problem-solving by animals. Examples abound of problem-solving abilities of non-human great apes, such as chimpanzees using boxes to climb up and reach bananas hanging high from a roof, or pouring water into a vertical clear tube containing a peanut, which makes it float upwards into reach.[12] Lower animals, particularly crows, have demonstrated some amazing problem-solving abilities. For example, crows have been observed to drop hard-shelled nuts on crossroads near traffic lights so that cars break the shells with their tires. The birds then wait for the traffic lights to change and pedestrians to cross so as to safely retrieve the edible nuts.[13] Such behavior demonstrates learning through observation, reasoning, inference, planning, adaptation to new circumstances, and exploitation of new opportunities.

It is also common observation that animals manifest feelings such as fear and anger. Witness a cat recoil in fear when cornered by a dog, arching its back and retracting its mouth while uttering defensive cries; or the menacing anger of a watchdog confronting a stranger. When it comes to consciousness, animals have been shown to have self-awareness. In 1970 psychologist Gordon Gallup let some chimpanzees play with mirrors. Then he anesthetized them and painted red spots on their faces. When they looked at themselves in the mirror, they tried to rub the spots off their faces. This was considered evidence of their recognizing themselves in the mirror. Children develop this self-awareness at about 15 months of age. Since then, several animal species have passed the mirror test: elephants, dolphins, magpies, and even a species of fish have been claimed to have passed the test.[14] This self-awareness does not prove that animals are aware of themselves as unique conscious individuals in the same sense as humans. Rather, it may be simply indicative of having a body image. The self-awareness test was extended to other species using sense modalities other than vision – to dogs, for example, using the sense of smell. Bees, ants, and termites are said to possess a collective consciousness. The 2012 Cambridge Declaration on Consciousness asserts that: "Convergent evidence indicates that non-human animals have the neuroanatomical, neurochemical, and neurophysiological substrates of conscious states along with the capacity to exhibit intentional behaviors. Consequently, the weight of evidence indicates that humans are not unique in possessing the neurological substrates that generate consciousness. Non-human animals, including all mammals and birds, and many other creatures, including octopuses, also possess these neurological substrates."[15] The debate about whether animals, or indeed machines, have consciousness is fueled at least in part by the absence of a generally-agreed-upon definition of consciousness and its manifestations.[16] What concerns us here is the fact that animal behavior does indeed appear to simulate some micro-aspects of consciousness though nothing like the integrated and uniquely-individual conscious self of humans. Nonetheless, consciousness cannot be considered to be uniquely and exclusively human.

What about spirituality? Is there animal spirituality? Again, it depends on what is meant by spirituality. If it simply means some sort of non-materialistically oriented, contemplative-like experience then it can be argued that animal spirituality does exist. An often-cited example is the waterfall dance, or rain dance, or thunderstorm dance of chimpanzees that is usually performed individually or sometimes in small groups. Jane Goodall, the renowned English primatologist who has done extensive field studies on chimpanzees, describes these dances as follows:

> ...Deep in the forest are some spectacular waterfalls. Sometimes as a chimpanzee – most often an adult male – approaches one of these falls his hair bristles slightly, a sign of heightened arousal. As he gets closer, and the roar of falling water gets louder, his pace quickens, his hair becomes fully erect, and upon reaching the stream he may perform a magnificent display close to the foot of the falls. Standing upright, he sways rhythmically from foot to foot, stamping in the shallow, rushing water, picking up and hurling great rocks. Sometimes he climbs up the slender vines that hang down from the trees high above and swings out into the spray of the falling water. This "waterfall dance" may last for ten or fifteen minutes...It is not only waterfalls that can trigger displays of this sort. Chimpanzees "dance" at the onset of a very heavy rain, reaching up to sway saplings or low branches rhythmically back and forth, back and forth, then moving forward in slow motion loudly slapping the ground with their hands, stamping with their feet, and hurling rock after rock. Twice I have seen them perform thus during the first violent gusts of wind, presaging a storm.[17]

This of course could be merely an expression of joy for experiencing rain or natural marvels, much as humans sometimes do, or an expression of awe of nature. We can never know because chimpanzees cannot tell us what they are thinking. Chimpanzees have complex social behaviors, make tools, and teach their use across generations – something reminiscent of the rudiments of culture. But there is no evidence whatsoever of chimpanzee spirituality as defined herein, "a sense of connection to the supernatural, that is, to something greater than ourselves". No one has observed a chimpanzee kneel in prayer or plead in earnest piety toward the heavens. If the aforementioned dances are a precursor to the spirituality that is meant here, then why hasn't chimpanzee spirituality evolved over the past millions of years to something more religious as in the case of humans? Why are there no chimpanzee religious artefacts, relics, or places of worship? One cannot but conclude that chimpanzees do not have the spirituality defined herein.

It was argued in the preceding that animals do have cognition, feelings, and some consciousness. Language is highly developed in humans and has certain unique features that are not found in animal communication. Some have argued, however, that the main differences may have arisen under evolutionary pressures for reasons other than language.[18] In this sense, language cannot uncontroversially be said to be unique to humans.

On the other hand, spirituality as defined herein is uniquely human. As a distinct mental activity, it must involve some features of its own, as postulated at the beginning of this chapter. To be sure, spirituality necessarily requires cognitive processes such as imagination and abstract thinking. This is evident in the early belief system of animism, as mentioned previously. It takes considerable imagination and some abstraction to think that everything in nature – animals, trees, rocks, waterfalls, etc. as well as natural phenomena such as thunder, rain, and wind – has some sort of spirit or vital force that endows it with a will, desires, needs, and feelings. The most prevalent spiritual, or numinous, experiences quoted in the literature are the following:

> (1) a sense of special patterning of events in a person's life by a divine being; (2) an awareness of the presence of a divine being; (3) a sense of union with a divine being or

> the divine universe; (4) an awareness of receiving help in answer to a prayer; (5) an awareness of being looked after or guided by a presence of God; (6) an awareness of a divine presence in nature; (7) experiencing in an extraordinary way that all things are "One" with a divine being; (8) the sense of having touched the ultimate ground of divine reality; (9) the experience of timelessness and spacelessness; (10) feelings of positive affect, peace, joy and unconditional love; (11) a metacognitive (that is, thinking or reasoning about one's own thinking) shift in the relationship between thoughts and feelings—they come to be observed as arising phenomena instead of occupying full attention; and (12) blissful absorption into the present moment.[5]

These experiences can occur in any combination, spontaneously and unintentionally, outside any religious belief or practice, and in prosaic circumstances. Although these spiritual experiences require consciousness and cognition and involve feeling, yet they are of a very particular nature, which justifies considering them a distinct mental activity, as mentioned at the beginning of the chapter. They are unique compared to other mental activities in that they involve a belief in the existence of a divine being and a sense of connectedness to this being. In addition, they encompass more sublime feelings that transcend the mundane affairs of everyday life. The fact that many people do have these spiritual experiences means that humans *can* have them. Why most people don't have them is simply because they are conditioned to repress their spirituality, consciously or unconsciously, under social, educational, and cultural influences that relegate spirituality to the realm of superstition and label it as naïve, unsophisticated, and unscientific. Nevertheless, in moments of introspection, the "primordial spiritual drive" can surface as a feeling of inner void that cries to be filled by connecting with something outside ourselves in search for a meaning and purpose to our existence.

Need for Spirituality

Could the supernatural simply be a figment of our imagination? An artefact of this imagination, so to speak, that has no basis in fact or reality? Is spirituality merely a superfluous distraction that is not needed and that we're better off without? A relatively large percentage of people nowadays would answer in the affirmative to these questions, particularly among those considered to be enlightened and well-informed. Such an attitude is essentially grounded, consciously or subconsciously, in a human-centered philosophy of life, the best example of which is arguably humanism and its variants.

Humanism as defined by the American Humanist Association "is a progressive philosophy of life that, without theism or other supernatural beliefs, affirms our ability and responsibility to lead ethical lives of personal fulfillment that aspire to the common good."[19] In essence, humanists believe that rational thinking and human experience, knowledge, and judgement are all that is needed for moral conduct and a fulfilling life based on real human needs, interests, and aspirations. Science and its thought tributaries are the only trustworthy sources of knowledge about ourselves and the universe. There are no supernatural beings; the only existence is that of the material universe, governed by immutable natural laws. Death is the end; there is no continuity in any form of life after death. This life is the only one we have and should be lived in affirmation of human dignity, individual liberty, and freedom to shape one's life, with compassion and responsibility toward others and the environment.

An extension of humanism is transhumanism,[20] which seeks to overcome human physical, psychological, and mental limitations by means of science and technology. The aim is to enhance human physiology and emotional well-being, eliminate aging, extend the human life span, and expand the human intellect and intelligence by various means such as artificial intelligence, for example.

Human-centered philosophies of life such as humanism undoubtedly seem very sensible, worthy, and attractive. Outwardly, they appear to be sufficient to lead a satisfying, wholesome life. A deeper scrutiny, however, raises some problematic issues. First, there is the question of implementation. Can the lofty ideals of humanism be realized by all people in all circumstances? Would a laborer toiling for his daily living care much about the greater good or personal fulfillment beyond physical needs? What would be the motivation for abiding by the rules of ethical conduct under all conditions? Self-satisfaction? Conscientiousness? Would these provide vigilance for everyone in the face of temptations and other allures, considering human capriciousness and base instincts?

Second, is the question of the sufficiency or efficacy of a human-centered philosophy of life in catering to human psychological needs. Does such a philosophy allow individuals to better cope with the stresses of modern life, stresses that may be job-related or may have social, familial, or other causes? Does it assuage our inner fears and anxieties, fear of the unknown or anxiety about what the future might hold? Does it overcome feelings of emptiness and loneliness that plague many people at times? Does it help grapple with misfortune or debilitating ailments? Does it combat the depression that many experience in old age as they witness the waning of their physical and mental powers and they ponder the worth of their life achievements, many not feeling satisfied no matter what was achieved? Does it allay the fear of death by many, the fear of vanishing into nothingness? Is it conducive to long-lasting serenity and peace of mind? While some may experience serenity or ecstasy in special circumstances such as when listening to music, for example, or viewing a beautiful landscape, such feelings are ephemeral and fade away only too quickly.

Third, a human-centered philosophy of life does not even broach the mystery of our existence. Is there no meaning or purpose to this existence? Are we simply the result of a chance encounter between a sperm cell and an egg cell in a narrow, dark abdominal tube, which then almost miraculously develops into this wondrous human being? Our physiology is incredibly complex, beyond amazement. We are endowed with astonishing mental capacities that are stupendously beyond those of our closest biological kin: the ability to probe into the mysteries of physical phenomena to make astounding scientific discoveries; the creativity to produce indescribably beautiful works of art and the sense to appreciate the beauty in these works and in what is around us; the propensity to discern good from evil, what is moral from what is not; the freedom to at least try and shape our own lives; a mysterious, fathomless consciousness; and last but not least, the spiritual dimension that is uniquely human, as was previously discussed. Is our destiny simply to be born, live our lives, enjoy what our circumstances allow, achieve what we are able to achieve, then end up as a lifeless corpse to be disposed of one way or another? Is human life, at the bottom of it, just a matter of biological continuation of the species? Like human, like dog, or like rat? Does this make sense? Do not the exalted human sensibilities and intellect deserve a more sublime purpose?

Human-centered philosophies seemingly place the human being in high regard. In actual fact they degrade humanness, for they ascribe only superficial and banal reasons for our existence, and they relegate humans to an ignominious end that is no different from that of lower animals. On the other hand, the advocated spirituality, discussed at length in Chapter 7, provides meaning and purpose to our lives, while providing immense psychological benefits and the firm foundations for virtuous conduct that would have tremendous social impact. Such spirituality would be the much needed antidote to the misery and stress that prevail in modern life – a life that is plagued by greed, envy, ruthless competition for empty and superficial rewards, mindless materialism and avaricious consumerism, hedonistic pursuits, selfishness and destructive individualism, injustice, oppression, exploitation, dishonesty, corruption, and many other forms of unrighteous conduct.

Even at the level of nations, as these develop beyond the state of struggling to meet life's basic necessities to a state of relative comfort and affluence, and in the absence of strong enough spiritual precepts, nations risk sinking into a predominantly materialistic mindset that only leads to decadence and eventual demise, as has often happened in history.

Speaking for Spirituality

Over the years, many writers, philosophers, and even scientists have maintained that spirituality is an innate human trait. Scientists who hold such beliefs tend to be rather circumspect about expressing them, for fear of disparagement or even ridicule. Some express them in a guarded manner, others become more outspoken further along in their careers.

Sir Fred Hoyle was a renowned English astronomer and cosmologist who developed the theory of supernova nucleosynthesis, according to which nuclei of elements of increasing atomic weight are formed inside stars and distributed through space by supernova explosions (see Chapter 4, Section "Miraculous Revelations, Item 1. Pulsars"). An atheist to begin with, he came to believe in some "intelligent design" in the universe. This is what he has to say about the religious impulse:

> This moral or religious impulse, whatever we choose to call it, is extraordinarily strong. When faced by opposition, and even by powerful political attempts at suppression, it obstinately refuses to lie down and die. One often comes on statements that religion is a primitive superstition that modern man can well do without. Yet if the impulse were truly primitive in a biological sense (as for instance patriotic loyalty to the group in which one happens to live is primitive) we would surely expect to see it in other animals. As far as I know, no-one has advanced any evidence for this idea. The religious impulse appears to be unique to man, and indeed to have become stronger in prehistory the more advanced man became in his intellectual attainments. Admittedly the trend has reversed over the recent past, but the change over the past two centuries may well prove to be impermanent.
>
> ...Stripped of the many fanciful adornments with which religion has become traditionally surrounded, does it (the religious impulse) not amount to an instruction within us that expressed rather simply might read as follows: You are derived from something "out there"... Seek it, and you will find much more than you expect.[21]

Sir John Eccles was a distinguished Australian neurophysiologist who was awarded the 1963 Nobel Prize in Physiology or Medicine for his pioneering work on synapses – the terminations of nerve cells on one another. Eccles was a Roman Catholic and a dualist, that is, a believer in the separation between mind and brain. On human uniqueness, Eccles explains:

> Since materialist solutions fail to account for our experienced uniqueness, I am constrained to attribute the uniqueness of the Self or Soul to a supernatural spiritual creation...I submit that no other explanation is tenable; neither the genetic uniqueness with its fantastically impossible lottery, nor the environmental differentiations which do not *determine* one's uniqueness, but merely modify it.[22]

On the human condition, Eccles states:

> I maintain that the human mystery is incredibly demeaned by scientific reductionism, with its claim in promissory materialism to account eventually for all of the spiritual world in terms of patterns of neuronal activity. This belief must be classed as superstition.[23]

This is absolutely contrary to what many people, including most scientists, believe: that it is all nothing more than random events, chance mutations, and evolutionary selection and adaptation, scientifically explained in terms of pure materialism. That would have been the case, were it not for unmistakable signs that it is not so. We will examine these signs in subsequent chapters as an essential part of a systematic building of a case for a spirituality that does not have the shortcomings of a purely human-centered philosophy of life.

In summary, humans are spiritual beings, whether we care to admit it or not. Those who choose to deny spirituality do so at their own peril while debasing what it truly means to be human. Those who choose to acknowledge, embrace, and cherish their spirituality are in a world of ever-fulfilling self-development and tranquility, as elaborated in Chapter 7.

But where does science and a scientific outlook fit into all this? That is the subject of the following chapter.

Chapter 2

What Science?

Theme: Present-day science can only give a tunnel view of the world.

Nature of Science

By tunnel view is meant the view through a tunnel opening from some distance inside the tunnel. It is a circumscribed, restricted view unlike the view from outside the tunnel, open in all directions.

This is by no means intended to disparage science. On the contrary, scientific thought and progress are assuredly one of the greatest achievements of humanity, if not the greatest. Apart from expanding knowledge, science – through engineering – has spawned technologies of immense benefit to humans, as in diagnostic and therapeutic medicine (MRI, X-rays, vaccines, medications, etc.), agricultural technologies (mechanization, increased crop yields, etc.), and industrial products (airplanes, cars, household appliances, computers, mobile phones, etc.). It is the fault of humans, not science, that some technologies have been abused, such as nuclear technology and genetic engineering.

Basically, science seeks to understand natural phenomena. According to the Science Council (UK), "Science is the pursuit and application of knowledge and understanding of the natural and social world following a systematic methodology based on evidence."[1] What distinguishes science from other means of acquiring knowledge is a systematic scientific method that, in essence, involves the following steps: (i) objective observation of a phenomenon, that is, observation that is not biased in any way; (ii) formulation of a hypothesis that provides a plausible explanation of the observed phenomenon; (iii) experimental, measurement-based testing of deductions and predictions that follow from the formulated hypothesis; and (iv) rejection, modification, or generalization of the formulated hypothesis based on the experimental results.

It follows that the phenomena that are amenable to scientific investigation must be observable and repeatable, eventually leading to an explanatory hypothesis that allows testable deductions and predictions, or falsification. Repeatability is required not only for enhancing the reliability of testing through repetition but also to enable other scientists to replicate the experiments and validate the results. However, this places a severe restriction on the range of phenomena that can be scientifically investigated. Evidently, science cannot prove or disprove the existence of a divine being, as neither assertion can be tested experimentally.

Consider consciousness. Its most basic level is that of awareness of the environment and the ability to respond to environmental stimuli. An unconscious person is not fully aware of the environment and responds to environmental stimuli in a limited fashion or none at all. This basic level of consciousness can be tested and catalogued in various ways, such as the Glasgow Coma Scale (GCS),[2] for example, which measures three functions – eye opening, verbal response, and motor response – and assigns a value to each function on a numerical scale. As it is based on test and measurement, the GCS is a medically acceptable and useful clinical tool for assessing brain injury and monitoring recovery. But the consciousness measured by the GCS is nowhere near in nature and scope to that of the conscious self, as mentioned in the preceding chapter, and which defines each human being as a unique individual having a very particular subjective worldview. Meaningful measurements of any elements of this subjective worldview – such as opinions, beliefs, attitudes, values, morality, and sense of appreciation of beauty – are beyond the realm of rigorous science. But their importance cannot be belittled. They are at the core of our humanness and central to our everyday experiences and interactions.

An intriguing aspect of consciousness was revealed by cerebral commissurotomy – the surgical procedure of severing the corpus callosum, which is a massive bundle of about 200 million nerve fibers that connect together the two hemispheres of the brain. The procedure was performed to alleviate the symptoms of severe, uncontrollable epilepsy and resulted in what is popularly referred to as a split-brain because of the disconnection between the two hemispheres. There remains, however, some interconnection between the two sides of the brain at the level of underlying brain structures on the two sides, including structures involved in movement (the motor system) and in various emotional and behavioral responses (the limbic system). Some psychologists had speculated that cerebral commissurotomy would result in a split-personality. In actual fact, it did not make any discernible difference in the normal daily activities of the subjects. In the late 1950s the American neuropsychologist, Roger Sperry, initiated a series of experiments on split-brain subjects for which he was awarded the 1981 Nobel Prize in Physiology or Medicine. By separating the right half of the visual field from the left half, Sperry and his co-investigators were able to communicate meaningful visual input, such as images or photographs, exclusively to one hemisphere and analyze the resulting behavioral responses. It turned out that the two hemispheres have different but complementary competencies. According to American psychologist Jerre Levy: "The right hemisphere synthesizes over space. The left hemisphere analyzes over time. The right hemisphere notes visual similarities to the exclusion of conceptual similarities. The left hemisphere does the opposite. The right hemisphere perceives form, the left hemisphere, detail. The right hemisphere codes sensory input in terms of images, the left hemisphere in terms of linguistic expressions."[3] What distinguishes the left hemisphere is that it contains the two language areas of the brain: the area involved in speech production (Broca's area) and the area involved in the comprehension of written and spoken language (Wernicke's area). It should be noted that the left hemisphere and the right hemisphere in the foregoing description refer to what is conventionally termed the dominant hemisphere and the minor hemisphere, respectively. The left hemisphere is in fact the dominant hemisphere in the majority of people – about 95% of right-handers but about 70% of left-handers.

What about consciousness? The role of each hemisphere in consciousness is more contentious, partly because of differences in the definition of consciousness. With more careful investigations, it is the consensus that both hemispheres have some awareness, including self-awareness, but the conscious self, in the sense described in the preceding chapter, is believed to be associated with the dominant hemisphere.[4] Why that should be so remains unexplained. It would seem that this has to do with the presence of the language areas. However, damage to these areas is known to produce severe difficulties in speaking and comprehending language, but does not seem to affect the conscious self.

Considerable research has been done, and is continuing, on the neural correlates of consciousness, that is, the neural activity or electrochemical processes in the brain that correlate with states of conscious experiences. Many such correlates have been proposed over the years, ranging from synchronized oscillations of electrical activity in the cortex of the brain, to interactions between electro-ionic activity and electromagnetic activity in the brain, to quantum-mechanical phenomena.[5] Continuing advances in neuroscience and other branches of science are expected to lead eventually to identifying physical processes that are associated with various aspects of consciousness. According to the Australian philosopher, David Chalmers, these are but the easy problems of consciousness.[6] Chalmers' hard problem of consciousness is *why* should these physical processes give rise to a subjective experience? If one looks at a red rose, for example, light of a certain frequency impinges on the retina and generates in some of the retinal cells electrical signals that travel to the brain along well-defined neural pathways. These electrical signals are processed in parts of the brain in a manner that is at present largely unknown, but which might well be known in the future. The resulting spatial and temporal patterns of neuronal activity and the accompanying electrochemical and computational brain activity are then associated with looking at a red rose. This is a subjective experience that is unique to every individual both in itself, that is, in how vivid is the red color, for example, or in the associations that it evokes, such as a bouquet of red flowers on a happy anniversary. But *why* should these physical processes give rise to any subjective experience at all? One might assert that the physical and computational processes *are* the subjective experience, so one need not look any further; case closed.

This view, known as the identity theory of consciousness, is held by many scientists. It is a purely materialistic theory – that everything is eventually explained by physics, chemistry, and neuronal computation. But this merely denies the question and does not answer it, namely, why do these purely physical processes give rise to something that is subjective, that is, nonmaterial, purely in the mind? Even if the neural correlates of all the distinct aspects of consciousness are identified, there still remains the question of how are they all combined in the unity of conscious experiences in each individual, and why are they unique to every individual? According to the American philosophy professor Alva Noë: "The idea that consciousness is a phenomenon of the brain, the way digestion is a phenomenon of the stomach, is as fantastic as the idea of a self-playing orchestra."[7] The musical instruments of an orchestra do produce the musical sounds, but the instruments are played by musicians – people outside the instruments – and the music is written by a composer; the instruments do not make the music by themselves. Noë recapitulates the quest to understand consciousness thus: "After decades of concerted effort on the part of neuroscientists, psychologists, and philosophers, only one proposition about how the brain makes us conscious – how it gives rise to sensation, feeling, subjectivity – has emerged unchallenged: we don't have a clue."[8]

The foregoing example on consciousness serves to illustrate that "science can give us the 'know-how' but it cannot give us the 'know-*why*'."[9] In all fairness, however, this statement should be qualified by applying it to present-day science, as it might well be that science in the future will be able somehow to provide at least some know-why. The characterization of present-day science is pursued in the following section.

Before ending this discussion on consciousness, it should be noted that there is also a practical aspect to the understanding of consciousness. There has been a lot of hype over the years, particularly in recent times, concerning the creation of supremely intelligent, god-like machines, or robots, having their own will, needs, and desires and which are able to exercise their own independent control over human affairs (which is reminiscent of animism, discussed in Chapter 1). Those who muse about such machines must not forget that in order for these machines to become a reality they must have human-like consciousness. This cannot happen before the nature of consciousness is understood, and it becomes possible somehow to instill this consciousness in machines. This is not only well beyond reach at present, but to add insult to injury, nobody has any viable ideas on how to go about it.

What Present-Day Science Is About

Physics is considered to be one of the most fundamental scientific disciplines, if not the most fundamental, as it studies matter – its composition and motion in space and time – energy and forces in their various forms, such as kinetic, gravitational, electric, magnetic, nuclear, etc., and their interactions with matter. Physics has a solid empirical foundation, that is, a foundation that relies on observation and experiment. What physicists say about physics is generally applicable to science in general in its most solid form.

A distinguished American theoretical physicist, John Wheeler, postulated three eras of physics.[10] Era I physics is that from earliest times to that of the Italian scholar Galileo Galilei who lived in the 16th and 17th centuries CE.

During this era natural phenomena were described, such as the attraction or repulsion between objects that were rubbed together, but without formulating the laws obeyed. Galileo made major contributions in the fields of physics, astronomy, cosmology, mathematics, and philosophy. He has been dubbed "the father of modern science" because he espoused the notion that experiment should be the only criterion for judgement in science, and not intuition or apparently obvious conclusions, or dictates by any authority. In discussing motion, Galileo stated in his book, *Dialogues Concerning Two New Sciences*, which appeared in 1638: "Imagine any particle projected along a horizontal plane without friction; then we know, from what has been more fully explained in the preceding pages, that this particle will move along this same plane with a motion which is uniform and perpetual, provided the plane has no limits."[11] This was in contradiction to the assertion by Aristotle, generally accepted at the time, that objects not acted upon by some force will come to rest. But Galileo did not propose any laws that govern the motion of objects. Galileo also asserted, although he might not have been the first to do so, that in the absence of air resistance, heavy objects will fall at the same rate as light objects.

In the year Galileo died, 1642, Isaac Newton was born in England. Newton is a towering figure in science, and is recognized as one of the most influential scientists of all time, with contributions in many fields, including mathematics, physics, astronomy, and theology. What concerns us here are his ideas about motion. He generalized and made more precise Galileo's insight about an object continuing to move horizontally at a constant rate when not subjected to an external force. This generalization was formally presented in Newton's book *Principia*

Mathematica Philosophiae Naturalis[12] in 1687 and became known as Newton's First Law of Motion, which is stated as: "Every object will remain at rest or in uniform motion in a straight line unless compelled to change its state by the action of an external force."[13] Newton, however, went much further. Inspired by a falling apple, according to legend, Newton realized that the apple's velocity increased as it fell, that is, its motion accelerated. In line with the first law, this required a force, which was nevertheless invisible. This contrasted sharply with Aristotle's view that objects fell because they were naturally attracted to earth, the center of the cosmos; no force was involved. Galileo did not challenge this view. On the other hand, not only did Newton postulate a force of gravity, based on knowledge accumulated hitherto, he argued in his aforementioned *Principia* that since heavy and light objects fall at the same rate, that is, they have the same acceleration, the force F must be directly proportional to the mass m, that is $F = ma$, where a is the acceleration. This became known as Newton's Second Law of Motion. Newton further proposed in his *Principia* what became known as Newton's Universal Law of Gravitation, because it applied to all objects, from apples to planets. According to this law, every object attracts every other object with a gravitational force that is directly proportional to the product of their masses and inversely proportional to the square of the distance between their centers. This is in fact an inverse square law of force, which means that if the distance between the centers of the two objects is doubled, the force between them is reduced to one quarter. Newton verified the laws he formulated by applying them to the motion of the planets, such as that described early in the 17th century CE by the brilliant German astronomer, Johannes Kepler. Newton found that he could reproduce the astronomical data using his equations.

Newton's work on motion and gravity was a monumental achievement whereby he went beyond a mere description of motion to formulating laws that governed the natural phenomena observed. Newton's work heralded what Wheeler has described as Era II physics, which continues to the present, and which is characterized by the formulation of laws that govern natural phenomena but without *explaining the meaning* – again the *why* – of these laws. It was sufficient that the laws made the correct predictions. When challenged to explain how his force of gravity could exert its influence through empty space, Newton's answer was *Hypotheses non fingo* (I make no hypotheses), which appeared in an essay appended to the 2nd edition (1713) of the *Principia*. This was a very telling response that is also embodied in a profound observation attributed to Niels Bohr, the distinguished Danish physicist who made foundational contributions to the theory of atomic structure and to quantum theory in the early 20th century CE. According to Bohr, "It is wrong to think that the task of physics is to find out how nature *is*. Physics concerns what we can say about nature."[14] This agrees with Wheeler's description of Era II Physics as not explaining the meaning of physical laws; explaining this meaning is tantamount to finding out how Nature is, that is, understanding and explaining Nature.

Explanations about how gravity acted were put forward since Newton's time. One was the concept of a field, which was first elaborated by the Scottish scientist James Clerk Maxwell in the 1860s and early 1870s in connection with his seminal work on electromagnetism, and was extended in the late 1920s to quantum fields. The concept of a field encompasses not only the gravitational field but also the electromagnetic field, which includes electric and magnetic fields. The field came to be regarded as a physical entity that carries energy and momenta across space. But how does it do that? And *why* do the phenomena associated with the field, whether gravitational or electromagnetic, act in this way and in no other?

Newton's laws of motion and gravity reigned supreme for more than two hundred years and formed the foundation of what became known as classical mechanics. But they were not absolute. For example, it was noted that the motion of planet Mercury deviated slightly from the predictions of Newton's laws. These deviations were later accounted for by the general theory of relativity, or general relativity, enunciated by Einstein in 1915. According to general relativity, gravity is a warping, or deformation, of space-time. The effect is analogous to a heavy object denting a tarpaulin on which it is placed, as in a trampoline. A less massive object on the tarpaulin will be attracted to the more massive object and will move toward it because of the deformation of the tarpaulin fabric by the larger object. But what is space-time? It is a conceptual model that combines the single dimension of time with the three dimensions of space to give a four-dimensional space-time. But how does this abstraction act like a tarpaulin fabric that is dented by a physical object? General relativity has explained phenomena at the cosmic level that could not be explained by classical physics. In terms of Bohr's observation, general relativity is a description of what Einstein has to say about gravity, but it does not explain *why* gravity acts in this and no other way.

Classical physics, including classical mechanics, failed at the atomic level and was supplanted at this level by quantum theory early in the 20th century CE. Quantum field theory explains gravitational attraction in terms of virtual particles that form for extremely short periods of time and then disappear again, even in a perfect vacuum.[15] However, the reality of these virtual particles remains controversial.[16]

Einstein was an early contributor to quantum theory and applied it in 1905 to derive the laws that govern the photoelectric effect, which is the emission of electrons from a material exposed to electromagnetic radiation such as light. Einstein was awarded the Nobel Prize in Physics in 1921 for his discovery of the law of the photoelectric effect and for his contributions to theoretical physics. But Einstein was quite disturbed by the implications of quantum theory, particularly the most common Copenhagen interpretation championed by Niels Bohr and his associates. According to this interpretation, observation creates reality, that is, nothing is real until it is observed (at least for isolated objects in the microscopic realm). "I like to think the moon is there even if I am not looking at it,"[17] Einstein is quoted as saying. Einstein believed in an objective reality that exists independently of any act of perception. But no matter how hard he tried to dispute the correctness or completeness of quantum theory he was unsuccessful. The predictions of quantum theory have always been correct no matter how weird they seemed.

In the spirit of the ultimate goal of science, Einstein sought to understand Nature: "I want to know how God created this world. I am not interested in this or that phenomenon, in the spectrum of this or that element. I want to know His thoughts; the rest are details."[18] According to Wheeler, Era III physics is the meaning physics, or the recognition physics which deciphers physical law that is, understands and explains the *why* of physical phenomena. But Era III physics in Wheeler's view is yet to come. It is still beyond present-day physics.

Both Bohr and Einstein were in a sense right about

physics, and implicitly science in general. Bohr was really talking about present-day physics, Era II physics that describes what we can say about Nature but does not explain it. Einstein was thinking of Era III physics, whose ultimate goal is to understand and explain Nature.

Scientific Theories Are Fragmented

The behavior of objects in the physical world is governed by three sets of laws depending on scale. At the microscopic level, quantum mechanics, based on quantum theory, reigns supreme. Its predictions that can be verified experimentally have been verified. At the cosmic scale general relativity reigns supreme. Again, its predictions that can be verified experimentally have been verified. At the ordinary macroscopic scale in between, the motion of objects such as projectiles, billiard balls, and falling apples, can be described by classical mechanics to a high degree of accuracy.

The three sets of laws appear very different. Classical mechanics is deterministic, that is, starting from the given state of an object, its future states can, at least in principle, be completely determined by the forces acting on it. Quantum mechanics, according to the Copenhagen interpretation, is intrinsically probabilistic. It deals only with the probability of finding a particle at a particular location; the actual location is determined only when the particle is observed. General relativity deals with space-time. As Wheeler put it, "Space acts on matter, telling it how to move. In turn matter reacts back on space, telling it how to curve."[19] However, general relativity is not considered complete, for it cannot adequately describe the gravitational field inside a black hole, for example (see Chapter 4, Section "Miraculous Revelations, Item 1. Pulsars"). But as all material objects have the same constituents, one would expect the same set of laws to apply at all scales. Physicists have been trying hard to reconcile quantum mechanics and general relativity but with no definitive results so far.

In both general relativity and quantum theory, the implications can lead to paradoxes in thought experiments. In the twin paradox of relativity,[20] for example, one of two twins travels into space in a rocket at near the speed of light and returns to earth to find that his twin who remained on earth has aged more because of time dilation in the fast-moving rocket. That is, a clock on the fast-moving rocket will run slower than a clock on earth, so that if the clock on the rocket registers one year for the trip, for example, the clock on earth would register ten years or more. Time dilation has actually been verified experimentally. If one travels at the speed of light, which is physically impossible, time would come to a standstill – the present becomes eternal.

Erwin Schrödinger was a renowned Austrian physicist who made major contributions to quantum mechanics. He derived the equation that bears his name and which constitutes the equation of motion in quantum mechanics. Even then, he realized the absurdities it can lead to. In a thought experiment, referred to as Schrödinger's cat paradox,[21] a cat is in a box with a bottle of poisonous gas that has a certain probability of being opened, depending on some random effect inside the box. Schrödinger envisaged a very small amount of a radioactive substance that during the course of the experiment might have one of its atoms decay or might not. If the decay occurs, it is detected by a Geiger counter inside the box, which will then open the bottle of poisonous gas. According to the conventional interpretation of quantum theory, until the box is opened, the cat is in a state that is the superposition of the two possibilities; that is, the cat is *both dead and alive* until the box is opened and the cat is observed. According to conventional wisdom, something can be either dead or alive, or euphemistically as neither dead nor alive, but how can it be both dead and alive at the same time? This example also illustrates that reality, which in this case is the cat being alive or dead, is created by observation. Most physicists are not at all bothered by the philosophical implications and subtleties of physical theories. It is sufficient for them that the theory works, that is, it can be applied to particular problems to give the correct answers. As John Polkinghorne, the English theoretical physicist, remarked, "Your average quantum mechanic is about as philosophically minded as your average garage mechanic."[22]

Unifying seemingly disparate phenomena under one umbrella is a beautiful and satisfying achievement in science. In his theory of electromagnetism Maxwell brought together electricity, magnetism, and light as different aspects of the same phenomenon, that of electromagnetism. The electromagnetic spectrum, predicted by Maxwell's equations, has since been shown to extend from very-low-frequency radio waves, having a wavelength of more than 10^8 meters to gamma rays having a wavelength of less than 10^{-12} meters. For more than twenty years at the end of his career Einstein tried to unify the theory of general relativity with the theory of electromagnetism, to no avail. There have been ongoing attempts to unify gravitational and electromagnetic interactions with two other interactions at the atomic level: (i) the weak interaction that underlies some types of radioactivity, and (ii) the strong interaction that binds together particles in the nucleus of an atom. These two interactions exert their influence only over subatomic distances, but together with gravitational and electromagnetic interactions constitute the four fundamental interactions or forces known to exist in nature. The unification of these four types of interaction has proved elusive so far.

Even more elusive at present is the task of combining consciousness with quantum theory, prompted by the need for a conscious observer exercising free choice to resolve the outcome of a quantum experiment, according to the conventional interpretation of quantum theory. Stanford University physicist Andrei Linde wonders: "Will it not turn out, with further development of science, that the study of the universe and the study of consciousness be inseparably linked, and that ultimate progress in the one will be impossible without progress in the other?... Will the next important step be the development of a unified approach to our entire world, including the world of consciousness?"[23] Chalmers does not believe that a reductive explanation of consciousness is possible, that is, conscious experience cannot be expressed in terms of something simpler. He proposes instead that subjective experience be considered a fundamental entity, alongside mass, charge, and space-time, and that this can then lead to new fundamental laws, which would be embodied in what he refers to as psychophysics.[24]

What Present-Day Science Does Not Know

Based on observations published by the American astronomer Edwin Hubble in 1929, it was concluded that the universe was not static but was in fact expanding, that is, galaxies appeared to be moving outward making the universe larger and larger. In 1931 Georges Lemaître, a Belgian physicist and Roman Catholic priest, proposed that the expansion of the universe, if projected back in time, meant that at some finite time in the past (which was later estimated to be about 14×10^9 years ago) the universe was concentrated into an extremely dense and extremely hot point that underwent a tremendous expansion, which subsequently was referred to as the big bang. As the universe expanded, it cooled enough for subatomic particles to combine to form the atoms of the lighter elements, then heavier atoms, and eventually celestial bodies and galaxies (see Chapter 4, Section "Miraculous Revelations, Item 1. Pulsars", and "Item 4. Origin of the Universe"). Additional observations led in the 1960s to a general acceptance of the big bang theory of the origin of the universe.[25] But how did this point universe originate, what was there before it, and what caused it to expand remains conjectural.

A big bang expansion from a tiny thing would explain an expanding universe, as any expanding matter will fly outwards. The expansion would also be expected to slow down under the influence of the gravitational forces between the galaxies. However, in 1998 and 1999, two teams of astronomers concluded from their observations on supernovae (explosions of massive stars, see Chapter 4, Section "Miraculous Revelations, Item 1. Pulsars") that the expansion is not slowing but is in fact accelerating. To explain this surprising finding, it was proposed that a repulsive force is generated somehow in what had hitherto been considered as empty space. This repulsive force was ascribed to a dark energy, where the adjective dark denotes something mysterious or unknown.

To complicate matters further, it would be expected based on physical laws that a star orbiting around the center of a galaxy, which contains a high concentration of mass in the form of stars, would experience two forces that balance one another: a gravitational pull toward the center of the galaxy, and a centrifugal force that tends to make the orbiting star fly outwards because of the rotary motion. This is the force in a spin dryer, for example, that throws the clothes against the spinning, perforated drum of the dryer and that drives water out of the clothes through the perforations in the drum. This centrifugal force decreases with decreasing speed of rotation, whereas the gravitational pull decreases with increasing distance from the center of the galaxy. The orbiting speed of the star should therefore decrease with the distance from the center of the galaxy, if the star is to remain in orbit under the influence of the gravitational pull and not fly away from the galaxy because of a high orbiting speed. Yet, the orbiting speed of a star was observed to be more or less the same regardless of its location in the galactic disc. This led to postulating a gravitational effect due to some dark matter in the outer regions of galaxies and their surroundings, thereby increasing the speeds of stars located further out from the center of the galaxy. This would also explain the distortion and magnification of light that is sometimes observed as it travels in the vicinity of a galaxy and which can only be ascribed to the gravitational effect of massive clouds of dark matter. Although dark matter exerts a gravitational attraction, it does not emit, absorb, or reflect electromagnetic radiation, including light, which makes it almost impossible to detect, and therefore dark. The great surprise was when estimates were made of the amount of dark energy and dark matter that would account for the observations. It turned out that the mass-energy of the universe consists of about 70% dark energy, about 25% dark matter, leaving about 5% for *all* the observed mass and energy of the universe, including Earth and all life on it.

This is really astounding when you come to think of it. It means that present-day science for all its glory is concerned with a mere 5% or so of physical reality in terms of matter and energy that have been postulated, and offers no generally accepted view of the remaining 95% percent. Dark energy and dark matter might not even exist; there may be alternative explanations for the observed anomalies. Even then, it would be some solace if present-day science could explain everything there is to know about the 5%, but sadly this is not the case. So much is still unknown about us, human beings, and the tangible world around us, and many observed phenomena in this tangible world simply do not have a scientific explanation. A fundamental question, for example, is what is life? Many definitions have been given in terms of structure, function, and operation, such as living matter is composed of cells and is characterized by metabolism, homeostasis, growth, a life cycle, reproduction, response and adaptation to environment, and evolution, without a general agreement on even such a purely descriptive definition. But what is the essence of life? If all the molecules of a cell are synthesized and assembled in place, will the cell spontaneously become alive? Would it be possible to bring a dead cell back to life somehow?

Leaving aside such knotty issues like life and consciousness, there is much that we still know little about. Consider the human brain, for example. It has been the subject of intense research and investigation for at least a century, and continues to be, with increasingly powerful tools being used to study its structure and operation such as electron microscopy in its various forms, functional magnetic resonance imaging (fMRI), calcium-ion imaging, electrophysiology, optogenetics, computer simulation, and mathematical modeling. A tremendous amount of knowledge has been accumulated about structures in the brain and the operation of its various constituents, but no coherent theory has yet emerged about brain functions. In fact, more is known about the cosmos and about subatomic structure than about the workings of the human brain. It is still not known, for example, exactly how movement is initiated and controlled by the brain, even though the end result, which is motion, is amenable to precise measurement of force, trajectory, velocity, etc. In contrast, cognition and perception are more elusive functions still, because their end effects are much harder to measure and quantify. Our everyday behavior is based on our memory of past experiences, activities, or events, and of acquired knowledge and skills. However, our knowledge of exactly how memories are formed in the brain, where and how they are stored, and how they are retrieved is quite sketchy at best.

It has long been assumed that memory is stored by some changes in the brain, referred to as memory traces or engrams. Yet, all attempts at definitive identification and localization of these memory traces have failed so far to give satisfactory and generally accepted results. Suggestions have ranged from specific types of macromolecules, to modifications of the connections or structure of synapses – the specialized endings of a nerve cell on other nerve cells – to reverberating neuronal circuits and neuronal assemblies. Working with rats, monkeys, and chimpanzees over a period of more than 30 years, the American neuropsychologist Karl Lashley attempted to locate the engrams for some specific types of learning, but without success. In a classical series of experiments, Lashley trained rats to run a maze. He then removed portions of their cerebral cortices and retested them to see if the memory of what they have learned was lost. To his surprise he found that no matter which part of the cortex he removed, the rats retained the memory, even with fairly massive removals, although the degree of impairment in maze performance increased with the amount of brain tissue removed.[26]

This suggested to the American neuroscientist Karl Pribram that memory was distributed in the brain and was of a holographic nature.[27] A hologram of a three-dimensional object is a two-dimensional recording, on a photosensitive plate or film, produced by a laser beam part of which is applied to the photosensitive medium and the other part is reflected by the object onto this medium. The two beams converging on the photosensitive medium interfere with one another producing an interference pattern that is recorded in the medium. When the same laser light used in the recording is shined on the recorded interference pattern a three-dimensional image of the object is reproduced. One can move around the image and view it from different angles, as with the real object. A remarkable property of the hologram is that a piece of the hologram can reproduce the image of the whole object, albeit with some blurring that increases as the size of the piece is reduced. This means that every part of the hologram contains information about the whole object, that is, the information about the object is distributed throughout the recording in a manner that allows any part of the recording to reproduce the image of the whole object. Technically, the holographic effect is due to a transformation from the spatial domain of the object to the frequency domain of the hologram, where the value of every point in the frequency domain is a function of the values of all points in the spatial domain, which means that a piece of the hologram (recorded in the medium in the frequency domain) contains information about the whole object (in the spatial domain). Pribram hypothesized that the holographic pattern arises from interference of the wavefronts due to electrical signals propagating along the fine branches of neurons in the brain, and that the brain performs the required transformations between the spatial and frequency domains. Although claimed to explain several aspects of memory, but in a general qualitative manner, this approach has not proved very fruitful. The search for the engram continues, as does the search for dark matter and dark energy.

Rupert Sheldrake, a one-time biologist at the University of Cambridge, has postulated the existence of morphic fields to explain some aspects of biological systems (see Chapter 6, Section "Maverick Views from Biology and Physics"). Memory according to Sheldrake is not in the brain at all but in the morphic field. Although such a field remains purely hypothetical, it is nevertheless an external agency that is being invoked to explain phenomena whose explanation has hitherto been confined, by conventional wisdom, to factors or elements within the organism itself, not outside of it. Bringing into play external factors is a whole new ball game that entails a radical paradigm shift.

Historically, it has been customary, for understandable reasons, to try to explain brain function mechanistically by analogy to prevailing technologies of the time. In the 17th century CE, the French philosopher, mathematician, and scientist René Descartes conceived of the nervous system as a hydraulic system. Animal spirits would flow from the ventricles of the brain through hollow tubes – the nerves – to muscles, filling them up and causing muscular contraction. After telephone exchanges became operative in the late 19th century CE, the brain was considered to act as a telephone switchboard that switches connections between incoming and outgoing pathways. With the advent of computers, the brain was likened to a computer performing some complex computations. Movement is thought to be executed as a sequence of commands in a motor program, similar to the set of instructions in a computer program. With the invention of holography, the brain was considered in terms of a hologram, as previously mentioned. But the mystery of brain function persists despite monumental efforts.

Another mystery is that of morphogenesis, that is, the development of form and structure during embryonic growth. How structure and form of the embryo become increasingly complex as the embryo develops is still an unsolved mystery. Genes code for proteins to be synthesized in a now well understood manner. During morphogenesis, cells differentiate, so that some cells become skin cells, for example, whereas other cells may become muscle cells or nerve cells. Different genes are expressed, that is, become active, in these different types of cells. But what directs this process? What directs the formation of whole organs, like the brain, or the heart, or the stomach? And what directs the form of a developing limb to be that of an arm or a leg, in the right position compared to other body parts, and as the mirror image of its counterpart on the other side of the body? Are the instructions for structure and form also coded in the genome? Materialists say: "Yes, but in a manner that is still undiscovered but certain to be discovered in the future." At least for now, this is clearly a matter of faith, not fact. This kind of assertion can be considered a case of counterfactual definiteness, that is, asserting the certainty of something that has not been proved for a fact. Counterfactual definiteness is inadmissible in the conventional interpretation of quantum theory,[28] or indeed science in general.

Another mystery of living organisms is that of regeneration of a lost limb or appendage, for example. It is well-known, for instance, that crayfish can regenerate lost legs or claws, and salamanders can regenerate entire limbs or tails. The most amazing feat of regeneration is found in planarian flatworms. If cut into pieces, each piece can regenerate into a complete organism.[29] This means that each piece has the blueprint for regeneration of the complete organism and can produce the required material. How is the wholeness of the organism encoded in each of its parts? This is again reminiscent of holography.

The great technical achievement of the Human Genome Project raised some troubling issues. For one thing, the number of human genes is estimated to be less than 25,000 – much less than the expected 100,000 or so genes. A sea urchin is reported to have about 23,300 genes.[30] The chimpanzee genome is so similar to the human genome that it is difficult, on the basis of the genome, to explain why we are so different from chimpanzees. It has also proved unexpectedly difficult to identify the genetic components of common traits, such as tallness, and diseases – the so-called missing heritability problem,[31] the fact that single genetic variations cannot account for much of the heritability of diseases, behaviors, and other phenotypes, that is, observable traits.

It is almost a truism that the more we know the more we become aware that there is a lot more that we do not know. To paraphrase Wheeler,[32] our knowledge is like an island surrounded by a sea of ignorance. As our island grows, so does our awareness of our ignorance (the perimeter of the island).

Generally Accepted Scientific Theories Are Not Absolute

It is to the credit of science that it is not dogmatic in the face of new evidence or knowledge. It does highlight the fact, however, that no scientific theory is final, but is subject to change or even rejection, despite a consensus of scientists about it at the time. In other words, science is, by its nature, a work in progress. The following two examples illustrate theories that were pervasive for at least two hundred years, and were accepted by prominent scientists of the time, up till early in the 20th century CE.

The first is Newtonian mechanics, which was unchallenged throughout the 18th and 19th centuries CE. It was universally accepted and greatly influenced scientific and even philosophical thinking. What lent more credence to Newtonian mechanics is that it provided a Universal Law of Gravitation that applied equally to gravitational phenomena on earth and to the motion of celestial bodies. Although some anomalies were noted, such as Mercury's orbit as mentioned earlier, these were considered minor and amenable to eventual explanation within the framework of Newtonian mechanics. Early in the 20th century CE Newtonian mechanics was shown to be an approximation to be superseded by general relativity on the cosmic scale and by quantum mechanics on the atomic scale, both of which were radically different from Newtonian mechanics in their theoretical foundations, as mentioned earlier.

The second example is that of the ether. Although the term was used in Greek and medieval times to denote a substance that was supposed to fill the whole world outside Earth, it was given a special meaning by Descartes in 1644 in order to explain action at a distance such as that between magnetized bodies or tidal motion due mainly to the Moon, and to a lesser extent, the Sun. He postulated an ether consisting of a whirlpool of rotating chains of particles that pervades all space and matter and which transmits actions between bodies that were not in direct contact. Newton in his early attempts to explain gravity invoked an ether that continually flowed downward toward the earth's surface because of an ether density gradient.

He also invoked an ether in explaining the radiation of heat and the propagation of light, which he considered to be corpuscular, that is made of tiny particles. More than two hundred years later, the concept of an ether was still pervasive. In his early work on electromagnetism Maxwell used the concept of lines of force that was introduced by the English scientist Michael Faraday to explain the forces exerted by electric charges and magnetic poles. Maxwell envisaged these lines of force being partly made of ether and partly made of ordinary matter. He believed that the propagation of light through empty space required a luminiferous aether (that is, a light-bearing ether), which also had to be stationary and form an absolute and unique frame of reference for his equations of electromagnetism. Although the theory of the ether was deeply entrenched for about two-and-a-half centuries, it was abandoned early in the 20th century CE as the postulated properties of this ether became increasingly untenable. Ether had to be fluid enough to fill the smallest space yet have a high rigidity like a solid in order to support the propagation of the high frequencies of light. It was transparent, did not disperse light, had no mass or viscosity, and was incompressible. Even in the face of experimental observations that did not support its existence, ether was strongly defended by some prominent scientists such as the English scientist Lord Rayleigh and the Dutch physicist Hendrik Lorentz whose famous transformation equations were later shown by Einstein to be in accordance with his theory of special relativity. But according to this theory, advanced by Einstein in 1905, ether was not required for the propagation of electromagnetic waves through space in accordance with Maxwell's equations.

Although the concept of ether was abandoned, empty space still has to have some physical properties according to theories that are generally accepted at present. Thus, according to general relativity, space-time is warped by gravity, which endows space with some physical properties, as mentioned earlier. According to quantum field theory, force is mediated by virtual particles that continually appear and disappear even in empty space, as mentioned earlier.

An idea may be ridiculed by scientists for a long time, before it becomes scientific. A good example is the postulate by ancient Greeks that disease can spread from a sick person to a healthy one by some invisible seeds of plague. That was considered ridiculous. How can any sane person believe that disease can spread by something intangible and invisible to the naked eye? It sounded more like sorcery. More than two thousand years later, in the 19th century CE, the germ theory of the cause of disease was accepted following the work of pioneers such as the German physician Robert Koch and the French chemist Louis Pasteur.

Are We Able to Understand It All?

A basic question is whether or not humans have the mental capacity to understand everything about Nature. Our physical senses, for example, are surpassed in some animals. The sense of smell is much stronger in dogs. Hawks and eagles have superior visual acuity; an eagle can spot a rabbit 3 km away. Birds not only perceive color but, unlike humans, can also perceive ultraviolet light. A rattlesnake can detect temperature changes of 0.003°C or less. Normally, humans can hear sounds in the range 20 Hz to 20,000 Hz. Mice can hear sounds at frequencies as high as 100,000 Hz, and elephants can hear sounds of lower frequencies than humans. Some animals have senses that humans don't have. Sharks and some fish can detect electric fields, and migratory birds can sense magnetic fields. Animals seem to be able to sense earthquakes well before humans. As for physical strength, chimpanzees, whose size is comparable to that of humans, are at least twice as strong on the average.

If our physical endowments are limited, why should our mental capacities be considered unlimited? The basic structure of the human brain is the same as that of the lowest vertebrates. It mainly grew in size and complexity of interconnections in higher vertebrates and mammals, culminating in the human brain having a cortex of about 16×10^9 nerve cells and the chance mutation that affected the brains of *Homo sapiens*, as noted in Chapter 1. The human brain endowed humans with imagination, abstract thinking, elaborate linguistic skills, exquisite manual dexterity and presumably a higher state of consciousness. But is this enough to enable humans to understand everything about Nature? Can the operation of the human brain be understood using the brain itself, or is something of a higher order of capacity required?

If human mental capacities are limited, then any science that humans are capable of producing will necessarily be of limited scope and incapable of unraveling all of Nature's mysteries. Yet, there is a general conviction particularly among scientists that science will eventually be able to figure it all out. That might be the case, but on the other hand it might not. It is an open question that cannot be settled with certainty either way, not the least scientifically, until it happens, if ever. To assert that science will be able to explain everything is a comforting thought but is not on solid grounds. This assertion is more a matter of faith, much like religious faith which most scientists reject as being unsubstantiated. It can be considered an example of counterfactual definiteness, which is inadmissible in the conventional interpretation of quantum theory, and science in general, as mentioned earlier. The assertion is mainly based on extrapolation of scientific achievement – which has unquestionably been great – into the vast unknown. However, extrapolation that does not have a solid foundation can be quite misleading, as illustrated by the following historical example.

In 1791, Luigi Galvani, an Italian doctor, Professor of Anatomy, and researcher, postulated the existence of animal electricity based on his investigation of the contraction of frogs legs when exposed to a source of electricity. His nephew, Giovanni Aldini, who was also his research assistant, was a bit of a showman. He travelled all over Europe demonstrating to the public how a fresh corpse could be made to jerk an arm or a leg upon application of a sufficiently high voltage – the familiar electric shock that people experience when they accidentally touch a conductor at the mains voltage, for example. Audiences were enthralled by these demonstrations. Here was a dead body moving its arm or leg under the influence of electricity; surely, it was only a matter of time, it was thought, before the dead body would be made to come back to life, that is, humans could be raised from the dead. People were extrapolating from what they could see with their own eyes to what they imagined could happen, but without knowledge of what is really involved in this extrapolation. It was of course wishful thinking that has not yet been realized and is unlikely to be realized in the foreseeable future. All sorts of similar extrapolations are currently being made about new forms of life to be produced in the laboratory, or about bringing back to life dead human bodies that have been kept at extremely low temperatures for this purpose, or about robots having human-like consciousness, as previously mentioned. Life cannot be created from inanimate objects, nor can be it restored after death until the nature of life is understood and the technology is available to apply this understanding. As in the case of consciousness and human-like robots, not only is this understanding beyond reach at present, but nobody really has any viable ideas on how to gain this understanding or how to apply it.

That our mental capacities may not be without limit should not of course stand in the way of our trying to understand everything about the universe. But to imply with some confidence that we will be able to do so smacks of a high degree of conceit.

Is It All a Matter of Chance?

It is popular among most scientists to ascribe matters to chance, such as chance encounters by atoms and molecules under appropriate conditions to produce life, chance mutations of genes, etc. This seems like a satisfying and convincing explanation, but is it? What is the nature of chance?

Let us consider a classical example of a chance event, the tossing of a coin. The probability of the outcome of any given trial being a head or a tail is considered to be 0.5. This means that in a large number (theoretically infinite) of trials, half the outcomes will be heads, the other half tails, ostensibly as a matter of chance. But is it possible in any given trial to determine with certainty whether the outcome is a head or a tail? The answer is yes in principle if all the factors affecting the outcome can be accounted for. These factors would include, for example, the angle at which the coin is initially placed over the thumb, the force with which it is tossed, the air resistance encountered, how the coin tumbles during its upward and downward motion, and how the coin is brought to rest. If all the factors affecting the outcome can be accounted for, the outcome is determined with certainty. In principle, this can be done, which means there is nothing *intrinsically chancy* about the outcome of tossing a coin.

Ascribing events to chance in such cases is not because chance is a fundamental mainspring of these events. Rather, it is essentially a means of avoiding having to consider influencing factors that are difficult to account for, or bypassing unknown factors altogether. A beautiful and extensive mathematical theory of probability has been developed for this purpose. This is the classical probability applied at the macroscopic scale. However, it may be argued that interactions at the atomic and subatomic scales are governed by quantum effects, in accordance with quantum theory. According to the Copenhagen interpretation, quantum theory is intrinsically probabilistic, unlike classical probability, as argued earlier. Einstein was troubled by this aspect of quantum theory, as expressed in his famous quotation, "God does not play dice."[18] But quantum theory currently has at least ten interpretations, not just the Copenhagen interpretation. In the interpretation of David Bohm, the renowned American theoretical physicist, the world is physically real and deterministic without intrinsic probability.[33] More will be said about Bohm's interpretation in Chapter 6, Section "Maverick Views from Biology and Physics". The criticism still holds, therefore, that relegating such matters as origin of life and mutation of genes to pure chance really reflects a lack of knowledge as to what the contributing factors might be and how they would exercise their effects. Moreover, ascribing such matters to chance has an air of finality that is almost anti-scientific in that it stifles the search for alternative explanations.

Where do We Go from Here?

In corroboration of the theme of this chapter it was argued that:

- Science only deals with a restricted range of physical phenomena that are observable and repeatable, leading to hypotheses that allow testable deductions and predictions, or falsification.
- Present-day science is about what we can say about Nature in the form of theories and laws. It does not explain the meaning of these laws, the *Why?*
- Present-day scientific theories are fragmented. They lack unity in many important respects. In this sense, they are incomplete.
- The theories and laws of present-day science have only dealt with a small fraction of presumed matter and energy in the universe.
- Scientific theories are never final but are subject to change or even rejection, although they may be embraced by almost all scientists for a very long time.
- Human mental capacities are not without limits, which severely constrain what science can achieve.

The pursuit of science is a very worthy endeavor. However, in view of the aforementioned limitations, present-day science cannot and should not be the beacon to guide one's life and shape one's philosophy of life, one's worldview, and one's conception of the meaning and purpose of our existence. The light of this science beacon is rather feeble and of limited reach, leaving an immense expanse of the unknown around it. However, science cannot and should not be ignored or simply swept aside. One would then be left in total darkness.

Once we appreciate the limitations of science, it becomes natural to look beyond science with an open mind. This is not depreciating science but more like using it as a springboard to what is beyond the scope and reach of present-day science. The supernatural should not be dismissed outright because it is not explainable by one's worldview, or as being too bizarre and unworthy of scientific minds. Repudiating the supernatural in the name of science is like a blind man denying the existence of what he cannot see.

However, in venturing beyond science into the supernatural one must not stumble into a realm of superstition, mindless dogmatism, stubborn denial, and anti-science. How can this be done? The question is addressed in the following chapters.

Chapter 3

What Is the Quran?

Theme: The Quran exhorts to exerting one's intellect and is inimitable in its language and style.

The chapter presents some characteristic features of the Quran that are relevant to our discussion on spirituality, namely, the language of the Quran, the authenticity of the Quranic text, the emphasis in the Quran on exercising one's intellect, and the Quran's linguistic and literary inimitability. This introduction on the Quran is a necessary prelude to the discussion of Chapter 4 on the Divine origin of the Quran as evidence for the existence of The Almighty, which is the major step in building up the case for the advocated spirituality (see "Translation of Quranic Text" in Conventions for the use of "The Almighty" in other than verses of the Quran).

Language

The Quran was revealed to the Prophet Muhammad through the angel Gabriel at intervals over a period of 23 years, starting in 609 CE when The Prophet was 40 years old and culminating in 632 CE, the year of his death. The Quran was revealed in Arabic, a rich, root-based, structured language having an elaborate syntax and word derivation.[1] In the words of the prominent Orientalist, Edward A. van Dyck: "The Arabic language is one of the finest languages of our globe, and this in two respects; first as regards the richness of its vocabulary; and second as regards the fullness of its literature."[2]

Two peculiarities of Arabic are important in the context

of the Quranic text. One is that Arabic is a highly expressive language that can convey very precise meaning. This is because: (i) Arabic allows a relatively large number of derivatives from a root, each derivative having a different shade of meaning, and (ii) what was of special relevance for the Arabs could be described by a large number of words, each word referring to a particular attribute or state. A sword, for example, is said to have more than one thousand descriptive words[3] that could be an indication of whether the sword is wide or narrow, or how well polished, or how sharp, or where it was made. The second peculiarity of Arabic is that most words in classical Arabic have quite a number of different meanings. The noun *ʿayn*, for example, has more than forty-seven meanings;[4] the ones commonly used are: "eye" and a "water spring". A root or its derivatives can have a number of meanings as a noun or as a verb depending on the diacritical vowel marks used. For example, the three-letter root *f-l-k* can be read as *fulk*, meaning an ark or ship, or as *falak*, meaning the orbit of a celestial body. In the Quranic text the meaning of such words is generally unequivocal, based on the context. But there are cases where different meanings are valid. For example, the verb *kafata* has several meanings:[5] (i) "to bring together", (ii) "to draw things toward self", and (iii) "to move swiftly", among other meanings. The Quranic verse: **"Did we not make the Earth *kifāta*..."** (77:25) can be interpreted as referring to: (i) the earth being a homestead,[6] or (ii) the gravitational pull of the earth,[7] or (iii) the motion of the earth in space.[7] According to author Paola Garcia: "In Arabic, each word has multiple layers of meaning and depth, often irreducible to their English or other European (purported) equivalences."[8]

Apart from the meaning of individual words, there are verses whose meaning was not clear at the time of the

Prophet Muhammad but which was clarified by scientific knowledge in modern times. Examples of these verses are given in Chapter 4, Section “Miraculous Revelations”. It is noteworthy that there are still many verses in the Quran whose meaning is not yet understood in the light of present knowledge. For all the aforementioned reasons, the only Quranic text that is officially recognized by Islamic authorities all over the world is the original Arabic text. No translation of the Quran to any language is recognized as official, because a translation only reflects the meaning of verses as understood by the translator.

Authenticity[9,10,11,12]

It is widely believed, though disputed by some, that the Prophet Muhammad could not himself read or write, lest he be accused of writing the Quran with his own hands, as the Quran says is true of other scriptures ((2:75), (2:79), and (4:46)). As soon as he received a revelation, the Prophet recited it to his attendant Companions (close followers who were frequently in his company), and it was recorded right away by scribes on material customarily used at the time, such as parchment, leather, palm stems, camels’ scapulae, wooden tablets, and soft stone. It should be noted that poetry was highly exalted in the Arabian Peninsula at the time (see the Section, “Linguistic and Literary Inimitability” later in this chapter), and Arabs generally had prodigious memories that allowed an individual to commit thousands of verses to memory, as most Arabs did not read or write. The Prophet himself and a large number of his Companions and those around them memorized the hitherto revealed verses of the Quran and would recite them often, particularly in prayers and during the holy month of Ramadan. The gradual revelation of the Quran over a period of twenty-three years no doubt facilitated its commitment to memory. Even today, the 6236 numbered verses of the Quran can be recited from memory by at least many hundreds of Muslims. Professional reciters regularly recite memorized verses from the Quran on radio, television, during prayers, or in special events such as mourning. The Quran itself claims to have been made easy to remember: **"And indeed We have made the Quran easy to remember; so is there any who will be mindful?"** (54:17) This is undoubtedly due to the poetic rhyme of many passages, as well as the choice of words and the way they are strung together in verses, but leaves open the possibility of other presently unknown ways.

At the time of the Prophet's death the entire Quran was memorized by at least a few thousand Companions and followers. The arrangement of the Quran in 114 chapters and the arrangement of verses in each chapter was not chronological, according to the time of revelation, but was directed by the Prophet himself under Divine guidance, as stated in one of the earliest revelations: **"Surely on Us rests the collecting of it and the reciting of it."** (75:17) The word *jam'* in the verse in Arabic implies both collection and arrangement. Indeed, the fact that the Prophet, his Companions, and other devout Muslims memorized the Quran and recited it frequently means that the verses of the Quran followed a definite and settled order from the time of the Prophet. Otherwise, it would be inconceivable for the Prophet to recite the verses in a certain order and for others to follow a different order. It should be emphasized that the arrangement of Quranic verses and the division of the Quran into chapters are most relevant to the numerical relations that will be discussed in the following chapter.

Although it was memorized in its entirety in a definite order, the entire Quran was also written, but only portions of it existed in any one place. Indeed, it would not have been possible to have a final and complete collection of the Quran in written form while the Prophet lived, because he continued to have revelations till the year of his death, and revealed verses were to be inserted, upon his instructions, in different locations between verses already revealed. Within six months of the Prophet's death, the first Caliph, Abū Bakr al-Ṣiddīq, who ruled for about two years and died in 634 CE, ordered the collection of the entire written Quran. This was in order to have a more permanent record than in human memory and to have a reference that facilitated circulation and consultation of the Quran. Abū Bakr entrusted one of the Companions, Zayd ibn Thābit, with the task, because Zayd had scribed most of the Quran during the last ten years of the Prophet's life. Zayd was most scrupulous. He collected only those writings that were a direct, not through hearsay, recording by the scribe of what was actually uttered by the Prophet. That the recording of the scribe was direct had to be confirmed by two witnesses. The written text from any one scribe corroborated the text from other scribes and what he and other Companions had committed to memory. It should be noted that Zayd was not asked to simply make a compilation of the Quran, which he could have done by getting a few reciters together, write down what they dictated and have it approved by the Companions. Zayd had to gather *original* writings of what the Prophet had in fact uttered, and in the presence of witnesses. This ensured a high degree of accuracy and is an indication of the extreme meticulousness and scrupulousness with which the Quranic text was treated. There can be no doubt that the collection of the Quran under Zayd's supervision had exactly the same wording and ordering of verses and chapters as in the time of the Prophet. This collection, or codex, of the Quran, remained in the custody of Abū Bakr and was transferred after his death to the custody of the second Caliph, ʿUmar ibn al-Khaṭṭāb.

During the rule of ʿUmar, which lasted nearly ten years until his death in 644 CE, Islam spread widely to neighboring lands and was embraced by people whose native language was not Arabic. Some differences in the reading of certain words in the Quran had been allowed by the Prophet because some Arab tribes spoke a dialect that was slightly different from that of Quraysh, the Prophet's tribe in whose dialect the Quran was revealed. These tribes could not pronounce certain words in the same manner as Quraysh, so they were allowed by the Prophet to pronounce them differently, but the meaning was the same. With the spread of Islam to non-Arabs, differences in reading became more common. It was feared that such differences if allowed to continue would appear in unofficial copies of the Quran and would eventually become serious enough to pose a threat to the integrity of the Quranic text. When this matter was brought to the attention of the third Caliph, ʿUthmān ibn ʿAffān, who ruled from 644 CE to 656 CE, he was prompted to take action. He requested a group of scribes, including the same scribe, Zayd ibn Thābit, who was entrusted by Abū Bakr to prepare the first codex of the Quran, to make copies of the Quran that were sent to the provincial capitals of the newly conquered lands. This now became the official codex of the Quran. ʿUthmān ordered that all other collections be destroyed so that the Quran could only be written and read in the dialect of Quraysh. In this way, the purity and integrity of the Quranic text, including its arrangement of verses and chapters, was conclusively assured to be the same as in the time of the Prophet Muhammad.

This, however, was not the end of the matter, because

the Quran was still written without diacritical and punctuation marks. Non-Arab Muslims, and even Arabs who were not as well versed in Arabic as the inhabitants of the Arabian Peninsula at the time of the Prophet, incorrectly read some words in the Quran, which changed the meaning of the verse involved. During the rule of the Umayyad caliph, ʿAbd al-Malik ibn Marwān, from 685 CE to 705 CE, the governor of Iraq, al-Ḥajjāj ibn Yūsuf, commissioned a select group of prominent reciters, scribes, and grammarians to add diacritical marks and text separators so as to facilitate the reading of the Quran.[13] Except for some additional diacritical and punctuation marks as well as a more readable calligraphy, this Quranic text, which dates from the beginning of the 8th century CE, is essentially the same Quranic text that is at present officially adopted by Islamic authorities all over the world.

It is evident from the preceding that there can be no doubt that the Quranic text, in wording and arrangement, is exactly the same as in the time of the Prophet Muhammad. The Quran itself assures:

It is certainly We Who have revealed the Reminder (the Quran), and surely We are its Preserver. (15:9)

The verse is considered an affirmation by The Almighty that He will protect the Quran from any alterations, additions, or corruption. English author Reginald Bosworth Smith states: "In the Qur'an, we have beyond all reasonable doubt, the exact words of Mohammad without subtraction and without addition."[14] According to Stanley Lane-Poole, the 19th century CE British Orientalist: "It is an immense merit in the Ḳur-án that there is no doubt as to its genuineness. The 'Word of the Lord' came to

Moḥammad, and he uttered it, and the people wrote it down or committed it to memory; and that very word we can now read with full confidence that it has remained unchanged through nearly thirteen hundred years."[15] Sir William Muir, the 19th century CE Scottish Orientalist and an avowed critic of Islam, declares: "Contending and embittered factions, taking their rise in the murder of ʿOthmān (the third Caliph, ʿUthmān ibn ʿAffān) himself within a quarter of a century from the death of Moḥammad have ever since rent the Moḥammadan world. Yet but ONE ḲOR'ĀN has been current amongst them; and the consentaneous use by all of the same Scripture in every age to the present day is an irrefragable proof that we have now before us the very text prepared by the command of the unfortunate Caliph. There is probably in the world no other book which has remained twelve centuries with so pure a text. The various readings are wonderfully few in number, chiefly confined indeed to differences in the vowel points and diacritical signs. But these, invented at a later date, can hardly be said to affect the text of ʿOthmān."[16]

Muir makes an important point. Despite bitter enmity between various Islamic factions over the years, the contentions were all about interpretations of some of the Quranic text, not about the text itself. This can be ascribed to the uncontestable preservation of the Quranic text from the time of the Prophet till the time of the third Caliph, ʿUthmān, and its subsequent finalization in form at the beginning of the 8th century CE.

It should be explained that although the skeletal form (*rasm*) of the Quranic text was the same, some differences in the reading of words arose later on, such as those involving diacritical symbols for extended vowel sounds, that led to differences in meaning as interpreted by different schools of Islamic jurisprudence. Even today, there are different schools for the recitation of the Quran, according to which some words are pronounced differently but without change in the meaning.

Resort to Rational Thinking

A most important and distinguishing characteristic of the Quran is its exhortation to resort to reason, judgement, knowledge, evidence, and contemplation in appreciation of the signs and wonders of The Almighty. Some illustrative verses will be cited in what follows by way of example.

1. **Truly in the creation of the heavens and the Earth and the variation of the night and the day are signs for the possessors of intellect.** (3:190)
2. **And among His Signs is the creation of the heavens and the Earth and the variation in your tongues and colors. Truly in that are signs for those who know.** (30:22)
3. **And among His Signs is that He shows you lightning, arousing fear and hope, and that He sends down water from the sky, wherewith He revives the earth after its death. Truly in that are signs for a people who understand.** (30:24)
4. **And in the Earth are signs for those possessing certainty. And in yourselves. Do you not see?** (51:20-21)
5. **We shall show them Our Signs upon the horizons and within themselves till it becomes clear to them that it is the Truth. Does it not suffice that thy *Rabb* is a Witness over all things?** (41:53)

The preceding verses emphasize knowledge and reason as the rational basis for the belief in The Almighty through comprehending His Signs in the wonders of creation. The first two verses are inclusive of all creation in the cosmos, with specific reference in the first verse to the implications of the alternation of night and day. This alternation induces diurnal rhythms and cycles. Diurnal rhythm regulates the sleep/wake cycle, sleep being vital to our physical and mental well-being. Sleep influences a host of bodily functions, including hormone release, metabolic regulation, memory consolidation, and various healing, repair, and recovery processes. Sleep deprivation detrimentally affects cognitive abilities and psychological health. Diurnal cycles arising from day/night temperature variations impact air circulation, cloud formation, precipitation, and weather and climate patterns.

The second verse refers to human diversity as expressed in linguistic and racial differences. Human linguistic and racial diversity, manifested in cultural variety, is fascinating in its origins and implications. The aggregate of these interactions between diverse human groups enhances communication, promotes tolerance and understanding, generates new ideas and practices, broadens perspectives, and sheds more light on the human condition and what it means to be human; in short, human diversity should lead to the enrichment of human life and to the advancement of mankind.

The third verse specifically mentions lightning as a sign that instills awe of nature and portends rain, which almost miraculously brings dormant, or "dead", seeds to life and sprouts all kinds of vegetation that, directly or indirectly through herbivorous animals, is the primary food source for humans.

The last two verses are particularly significant in emphasizing that the cosmos, including planet Earth and "ourselves", both in body and mind, are full of His Signs.

"Those possessing certainty" in the fourth verse are those who are certain about their knowledge of these signs, through their research, and those who are certain that these signs attest His Existence. The last verse is in the future tense, which means that He will keep revealing, through expanding human knowledge, His Signs in everything outside the human being ("upon the horizons") as well as within the human being, until it becomes clear that He is the Truth. The "*Rabb* is Witness over all things" refers to His providing evidence to "His own Self-Disclosure and Self-Manifestation within each existent thing".[17] The Arabic word "*Rabb*", conventionally translated "Lord", is retained, as mentioned in Conventions and explained in Chapter 5, Section "The Image of God".

6. **The life of this world is naught but play and diversion. Better indeed is the Abode of the Hereafter for those who are pious. Do you not understand?** (6:32)
7. **And when it is said to them, "Follow what Allāh has revealed" they say, "Nay, we follow that wherein we found our fathers." What! Even though their fathers had no sense at all, nor did they follow the right path?** (2:170)
8. **Shame on you, and on what you worship instead of Allāh. Have you no sense?** (21:67)

The preceding three verses emphasize the ability to discern what is Right from what is not,[18] and also involve reasoning and judgement. The first verse invokes understanding in order to appreciate the frivolous nature of worldly life (see Chapter 7, Section "Formative Attitudes, Item 5. Frivolity of Life"). The reference in the last two verses is to the disbelievers, who at the time were Arabs who have not embraced Islam and who worshipped many gods, for whom they had statues. These verses are still relevant to modern times, for "polytheism" persists today, albeit in different forms. In fact, many people do "worship" various gods, such as the "god of money", the "god of greed", the "god of profit", the "god of consumerism", or what is sometimes referred to as the "God of Mammon". (For the meaning of "worship" compared to "Serving The Almighty" see Chapter 7, Section "Virtuous Conduct".) The second verse condemns blind and mindless imitation lacking in judgement and good sense. The third verse reprimands for senseless worship of other than The Almighty.

9. **...Thus does Allāh make clear unto you the signs, that you may reflect.** (2:266)
10. **And among His Signs is that He created for you, from among your selves, spouses that you may dwell in tranquility with them, and He has instilled love and mercy between you; verily, in that are signs for those who reflect.** (30:21)

The preceding two verses emphasize reflection on His Signs so as to comprehend their meaning and significance in bearing witness to His Existence. The word used, *tafakkur*, means deep, contemplative thinking that is both intellectual and spiritual in nature. The last verse refers to spouses being created from the same "selves" and joined in matrimony so they may find tranquility with one another and manifest love and mercy toward one another. The meaning of this verse is more fully explained in Chapter 7, Section "Virtuous Conduct", subheading "Marital Relations". That marriage is not only for procreation but also for emotional maturity and spiritual advancement is surely a sign that one should ponder of His Love, Mercy, and Knowledge of human nature.

11. **O you who believe, shun much conjecture. Indeed, some conjecture is a sin...** (49:12)
12. **Truly those who believe not in the Hereafter name the angels with female names. But they have no knowledge thereof. They follow but conjecture; and surely conjecture avails naught against the Truth.** (53:27-28)

The preceding verses admonish on conjecture. Assertions should be based on knowledge, facts, and certainty, not conjecture, which can cause mischief, misunderstanding, and conflict.

13. **...Is there a god alongside Allāh? Say: "Bring your proof, if you are truthful."** (27:64)
14. **Say (O Prophet): "Call on those whom you assert besides Him; they have neither the power to remove distress from you nor to change it."** (17:56)
15. **And they say: "None will enter the Garden unless he be a Jew or a Christian." Those are their fancies. Say: "Bring your proof, if you are truthful."** (2:111)

The first verse calls for proof to be provided by the disbelievers for the existence of gods besides The Almighty. The second verse instructs the Prophet Muhammad to ask the idolaters to beseech their gods to remove or alleviate their distress. Their inability to do so would then be proof of their impotence and hence their fraudulence. The third verse requests those who claim that only Jews or Christians will go to Heaven to back their claim with proof. These verses and many others emphasize providing proof to bolster claims and beliefs. Providing proof for claims being made is of course basic to the scientific way of thinking.

Of special interest regarding proof based on observation is the parable of Abraham's four birds:

> 16. **And when Abraham said, "My *Rabb*! Show me how you give life to the dead." Allāh responded, "Do you not believe?" Abraham replied, "Yes I do, but just so my heart can be reassured." Allāh said, "Then bring four birds, train them to come to you, then (having slaughtered them and cut them into pieces) place a part of them on each mountain. Then call them back, they will come to you in haste. And know that Allāh is Almighty, All-Wise."** (2:260)

Although there are several interpretations of this verse,[19] prominent exegetes agree that, as a prophet, Abraham could not have entertained any doubts about The Almighty's resurrection of the dead. However, his knowledge was on a theoretical level, based entirely on faith. Here Abraham's objective is twofold: (i) seeking knowledge at another level, that of seeing for himself the resurrection of the dead, not as a proof, because he already believed in this resurrection, but as an added reassurance based on actual observation, and (ii) gaining the immense satisfaction of being privileged to witness this awesomely miraculous and exclusively Divine Act of The Almighty. The parable is noteworthy in its explicit acknowledgement of a higher degree of certainty based on actual observation, which is a basic tenet of science, and in The Almighty acceding to

Abraham's request. This, in itself, is an affirmation of the importance of seeking evidence, particularly that based on direct observation.

Another aspect of the high regard for rational thinking, reasoning and judgement afforded by the Quran are the justifications given for Divine commands, as in the following:

17. **They ask you (O Prophet) about intoxicants and games of chance. Say, "There is great evil in both, as well as some benefit for people – but the evil outweighs the benefit..."** (2:219)
18. **...And to fast is better for you, if only you knew.** (2:184)
19. **...Indeed prayer deters (one) from indecency and abomination...** (29:45)

The preceding verses rationalize the Divine commands against intoxicants and games of chance and the ordaining of fasting and prayer. Significantly, the first verse acknowledges that intoxicants and games of chance do have some benefits but their harm outweighs their benefits. This is a very clear application of reasoning and judgement in deciding what is best.

The foregoing is but a sample of verses that illustrate the importance that the Quran attaches to rationality based on thinking, understanding, reasoning, knowledge, and providing evidence. The Quran invokes the intellect, reasoning, understanding, and contemplation in some one hundred verses, and refers to knowledge in even more verses. Disbelievers are described as lacking understanding and likened to cattle: **"Or do you suppose that most of them hear or understand? They are just like cattle. Indeed, more lost in their ways."** (25:44)

The verse is being fair in excluding some disbelievers, referring to most disbelievers. These are likened to cattle in that they do not listen to the message of The Almighty nor are they capable of thinking and understanding. They are more lost than cattle because cattle, by nature, know what is good or bad for them, unlike these disbelievers, who are completely averse to the truth, for they are **"... Deaf, dumb, and blind, so they have no sense."** (2:171) Being deaf, dumb, and blind is to be disconnected from reality and not able to comprehend anything.

According to Rosalind W. Gwynne, Associate Professor of Religious Studies: "Reasoning and argument are so integral to the content of the Qur'an and so inseparable from its structure that they in many ways shaped the very consciousness of Qur'anic scholars."[20]

Linguistic and Literary Inimitability

The following verse poses a challenge to the whole of mankind to produce the like of the Quran, even collectively:

> **Say: "Surely if mankind and jinn banded together to bring the like of this Quran, they would not bring the like thereof, even if they supported one another."** (17:88)

The challenge, which remains unmet to this day, was particularly provoking to 7th century CE Arabs, who were at the pinnacle of their linguistic and literary abilities. According to the linguistics expert Professor Hussein Abdul-Raof, "The Arabs, at the time, had reached their linguistic peak in terms of linguistic competence and sciences, rhetoric, oratory, and poetry."[21] Professor of Islamic Studies, Muhammad A. Draz asserts: "In the golden age of Arab eloquence, when language reached the apogee of purity and force, and titles of honour were bestowed with solemnity on poets and orators in annual festivals, the Qur'anic word swept away all enthusiasm for poetry and prose, and caused the Seven Golden Poems hung over the doors of the Ka'ba to be taken down. All ears lent themselves to this marvel of Arabic expression."[22] (The meaning of "jinn" is discussed in Chapter 7 under "Virtuous Conduct".)

The aforementioned Seven Golden Poems (also known as the Seven Odes or the seven *mu'allaqāt*) were seven selected and highly regarded long poems that were written in gold on special cloth and hung on the walls of the *Ka'bah*, which was the most holy site that housed statues of idols worshipped by the Arabs at the time. This was testimony to the great esteem that the Arabs placed on poetry. It is noteworthy that Labīd ibn Rabi'ah, considered as the most distinguished poet of the Seven Golden Poems, embraced Islam because of the inimitability of the Quran and, in veneration of the Quran, stopped composing poems thereafter. When asked why he stopped composing poetry, he replied: "What! Even after the revelation of the Qur'an?"[23]

Comparing the Quran to pre-Islamic poetry, Professor of Oriental Studies Martin Zammit states: "Notwithstanding the literary excellence of some of the long pre-Islamic poems…the Qur'an is definitely on a level of its own as the most eminent written manifestation of the Arabic language."[24] In the opinion of British Orientalist Arthur J. Arberry: "In making the present attempt to improve on the performance of predecessors, and to produce something which might be accepted as echoing however faintly the sublime rhetoric of the Arabic Koran, I have been at pain to study the intricate and richly varied rhythms which – apart from the message itself – constitutes the Koran's undeniable claim to rank amongst the greatest literary masterpieces of mankind."[25]

The Quran has proved to be linguistically and literarily inimitable. According to the English Orientalist, Edward H. Palmer: "That the best of Arab writers has never succeeded in producing anything equal in merit to the Qur'an itself is not surprising."[26] The reason for its inimitability is "because of its eloquence, its unique style, and because it is free of error."[27] The style of the Quran is in a genre of its own; it is neither poetry nor rhyming prose. As for being "free of error", the Quran posits:

> **Do they not contemplate the Quran? Had it been from other than Allāh, they would surely have found much inconsistency therein.** (4:82)

The fact of the matter is that the Quran remains to this day the ultimate reference and benchmark for all matters linguistic and grammatical in classical Arabic.

A most extraordinary aspect of the Quranic text, is that, "In the process of making good literature, editing and amending are absolutely necessary. No one can produce sophisticated literature 'on the go'."[28] Yet, the verses of the literary masterpiece that is the Quran were revealed in their final form when first uttered by the Prophet, not to be edited or reviewed later in any way, with their superb quality and freedom of error maintained over a period of 23 years.

The inimitability of the Quran is not of course a conclusive proof of its Divine origin, although a rational argument can be made for this on the basis of "inference to the best explanation"[29] considering the only alternative possibilities of the Quran being either authored by an Arab (other than the Prophet), or by a non-Arab, or by the Prophet himself, or the Quran being of Divine origin, bearing in mind that the Prophet was not known to have composed any poetry even before he received the first revelation at the age of 40. The inimitability of the Quran is presented here simply as a characteristic feature of the Quran. The Divine origin of the Quran is discussed in next chapter.

Chapter 4

Is the Quran of Divine Origin?

Theme: The Quran provides incontrovertible evidence for the existence of The Almighty.

On the Existence of the Supernatural

Numerous arguments and counter arguments for the existence of the supernatural have been presented over the years by philosophers, religious thinkers, and even some scientists. Of considerable interest in this regard is the Anthropic Principle,[1] a term coined by the Australian cosmologist Brandon Carter in 1974. One version of the Anthropic Principle is the Strong Anthropic Principle, an interpretation of which is essentially that the universe was created for human existence. Some would cite in support of this claim the extreme fine-tuning of the laws of nature, the values of the physical constants, and the initial conditions of the universe so that life as we know it can exist.[2] The odds in favor of having just the right conditions for the existence of life are exceedingly small. If the universe was created for human existence, then there must be some creating agency behind it all, which predicates the supernatural. According to Sir Fred Hoyle, the renowned English astronomer: "Once we see, however, that the probability of life originating at random is so utterly minuscule as to make it absurd, it becomes sensible to think that the favorable properties of physics, on which life depends, are in every respect deliberate… It is, therefore, almost inevitable that our own measure of intelligence must reflect higher intelligence – even to the limit of God."[3]

In another quote, Hoyle likens the probability of life of greater and greater complexity arising by chance to that of assembling a ready-to-fly Boeing 747 aircraft by a tornado tearing through a junkyard containing all the bits and pieces of the Boeing 747, disassembled and in disarray.[3]

A counter proposal to having a universe designed for human existence, is the multiverse theory,[4] according to which our universe is just one of a vast number, perhaps many thousands of millions, of universes each having different laws and physical constants, as chance might dictate. Our universe just happens to be the one with the right conditions for our existence. However, there is no empirical evidence for the existence of parallel universes. Moreover, as pointed out by the American philosopher Robin Collins, even if there were such universes, this would not negate the existence of an Omnipotent God who created them all for His Purpose.[5]

The evidence for the supernatural that is considered in this chapter is derived from the Quran, the Holy Book of Islam, as explained in the Preface. Maurice Bucaille, a famous French medical doctor, spent many years researching the relation between modern science and scriptures, culminating in 1976 in the publication of his acclaimed book, *La Bible, le Coran et la Science*. Translated to many languages including English, the book was influential enough so that the movement to relate science to religion became known as "Bucailleism". At the end of the introduction to the section in the book entitled "The Quran and Modern Science", Bucaille states: "The ideas in this study are developed from a purely scientific point of view. They lead to the conclusion that it is inconceivable for a human being living in the seventh century A.D. to have made statements in the Quran on a great variety of subjects that do not belong to his period and for them to be in keeping with what was to be known only centuries later. For me, there can be no human explanation to the Quran."[6]

Since then, there has been an explosion of claims of the miraculousness of the Quran aiming to prove its Divine origin. These claims can be divided into two broad categories: (i) references to physical phenomena that have since been confirmed by modern science, as in Bucaille's book, and (ii) special numerical relations in various forms that have been discovered more recently. In their overzealousness to bolster their point of view, some proponents of the Divine origin of the Quran have made exaggerated and not well-substantiated claims that detractors were bound to pick on. Some miraculous references to physical phenomena in the Quran are considered in the following section together with a brief, relevant scientific background in each case.

Miraculous Revelations

The Quran refers to physical phenomena in many verses, not only as Signs of His Existence and His Omnipotence, but also as evidence that the Quran is of Divine origin. It is important to appreciate that the wording of many Quranic verses that are concerned with physical phenomena is carefully crafted so as to have layers of meaning in order for it to be understood somehow by illiterate Bedouin Arabs of the 7th century CE, but at the same time have other meanings that unfold with time and as human knowledge expands. These new meanings serve as a testimony to the Divine nature of the Quran. In some cases, the wording is such as not to be blatantly in contradiction with prevalent beliefs, lest the Quran be ridiculed and shunned as a book of faith – which is its major import – but at the same time be consistent with future scientific facts. The Arabic language is well suited for these purposes, as noted in Chapter 3.

Some examples are given in this section of Quranic verses that cannot be explained away as being of human origin.

1. Pulsars

All stars, including our Sun, generate their energy by nuclear fusion reactions that begin by fusing hydrogen atoms to produce helium atoms, with release of energy through conversion of mass to energy, although the primary chains of hydrogen fusion reactions that take place differ somewhat in stars such as the Sun from those in more massive stars. The fusion reactions occur in the central region of the star, which is its hottest part, at a temperature of more than 10 million degrees Celsius. The heat generated by the fusion reactions causes expansion and results in an outward pressure that is balanced by an inward gravitational force due to the mass of the star. The fusion reactions produce a helium core surrounded by an envelope of hydrogen gas. In less massive stars these conditions persist until the hydrogen fuel is nearly depleted, as elaborated later in Item 2.

If the star is more massive than about 8 solar masses, where a solar mass is the mass of the Sun of almost 2×10^{30} kg, the density of the helium core increases and its temperature rises sufficiently to start a new fusion process that converts helium to carbon. This produces a carbon core surrounded by helium then hydrogen, the fusion reactions occurring at the boundaries of the layers. If the star is massive enough this process continues, fusing carbon into oxygen and then through successively heavier elements until iron is produced. As iron fusion consumes rather than releases energy, the outward pressure of the core is reduced. The gravitational force dominates, causing the massive star, which could have a mass that is several million times that of the Earth, to collapse very quickly, in a matter of 15 seconds or less. The resulting compression of the core compacts atoms to the point where electrons combine with protons in their parent nuclei to form neutrons and release neutrinos – subatomic particles that are similar to electrons but without an electrical charge. The neutrinos and the enormous shock waves produced by the collapse explode the outer part of the star. This explosion is a type of what is referred to as a supernova, where a supernova is the explosion of a dying star and is one of the most violent explosions that can be observed in the universe. The exploded outer part of the star becomes a type of nebula referred to as supernova remnants, where the word "nebula" refers quite generally to a cloud of gases and tiny particles of matter, or dust.

If the core of the collapsing sun is between about 1 and 3 times the solar mass, the newly-created neutrons, together with nuclear repulsive forces, can stop the collapse, leaving behind a neutron star that is some 20 km in diameter. The neutron star is one of the densest objects known; a teaspoon-full of neutron star material would weigh about a thousand million tons. If the core of the collapsing star is more than about 3 solar masses, it will continue to collapse into a black hole.

Stars are formed from huge clouds of interstellar gas and dust – a type of nebula – when enough hydrogen collects in one place so that the gravitational pull, including that due to dark matter (see Chapter 2, Section "What Present-Day Science Does Not Know"), compresses a mass of hydrogen and raises its temperature high enough to start a fusion reaction, as mentioned earlier. The constituents of these star-forming clouds are in motion, and would have some small rotation about the central part where the core of the star is forming. As the star-forming cloud contracts in volume, this rotation increases in speed and becomes a spin of the star around its axis. The effect is similar to the increase in the spinning speed of an ice skater as she draws in her arms and reduces the outward extent of her body.

The interiors of stars consist of ionized gases at very high temperatures, which are good conductors of electricity. As the star spins, the movement of charged particles produces a magnetic field around the star, just like a current in a coil produces a magnetic field inside and around the coil. This magnetic field, like that of the Earth, emanates outside the star from a magnetic north pole and terminates on a magnetic south pole, just like an ordinary magnet. When the star collapses, the same magnetic flux (that is, the totality of the magnetic field) around the much smaller core results in an intense magnetic field that is about 10^{10} times stronger, which makes the magnetic field between 10^8 and 10^{15} times stronger than that of Earth. The spin rate also increases by the same factor as the magnetic field strength, but the rotating magnet generates a huge amount of low-frequency energy that slows down the spin with time. Electrons are trapped in the polar regions of the magnetic field and are magnetically accelerated to very high energies, thereby resulting in high-frequency radiation. This radiation interacts with the magnetic field in a rather complex manner to produce more high-frequency radiation. The end result is two beams of high-frequency radiation that emanate from the polar regions of the neutron star along the magnetic axis, as illustrated in Figure 4.1.

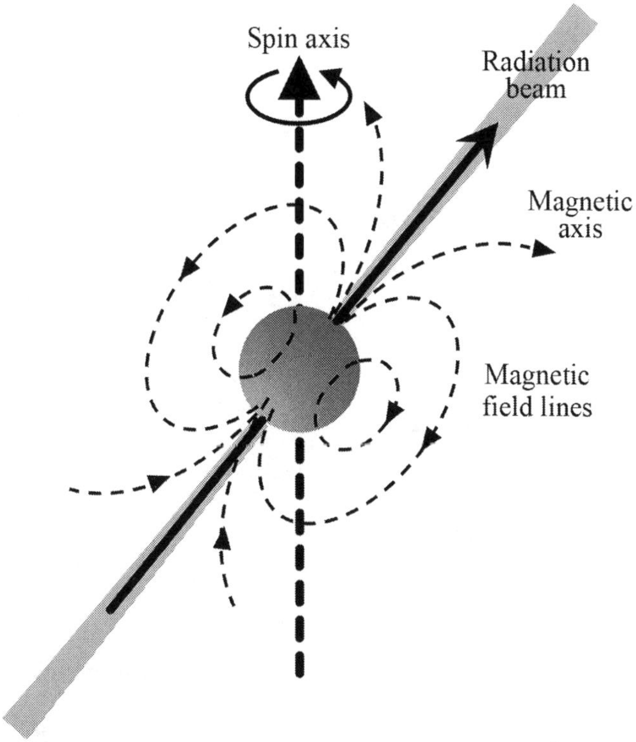

Figure 4.1 Spinning neutron star with beams of high-frequency radiation emanating along the magnetic axis

In general, the magnetic axis does not coincide with the spin axis, or axis of rotation (Figure 4.1). The beams therefore sweep through space as the star spins around its axis. If the path of the beams crosses Earth, pulses of high-frequency radiation are detected, just as the continuous, rotating light beam from a lighthouse is perceived by a ship approaching land as a source of light pulsating in the darkness. Such a neutron star is referred to as a pulsar,[7] first discovered in 1967. The intervals between pulses range between 1.4 ms and about 10 s, with most pulsars having pulse intervals between about 0.2 s and 2 s. If the pulses are applied to a sound system with a loudspeaker the slower pulses can be distinctively heard as a repetitive "knocking" sound.[8]

One might ask, what does all this have to do with the Quran? Chapter 86 of the Quran opens with the following verses:

> **By the heavens and the knocker. But how can you know what is the knocker? The piercing star.** (86:1-3)

The root word at the end of the first verse is the verb *ṭaraqa* whose primary meaning is "to pound" or "to knock". To be sure, the word "knocker" was used by the Arabs to refer to a night visitor who knocks on the door that is shut at the time.[9] For this reason, the title of Chapter 86 is conventionally translated as "The Comer by Night", "The Night Visitant", or suchlike. But what does the night visitant have to do with the oath "By the heavens" at the very beginning of the first verse? The reference to the heavens together with the third verse, "The piercing star", clearly affirms that the reference is to a star, not a person. Metaphorically, the morning star – usually Venus – was also referred to by the Arabs as the "knocker" because it is seen at the end of the night, just before sunrise.[10,11] The second verse, however, clarifies that the reference is not to any particular star known to the Arabs. In Arabic, the question phrase of the second verse is commonly used to signify that there is more to know about the subject at hand than meets the eye. The phrase occurs in the Quran some 15 times. If the first verse was meant to refer to a particular star that was well known to the Arabs, the second verse would be rather superfluous. Moreover, the third verse indicates that the "knocker" is a piercing star. The root verb in the third verse is *thaqaba* whose primary meaning is "pass through, perforate, or pierce".[12]

This verse is conventionally interpreted to mean piercing through the dark, and metaphorically as overcoming ignorance.[11] But the verb "to pierce" if applied to light would more accurately imply a light beam, such as that of a flashlight, rather than the diffuse light of visible stars. The light beam will serve to illuminate a target rather than dispel a surrounding darkness. The only star that is bright enough to dispel the darkness surrounding the Earth is the Sun, which is described in the Quran as a "radiance" or "shining brightness": **"He it is Who made the Sun a shining brightness, and the Moon a light..."** (10:5) "The piercing star" would then hardly be an apt description of a morning star, whose light is not only diffuse but is also not bright enough to dispel the darkness. Besides, the morning star is visible at the end of the night, just before sunrise, when the darkness is waning anyway.

Evidently, the "knocker" in the first verse refers to a "knocking star", which according to present-day knowledge, can be identified as a pulsar. The second verse asserts that there is more to know about this "knocker", which is true even today. "The piercing star" can then be understood in terms of the high-frequencies emitted by pulsars, which range through the electromagnetic spectrum from radio broadcast frequencies, to the frequencies of visible light, to X-rays, and to gamma rays.[13] The more appropriate interpretation of "piercing" is therefore in terms of the penetrating power of the higher-frequency radiation of a pulsar such as X-rays, which can pass through matter and the human body as in X-ray imaging. If intense enough, X-rays can literally burn a hole in tissues they pass through. Gamma rays from pulsars are also highly penetrating.

Quranic verses such as these are remarkable in that they had to have some meaning for illiterate Bedouin Arabs of the 7th century CE, as mentioned earlier. The meaning could be somewhat vaguely associated with something they are familiar with or can understand. Yet, the precise meaning can only be understood in later times such as ours, and in the light of unfolding knowledge, as sure Signs of The Almighty.

The Quran unmistakably refers to pulsars that were discovered more than twelve centuries later. Neither the Prophet Muhammad nor any other mortal before the 7th century CE, when the Quran was revealed, could have possibly concocted all this. So how can the Quran be of other than Divine origin?

2. Planetary Nebulas

When the core of a star whose mass is comparable to that of the Sun runs out of hydrogen, fusion stops and the core contracts under gravity. As the contracting core heats up, the rise in temperature causes expansion of the shell of hydrogen surrounding the core and supports hydrogen fusion in this shell, which produces much energy. The star expands over time to hundreds of times its original size and glows red, becoming a red giant. Meanwhile, temperature and pressure in the contracting core increase sufficiently to start fusion of helium to carbon. The generated energy temporarily stops the contraction of the core. Eventually, the helium in the core is depleted and fusion stops. The star shrinks again until a new helium shell from the outer layers reaches the core and begins fusing. At the same time hydrogen may begin fusion in a shell just outside the burning helium shell. The outer layers of the star are ejected in a huge cloud of gas and dust known as a planetary nebula, composed mostly of hydrogen and some helium. The core cools into a hot and dense white dwarf. Eventually, the expanding outer layers disperse, leaving an exposed core that cools to form a black dwarf that does not emit any significant heat or light. The whole process can take a thousand million years or more.

Remarkably, some of the planetary nebulas have a rose-like appearance, shaped by how they were formed and the cosmic influences they have been subjected to. One such nebula is the famous Cat's Eye Nebula,[14] also known as the Sunflower Nebula. It is a rather complex nebula having a core radius of nearly 0.2 light years and is about 3300 light years from Earth, where a light year is the distance travelled by light in a vacuum in a year and is equivalent to 9.46×10^{12} km. A high-resolution image of the nebula taken by the Earth-orbiting Hubble Space Telescope is shown in Figure 4.2.[15]

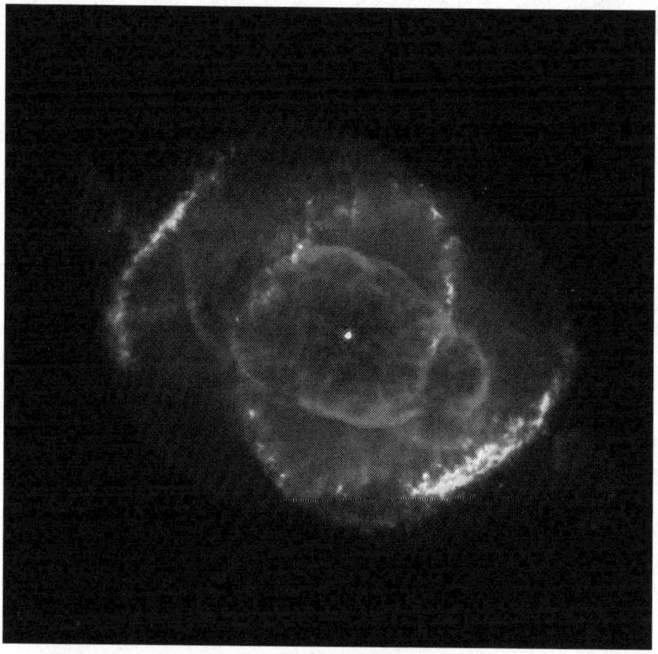

Figure 4.2 Cat's Eye Nebula
(Credit: The Space Telescope Science Institute, USA)

Another rose-shaped nebula is the Rosette Nebula[16] shown in Figure 4.3 and described on the APOD website as: "The Rosette Nebula, NGC 2237, is not the only cosmic cloud of gas and dust to evoke the imagery of flowers, but it is the most famous. At the edge of a large molecular cloud in Monoceros some 5,000 light years away, the petals of this cosmic rose are actually a stellar nursery. The lovely, symmetric shape is sculpted by the winds and radiation from its central cluster of hot young, O-type stars."[17]

Figure 4.3 The Rosette Nebula
(Credit: Dr. Jean M. Dean, FRAS)

What does this have to do with the Quran? The Quran states:

> **When the sky splits, so it becomes a rose, varicolored like ointments.** (55:37)

Due to lack of pertinent knowledge about cosmology, the early commentators (exegetes) of the Quran invariably interpreted cosmic events such as the "splitting of the sky" as occurring at the end of the world, or the Day of Resurrection (see Chapter 6, Section "The Afterlife"). It is now well established of course that cosmic events such as supernova explosions or the formation of planetary nebulas have been occurring for at least many hundreds of millions of years and are ongoing. The root verb at the beginning of the verse is *shaqqa* whose primary meaning is "to split with or without separation".[18] Evidently, only material objects can be split, so the "splitting of the sky" cannot occur in the "void" of the sky but must occur in celestial bodies such as stars. The word *al-dihān* at the end of the verse means ointments in this context.[19] Various ointments of different colors were used by the Arabs at the time for medicinal or cosmetic purposes,[20] so the reference to the colors of ointments was meaningful to them.

The Quran unmistakably refers to roses in the sky that are caused by some splitting, and that is some twelve centuries before these rose-like formations could be observed in detail using powerful telescopes. Did the Prophet Muhammad or other mortals before the 7th century CE see these roses thousands of light years away with telescopic naked eyes? So how can the Quran be of other than Divine origin?

3. The Expanding Universe

When applying his theory of general relativity to the whole universe, Einstein found that his equations predicted an unstable universe that would either expand or contract. The prevalent thinking at the time was that the universe was in a steady state, that is, neither expanding nor contracting, which seemed reasonable, intuitive, and had been more or less taken for granted. In order to satisfy this steady-state condition, Einstein introduced into his equations a term having a constant that became known as the cosmological constant.

About 12 years later, in 1929, the American astronomer Edwin Hubble made the observation that the red shift of the light emitted from galaxies was directly proportional to the distance of the galaxy from Earth, which meant that galaxies farther away from Earth were moving away faster. In other words, the universe is expanding.[21] The expansion of the universe is in fact an expansion of space itself, which stretches light waves, thereby increasing their wavelength and reducing their frequency toward the red end of the visible spectrum, hence the red shift.[22]

Hubble's observation is considered as one of science's greatest discoveries, as it marked a turning point in our understanding of the universe and inaugurated the field of observational cosmology that led to hypotheses on such matters as the age of the universe and the existence of dark energy and dark matter that were mentioned in Chapter 2. The expansion of the universe was promptly embraced by the scientific community. Einstein is said to have referred to his introduction of the cosmological constant to accommodate a non-expanding universe as his "biggest blunder".[23]

Evidently, Einstein did not read the Quran in Arabic. Had he done so, he would not have made this "blunder".

The Quran plainly states:

> **The universe We have built with forces, and verily we are expanding it.** (51:47)

The reference to expansion is the end word *musi'ūn*, derived from the verb *awsa'a*, whose primary meaning is "to make more spacious, to extend, to expand." Critically, the word *musi'ūn* is in the present continuous tense, indicating that the expansion is ongoing, and not a vastness that is over and done with. The verse states that The Almighty built the universe with *aydin*, the plural of *yad*, which is literally a hand, but signifies power in Arabic. It has been rendered in translations of the Quran as power, strength, and might. In the context of building the universe, it is more likely referring to the physical forces acting on the celestial bodies.

Understandably, the older commentaries, or exegeses, of the Quran did not interpret *musi'ūn* in terms of an expanding universe because of the lack of cosmological knowledge. Most came close by referring to the vast extent of the universe, so that the verse has been translated as: **"And the sky We established with might; truly We make vast!"**[11] or as: **"And the heaven, We raised it high with power, and We are Makers of the vast extent,"**[24] or as: **"We have built the heaven with might, and We it is who make the vast extent (thereof),"**[25] and **"With the power and skill did We construct the Firmament: for it is We who create the vastness of space."**[26] Other commentaries and translations based on them have used more metaphorical meanings of the verb *awsa'a* such as "giving generously", or "being able to do". But for "being generous" the Quran uses the verb *akrama* and its derivatives in more than 7 verses, and for "being able to do" the Quran uses words such as *qādir*, *muqtadir*, and their variations in more than 25 verses, but *musi'ūn* is used only once, in this verse. It is extremely unlikely, therefore, that the true meaning is other than expansion of the universe. More recent translations mention expansion of the universe, as in: **"And it is We who have built the universe with (Our creative) power; and, verily, it is We who are steadily expanding it,"**[27] or: **"We built the universe with great might, and we are certainly expanding it."**[28] The interpretation in terms of an expanding universe is also adopted in books on science and the Quran.[29,30]

The Quran states that the universe is being expanded. This could not possibly have been concocted by the Prophet Muhammad or by any mortal before the 7th century CE. The expansion of the universe became a scientific fact more than twelve centuries later. So how can the Quran be of other than Divine origin?

4. Origin of the Universe

It was mentioned in Chapter 2 that Georges Lemaître proposed in 1931 that the expansion of the universe, if projected back in time, meant that at some finite time in the past (estimated at nearly 14×10^9 years) the universe was concentrated into an extremely dense and extremely hot point that underwent a tremendous expansion, which subsequently was referred to as the big bang. Since then, this proposal has been generally accepted as it was consistent with a range of observable phenomena such as the formation of the light elements – mainly hydrogen and helium – and the existence of cosmic microwave background (CMB) radiation.[31] The extrapolation back in time from an expanding universe was based on general relativity and led to the conclusion that at this extremely dense and extremely hot point the curvature of space-time becomes infinite, a state referred to as a cosmological singularity. This singularity, therefore, not only marks the beginning of all matter and energy but also the beginning of space and time. Neither general relativity nor quantum mechanics are applicable to the singularity or to the earliest moments of the big bang.

According to the big bang model, the universe cooled sufficiently because of its initial expansion to allow the formation of some subatomic particles, and later, neutral hydrogen atoms and some helium, with traces of other elements. Giant clouds of these mostly hydrogen with some helium atoms, later coalesced through gravity to form stars and galaxies. Dark matter is believed to have contributed much to this gravitational pull. The big bang model does not address such questions as how this extremely dense and extremely hot point arose in the first place, what preceded it, and what caused its tremendous expansion. Nevertheless, the big bang is currently the best model available for the origin of the universe. It is continually being refined but may yet undergo drastic modifications or be superseded by another model altogether.

The Quran states:

> **Do the disbelievers not realize that the heavens and Earth were a closed-up mass, but We rent them asunder, and made from water every living thing. Will they not believe?** (21:30)

The first keyword in this verse is derived from *ratq*, which means "closed up, without any interstices".[32] This keyword was translated in the aforementioned translations of the Quran as "sewn together", "closed up", "of one piece", "joined together", "one single entity", and "one mass". The second keyword is *fataqnāhumā* which means "we rent them asunder".[33] The words *ratq* and *fatq* are antonyms. Having the heavens and Earth in one mass does not mean that they were joined together as such, that is, as separate entities having their different compositions. The meaning in the context of Quranic expression is that the heavens and Earth were an undifferentiated mass from which they were subsequently formed.[34]

Another meaning of the word *ratq* is darkness,[35] so that the closed-up mass was also dark. But there was also a period of darkness in the evolution of the universe. In the chronology of the universe,[36] it is believed that various subatomic particles were formed immediately after the big bang, resulting after about 1 second in photons, electrons, protons and neutrons. After about 10 seconds, at a temperature of approximately a thousand million degrees Celsius, protons and neutrons began to fuse together to produce some forms of hydrogen and helium nuclei. By about 20 minutes, this fusion stopped because of cooling to about 10 million degrees Celsius, leaving the universe in a state of plasma, consisting mostly of ionized hydrogen, with some helium, and electrons. Photons, which are the elementary particles of electromagnetic radiation, including light, could not travel significant distances without interacting with electrons and protons of the plasma. This made the plasma opaque.

After about 18,000 years, the temperature dropped to several thousand degrees Celsius, which allowed electrons to bind to nuclei to form neutral atoms, which were mostly hydrogen and some helium, with traces of other light elements. This continued till about 370,000 years after the big bang. Photons could now travel throughout the universe almost unimpeded, which made the universe transparent. The photons that could travel unimpeded are the origin of the cosmic microwave background (CMB) radiation referred to earlier and would have given the universe an orange glow at first. With further expansion, this light was stretched, shifting to lower frequencies, as explained earlier, until it became no longer visible after several million years. The universe again became dark until stars began to form some hundreds of millions of years later.

The most common everyday usage of the words *ratq* and *fatq* is in connection with fabric sheet material made of filaments. Amazingly, according to modern cosmology, the hydrogen gas that began to appear about 370,000 years formed colossal sheets which then broke apart to form the filaments of a vast cosmic web.[37] Hence, *ratq* could also refer to the initial sheets and *fatq* to their breaking apart into filaments. More will be said about the cosmic web later under "Item 5. Evolution of the Universe". Hence, darkness could also refer to the period when the radiation became invisible and until the formation of stars.

To be sure, some ancient myths in the Middle East and the Far East alluded to the separation of the Earth and heavens but in very different contexts.[38,39] In the Polynesian myth, for example, there were primeval waters covered in darkness until they separated when light appeared, thereby producing heaven and Earth. In the Egyptian myth there was also a primeval sea teeming with demi-gods, who produced an original mound of earth, and a Sun goddess from whose tears humanity was born. There is also a child-god whose eyes, when open, gave light to the world. In the Sumerian myth there was a primeval sea that begot a mountain consisting of heaven and Earth united, and there was a union of the god of heaven and the goddess of Earth that gave birth to the air god. In the Babylonian myth,[40] there is in the beginning only undifferentiated water swirling in chaos, out of which a god and a goddess emerged. The union of these gods gave birth to younger gods whose skirmishes eventually ended in the killing of the goddess. The Tigris and Euphrates rivers flowed from the eyes of this goddess, and heavens and Earth were created from her corpse.

A primordial body of water is common to all the myths of the Middle East about the origin of the universe. Even in the Old Testament there was water to begin with: "In the beginning when God created the heavens and the Earth, the Earth was a formless void and darkness covered the face of the deep, while a wind from God swept over the face of the waters" (Genesis 1:1-2). If the Prophet Muhammad were to plagiarize the origin of the universe, he would surely have included a body of water, perhaps with some embellishments, to make it more palatable and alluring. Yet, the Quranic reference to the creation of the universe is concise, sober, and consistent with modern scientific cosmology that emerged thirteen centuries later, including the filamentous nature of the early universe. So how can the Quran be of other than Divine origin?

This same verse on the origin of the universe is also concerned with the origin and basis of life: **"…and (We) made from water every living thing…,"** as will be considered later under "Item 13. Water and Life".

5. Evolution of the Universe

In ancient times, the prevalent view was Aristotle's, namely, that the universe was unchanging. It always was and will continue to be without change. The Quran sees it differently:

> **So when the stars will lose their light.** (77:8)

> **And when the stars spill out.** (81:2)

The verb in the first verse is *ṭamasa*, which means "to be obliterated" and for a star, "to be deprived of its light".[41] The verb in the second verse is *kadara*, which means "to spill out, as a container spills out when it is broken",[11] or "scatter", or "dart down", or "become dusky and dingy".[42] These verses are a clear reference to the evolution of stars, as they fade, change color, and shed some of their material. There are also references to the fate of the Sun in particular:

When the Sun is wound around (with darkness). (81:1)

And the Sun runs its course to a settled place. That is the decree of The Almighty, the All-Knowing. (36:38)

The verb in the first verse is *kawwara*, whose original meaning is to coil or wind a turban around the head, hence this translation.[43] The second verse states that the Sun is moving to a destination. According to modern cosmology, the Sun and the solar system are moving at approximately 17 to 22 km/s relative to the Local Standard of Rest (LSR), the Sun's velocity being directed toward a point, known as the solar apex, in the constellation of Hercules.[44]

Another amazing revelation of the Quran is the intergalactic structure, which according to computer simulations is a cosmic web consisting of filaments hundreds of millions of light years in length, and about 20 million light years in thickness, and made up of thousands of galaxies. Galaxy superstructures are found at the intersections of filaments[45] (Figure 4.4).

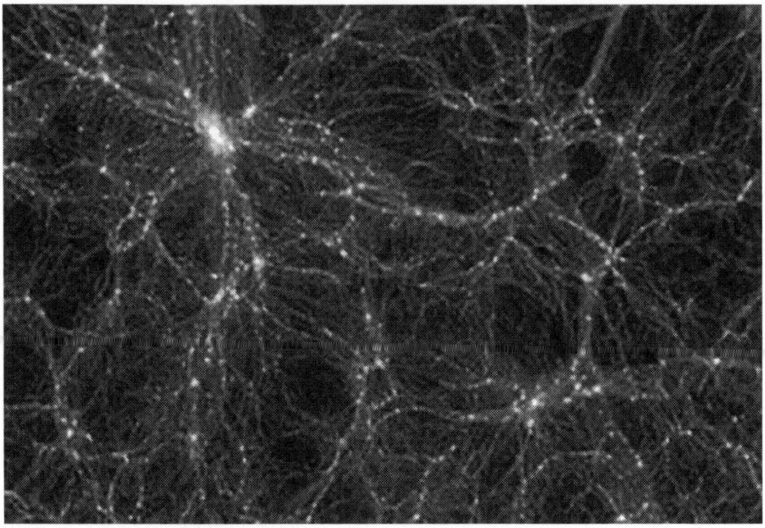

Figure 4.4 The cosmic web (Credit: Professor V. Springel & The Virgo Consortium, Max-Planck-Institute for Astrophysics, Germany)

Observational evidence for the cosmic web was reported in 2019.[46] Incredibly, the Quran states:

> **By the heaven that is woven well and firmly.** (51:7)

The verb *ḥabaka* means "to weave well and firmly".[47] The conventional translation of *ḥubuk* is "paths", and in a recent translation, "wondrous mazes",[48] as the early exegetes of the Quran had no knowledge of the cosmic web. But *ḥabaka* is conventionally used in connection with cloth and the weaving of threads or filaments.

The end of the universe is mentioned in the following verses of the Quran:

> **The day when We roll up the heavens like the rolling up of scrolls for writings. As We began the first creation, We shall reproduce it. A promise binding**

on Us. Surely We shall do it. (21:104)

And the Sun and the Moon are brought together. (75:9)

According to the first verse, the universe will be collapsed and produced again. The collapse will join the Sun and Moon together, as stated in the second verse. This joining together could come about when the Sun becomes a red giant, as explained earlier, and expands to engulf the Moon and maybe the Earth as well. As for the end of the universe, one of the current theories is the Big Crunch, which postulates that the universe will stop expanding and will contract again to a singularity, after which a new big bang might occur.[49]

The Quran clearly refers to evolution of stars and their death and the motion of the Sun to a destination, which have become accepted by science since at least the 18th century CE. The cosmic web structure expressed in the Quran was observed in the 21st century CE. This could not possibly have been conceived by the Prophet Muhammad or by any mortal before the 7th century CE. So how can the Quran be of other than Divine origin?

6. The Protective Atmosphere

The Earth's atmosphere forms a protective layer, some 100 km thick, without which life on Earth would not exist. Besides harboring the oxygen we breathe, and creating the pressure that keeps water in liquid form at the Earth's surface, the atmosphere shields the Earth from harmful impingements from outer space. These include not only meteoroids but various forms of radiation as well, such as cosmic rays, gamma rays, X-rays, and ultraviolet radiation.

Radiation reaching the Earth from outer space originates

from sources such as solar flares, supernova remnants, huge clouds of particles being attracted by massive black holes, pulsars, and other galactic sources. Cosmic rays, which are highly energetic protons, with some helium nuclei, and a very small percentage of other nuclei, have a high penetrating power through the body, where they can damage DNA and increase the risk of cancer. They are largely prevented from reaching the Earth's surface by interactions with oxygen and nitrogen molecules in the atmosphere, although secondary products of these interactions may reach the Earth's surface. Gamma rays and X-rays are electromagnetic waves, like visible light but of much higher frequencies. They are absorbed by molecules in the atmosphere, mainly nitrogen and oxygen, resulting in low energy particles and radiation. Gamma rays are biologically hazardous and can kill cells, as used in radiotherapy for killing cancerous cells. X-rays also increase the risk of cancer, as a result of cell mutations, and can have harmful effects on living tissues.

Most of the ultraviolet radiation comes from the Sun. The high-frequency ultraviolet radiation which is very harmful to all living organisms is absorbed by the ozone layer, extending from about 15 to 35 km above the Earth's surface. The lower-frequency ultraviolet radiation reaches the Earth's surface and is beneficial to humans as well as birds and insects although overexposure is harmful, particularly to the skin and eyes.[50] Solar radiation also ionizes the upper layers of the atmosphere, beyond about 60 km from the Earth's surface, creating the ionosphere.

Meteoroids hurtling toward Earth are broken up and burned in the atmosphere. A high air pressure difference exists between the front of an advancing meteoroid and its rear, which forces air into any cracks in the meteoroid and may break it apart. The meteoroid or its fragments are burnt by the extreme heat generated by motion through the atmosphere. Were it not for the atmosphere, the Earth's surface would be almost incessantly bombarded by potentially injurious meteorites and would be pockmarked like the Moon's surface. Even then, large meteoroids are able to reach the Earth's surface, but only rarely.

In addition to the gaseous atmosphere, the Earth is protected by the magnetosphere, which is a giant magnetic bubble formed by the Earth's magnetic field. The magnetosphere deflects away from Earth most of the cosmic rays and the deadly plasmas, or solar wind, emanating from solar flares, as well as the continuous solar winds coming from the Sun. These solar winds consist of a stream of hot charged particles – mostly protons and electrons with some helium nuclei – released from the outer atmosphere of the Sun at high speeds. They would otherwise destroy the ozone layer and make Earth uninhabitable.

The following verses of the Quran assert the protective nature of the sky:

> **And We made the sky a roof preserved...** (21:32)

> **By the sky that returns.** (86:11)

The first verse describes the sky, that is, what is above the Earth's surface, as a roof, which proverbially affords safety and security. This roof is preserved by physical phenomena ordained by The Almighty. Thus, the atmosphere is held in place by the Earth's gravity. The ozone layer is regenerated and kept in a state of balance by the ozone-oxygen cycle.[51] The layer is protected by the Earth's magnetic field, as mentioned earlier.

The noun *raj'* in the second verse is derived from the verb meaning "to return" or "to send back". It was understood by some early exegetes to refer to rain "because the clouds raise the water from the seas and then return it to the earth".[52] Whilst true, this cannot be the only meaning. As is typical of the Quran when referring to physical phenomena, there can be several layers of meaning. If rain was the only intended meaning, it would have been explicitly mentioned, as in many other Quranic verses. It is now known that the sky returns other than water. As previously explained, when radiation from outer space interacts with the molecules of the atmosphere, lower energy particles and radiation are produced, some of which are returned to space. Of more significance perhaps is the greenhouse effect.[53] Earth is heated by the Sun's radiation during the day and radiates heat into the atmosphere at night. Some of this radiated heat is absorbed by greenhouse gases – mainly water vapor, carbon dioxide, methane, nitrous oxide, and ozone – and is re-emitted back into the atmosphere. It is estimated that this maintains the Earth's mean surface air temperature at about 14°C, instead of the -18°C that it would otherwise be, thereby allowing life on Earth. It may also be noted that radio waves of frequency less than about 30 MHz are reflected back to Earth by the ionosphere.

The Quran speaks of the protective sky and its "sending back" properties at least twelve centuries before these were elucidated by science. So how can the Quran be of other than Divine origin?

7. Recycling of the Earth's Crust

The Quran proclaims in two places:

> **Do they not see how We come upon the land, reducing it of its sides...** (13:41)
> **...Do they not see how We come upon the land, reducing it of its sides...** (21:44)

The early exegetes had some difficulty with this statement. It was metaphorically interpreted as Allāh giving the Prophet Muhammad victory over the Makkans and Makka's environs, or to mean that when Allāh comes upon the land of the heart of the sincere believer, He reduces it of its outlying regions, that is, the believer's concerns for things other than Allāh.[54] The direct meaning eluded them, for the verb is in the present continuous tense, which means that the action is ongoing. But what land is being reduced of its sides? And if this is continuous, wouldn't this land eventually disappear? More recent scientifically-minded commentators opined that these verses referred to erosion. To understand the direct meaning of these verses, some basic knowledge of modern geology is needed.

Earth can be divided into four main concentric shells (Figure 4.5):

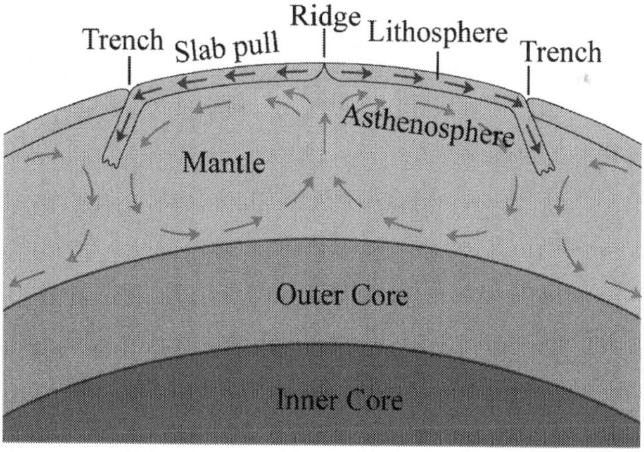

Figure 4.5 Earth layers and movement of tectonic plates

(i) a solid, or extremely viscous, inner core of about 1200 km radius made up of an iron-nickel alloy with some lighter elements, (ii) a surrounding, liquid outer core that is a spherical shell about 2300 km thick composed mostly of iron and nickel; the magnetic field of the Earth is generated by motion of this liquid core, (iii) a semi-solid mantle about 3000 km thick, composed mainly of iron, magnesium and silicon; the viscous, outer part of the mantle is at the temperature of molten rock, 700°C to 1300°C, whereas its temperature near the boundary with the outer core is about 4000°C, and (iv) an outermost crust that is partly oceanic, composed mainly of silicon and magnesium, and partly continental, composed mainly of silicon and aluminum. The oceanic crust is denser and thinner than the continental crust, its thickness varying between about 6 km and about 100 km, whereas the thickness of the continental crust is typically about 200 km, with considerable variation between basins and mountain ranges. The crust, together with the outermost part of the mantle that is in contact with it, form the lithosphere. The part of the mantle underlying the lithosphere is the asthenosphere. The lithosphere is solid, cold, and brittle whereas the asthenosphere is viscous, hotter, and mechanically weak.

The lithosphere is not a single continuous mass but is divided into 15 to 20 huge slabs referred to as tectonic plates that float over the asthenosphere and are jostled around mainly by the churning movement of material in the viscous mantle. This movement is due to the hotter and hence less dense material in the lower part of the mantle rising toward the upper part, then cooling and sinking back to the lower parts. As a result, the tectonic plates are pushed around in different directions at a rate in the range of 1 cm to 16 cm per year. Where tectonic plates meet, they could pull away from one another, or push toward one another, or slide past one another. These motions can result in earthquakes, volcanos, mountains, rifts, mid-ocean ridges, or oceanic trenches.[55]

Two tectonic plates are diagrammatically shown moving apart in the upper middle of Figure 4.5. As the plates slowly move away from each other, magma – that is, molten or semi-molten rock from the asthenosphere – rises up from within the mantle to fill the opening. This creates an elevation in the seafloor that eventually becomes a mountainous ridge, such as the Mid-Atlantic Ridge, which constitutes the longest mountain chain on Earth – about 80,000 km long. With mounting pressure from below, the crust cracks. The hot magma bubbles up to fill cracks and spills out onto the crust. As it comes into contact with the frigid seawater in the deep, the magma cools and forms new crust, in what is referred to as ridge push. The seafloor thus expands laterally on each side of the ridge, a process described as seafloor spreading. The spreading rate is about 2 cm to 5 cm per year for the Mid-Atlantic Ridge and 6 cm to 16 cm per year for the East Pacific Rise. Sometimes the cracks in the ridge are such that they result in small volcanos and earthquakes.

Where tectonic plates of different densities push toward one another, the less dense plate is lifted and the denser plate slips underneath it – a process referred to as subduction (Figure 4.5). The denser plate could be an oceanic plate and the less dense plate a continental plate. Or both plates could be oceanic or continental, with the younger plate being less dense. As the subducted plate moves into the asthenosphere its edges melt away, so that the Earth's crust is recycled in this manner. The melting at the edges of the tectonic plates is accurately described in the Quranic passage as "reducing the land of its sides".[56] The subducting plate also pulls on the slab – a process called slab pull – which is believed to be in fact the major force behind seafloor spreading. The process of seafloor spreading is also referred to in two Quranic verses:

And the earth We spread out... (15:19)

The earth We spread out... (50:7)

The earth is said to be spread out, where the Arabic verb used is *madda*, which means “to stretch”, “to extend by pulling”, “to lengthen”.[57] The verb is seen to be a very apt description of seafloor spreading, particularly with respect to the major force of slab pull. The remaining parts of the verses support the interpretation that it is the seafloor that is being referred to, as will be discussed next under “Item 8. Seamounts”.

The theory of plate tectonics was advanced in the early 20th century CE and became accepted about 50 years later based on extensive data collected particularly during and after World War II. The Quran referred to seafloor spreading some thirteen centuries before. Did the Prophet Muhammad have expert knowledge of geology in addition to cosmology? So how can the Quran be of other than Divine origin?

8. Seamounts

Seamounts are underwater mountains that typically rise 1 km to 4 km above the seafloor. They mainly occur in three forms:[58] (i) mid-ocean ridges, as described in connection with Figure 4.5 and which are associated with small volcanos and earthquakes, as mentioned earlier, (ii) near a subduction zone between an oceanic plate and a continental plate, where the oceanic plate slips beneath the continental plate whose edge is also elevated in the process (Figure 4.5); in addition, magma from the subducting (that is, sinking) and melting plate rises to the surface creating volcanos and seamounts, and (iii) isolated regions, or hotspots, in the tectonic plate where heat from deep down makes the magma in these regions hotter than surrounding magma. The hotter magma is able to break through the crust to form volcanos. It is estimated that there are more than 35,000 seamounts exceeding 1 km in height and more than 140,000 smaller seamounts.

The preceding two verses continue as follows:

> **And the earth We spread out, and cast therein seamounts, and We caused to sprout therein all kinds of things in due balance.** (15:19)

> **The earth We spread out, and cast therein seamounts, and caused to sprout therein every kind of delightful growth (in pairs).** (50:7)

The Quran uses two words for mountains: *jibāl*, the everyday word, occurs in the singular or plural in 39 verses and *rawāsī* in 10 verses. The latter word is from the root verb *rasā* whose primary meaning is "to become stationary, firm, or steady" and is commonly used with "ships at anchor".[59] *Rawāsī* is translated here as seamounts,[60] although it is conventionally translated as "firm mountains", as if mountains can be anything but firm, particularly as they have deep roots (see "Item 10. Mountains as Pegs"). It should be noted that in the two verses above, *rawāsī* follows the reference to seafloor spreading.

Further corroboration of seamounts being the intent is provided by the end parts of these verses. Seamounts shape ocean currents and direct deep, nutrient-rich waters up their sloping sides. Moreover, hydrothermal vents are found in the vicinity of seamounts and are the result of seawater percolating down through fissures in the ocean crust, becoming superheated to more than 400°C, and shooting out of the fissures at high speeds. The heat from volcanos and hydrothermal vents provides the energy to sustain, on and around seamounts, an unusually rich and varied marine life that is not based on photosynthesis, as is the case on land, but rather on microbes that convert sulfur compounds to organic material. The causing "to sprout therein all kinds of things in due balance" is a clear reference to ecosystems with their characteristic, balanced composition of various species. The biodiversity of these ecosystems is very striking: "Deep-sea corals that thrive on and around seamounts host more than 1,300 different species of animals; some are unique to seamounts themselves and some live only on a specific species of coral."[61] The animal species that strive in such environments include fish, eels, clams, mussels, crabs, octopuses, and giant tube worms. This explains the reference to "delightful growth in pairs". It should be noted that in the Quran the Arabic *anbata*, which is "caused to sprout", is not restricted to vegetation, as has been rendered in some translations, but is used in the sense of "allow to develop". Mankind is said to have been sprouted from earth: **"And Allāh has caused you to sprout as a growth from the earth."** (71:17)

The Quran also asserts:

And by the sea set on fire. (52:6)

The verb *sajjara* can mean "heated" or "kindled fire in it",[62] in addition to "filled" or "made to swell". Most translations of the Quran are based on the early exegeses that interpreted this verse to mean "swollen sea", since submarine volcanos were first observed in 1650 and hydrothermal vents discovered in 1977. So it was inconceivable to the early exegetes that the seas are heated or set on fire. However, the grammatical tense used is the passive participle, which does not refer to a future event, such as what might occur in the apocalypse at the end of the world (see Chapter 6, Section "The Afterlife"). At least one modern translation renders this verse as "seas set on fire".[28]

The Quran refers to seamounts, submarine volcanos, and deep sea habitats many centuries before they were observed by humans. Neither the Prophet Muhammad nor any mortal before the 7th century CE could have possibly known about them. So how can the Quran be of other than Divine origin?

9. Earthquake Dampening

The Quran affirms in three places:

> **And He cast seamounts in the earth, lest it quake with you...** (16:15)

> **...And He cast seamounts in the earth, lest it quake with you...** (31:10)

> **And We placed seamounts in the earth, lest it quake with them...** (21:31)

The word *rawāsiya* is used in these verses, which refers to seamounts as noted previously. The verb *māda* means "to be in a state of violent motion" or "to be inclined from side to side",[63] and is understood to refer to earthquakes. An important point to note is that these verses do not state that the seamounts stop the earth from "quaking" but rather that it stops the earth from "quaking with you" or "quaking with them" which means that the quaking will not be felt or the movement will be less than what it would have been without the seamounts.[60] The last verse addresses the disbelievers reminding them of the graces of The Almighty, among which is the lessening of earthquakes.

It is well established that the most destructive earthquakes occur at the edges of tectonic plates, where these plates push toward one another, or slide past one another, as mentioned earlier. The edges of these plates are naturally jagged, which prevents smooth sliding at these edges. The jaggedness would stop the movement at some point, but under the influence of the driving forces behind the movement, stresses build up at the points stopping the movement. Eventually, the mounting stresses overcome the causes of the stoppage, resulting in a sudden slippage that releases the pent-up stresses and which is felt as an earthquake. It has also been observed that the most violent earthquakes tend to occur at subduction zones (Figure 4.5) and that the presence of seamounts reduces the intensity of the earthquake: "The vast majority of subducting seamounts...cause numerous small earthquakes, but not large (M>7) ones."[64] And "...when underwater mountains – also known as seamounts – are pulled into subduction zones, not only do they set the stage for these powerful quakes, but also create conditions that end up dampening them."[65] The underlying mechanisms could be quite complex, but a suggested simple-to-understand explanation is that the subduction zone is reduced in extent to only the areas of contact between the tops of the seamounts and the upper tectonic plate, which prevents large stresses from building up and results in a smaller and less violent slippage.[66]

The Quran asserts that seamounts dampen earthquakes, thirteen centuries before this was confirmed by geological studies. Neither the Prophet Muhammad nor any mortal before the 7th century CE could have possibly conceived of that. So how can the Quran be of other than Divine origin?

10. Mountains as Pegs

Mountains are pretty massive structures that protrude above the surrounding land. The question is: how is the weight of these massive structures supported? Intuitively, one would imagine that the added weight of mountains is supported by the mechanical strength of the crust of Earth surrounding them. If one stands on a sufficiently thick wooden plank, for example, the plank might bend a little but is rigid enough to support the added weight. However, careful geophysical investigations since the 19th century CE have led to the conclusion that this is only part of the answer. It turns out that as mountains form they develop huge roots that project downwards into the Earth's mantle[67] (Figure 4.6).

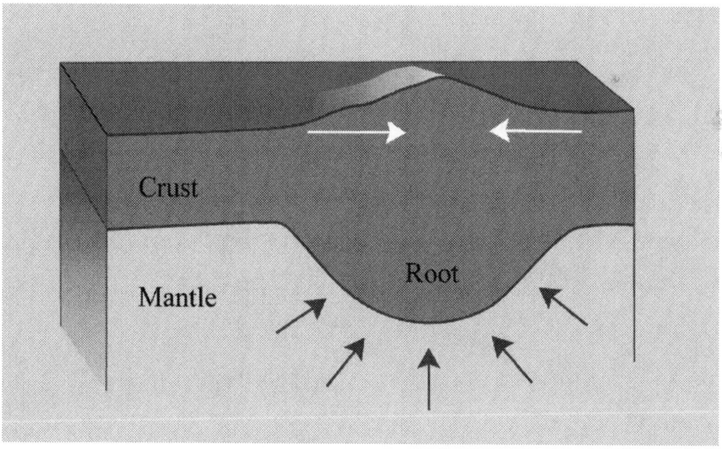

Figure 4.6 Root of mountain

Since the mantle is of higher density than the crust, including the root, there will be a buoyant force on the root that helps support the weight of the mountain, as indicated by the arrows in the figure. The effect is similar to a block of rather dense wood floating on water. Most of the wood will be submerged below the surface, so that the buoyant force on the submerged part supports the weight of the block. The peaks of the Himalayan mountains, for example, are less than 9 km high but their roots are more than 200 km deep.

The Quran states:

> **Have We not made the earth an expanse and the mountains as pegs.** (78:6-7)

The Arabs were well familiar with pegs that were driven into the earth and used for holding tents. Just like pegs, mountains are buried deeper into the earth, through their roots, than what protrudes above the surface. Functionally, the roots help support the weight of the mountain through buoyancy.

Neither the Prophet Muhammad nor any mortal before the 7th century CE could have possibly envisaged mountains having deep roots like pegs. Why would they? Surely mountains are secure enough and need no supporting roots. Yet the Quran refers to roots of mountains more than twelve centuries before they were postulated. So how can the Quran be of other than Divine origin?

11. Motion of Mountains

The Quran states:

> **And you see the mountains thinking they are standing still while they are moving like clouds, the work of Allāh Who does all things to perfection. Truly He is All-Experienced with whatsoever you do.** (10:88)

Mountains are icons of immovability. In fact, not only are

they moving, but their motion has several components: motion of tectonic plates, Earth spinning and orbiting the Sun, motion of the solar system within the Milky Way galaxy, and motion of this galaxy. The verse implies that motion is relative; although mountains are moving we do not see their motion because we are moving with them at the same velocity. The comparison with the motion of clouds has some interesting connotations: (i) since clouds move faster than tectonic plates, mountains are moving faster than tectonic plates, like clouds, which implies that Earth is itself moving, (ii) clouds are not self-propelled; they are driven by wind. The same is true of mountains; the tectonic plates, to which the mountains are anchored, are driven by the convection movements in the mantle, as previously mentioned. On the other hand, a planet such as Earth has a motion of its own that originated since its formation, and is subject to gravitational forces, mainly from the Sun. Such motion is described in the Quran as "swimming in an orbit" (see verse (36:40) below) since swimming is a more active movement that is different from being carried along as in the case of clouds; and (iii) a uniform cloud cover appears stationary, just like mountains, when in fact it is moving with the wind.

In Aristotle's view, Earth was at the center of the universe and was unmoving. The planets and the Sun moved in circles centered on Earth. This view was later modified by Greek astronomers and by Ptolemy, the highly influential Egyptian astronomer of Greek descent, but the Earth remained stationary. At the time the Quran was revealed this was the prevailing view. Rather than refer to the motion of Earth directly, and hence subject the Prophet Muhammad to the ridicule of his opponents, the Quran refers to the motion of the Earth less obtrusively. The verse was interpreted by the early exegetes to refer to the Day of Resurrection, although the verb concerning motion is in the present continuous and not the future tense. Besides, will any human stop and watch the mountains moving on this most terrifying Day of Resurrection? (See Chapter 5, Section "The Afterlife".)

To be sure, the Pythagoreans, around the 6th century BCE and almost a century-and-a-half before Aristotle, believed that the Earth rotated on its own axis. The Prophet Muhammad could not have possibly derived the motion of the Earth from the Pythagoreans, for these also believed that the Sun was fixed in space at the center of the universe. Yet the Quran clearly refers to the motion of the Sun, as mentioned earlier under "Item 5. Evolution of the Universe", verse (36:38), and in:

> **It is not for the Sun to catch up with the Moon, nor does the night outrun the day. Each is swimming in an orbit of their own.** (36:40)

Moreover, the Quran does not explicitly speak of the rotation of Earth around its axis as did the Pythagoreans. Rather, a more general motion of Earth is implied, which is inclusive of several components of motion, as explained earlier. The motion of Earth that is consistent with the present-day view of planetary motion was proposed by Copernicus about nine centuries later. So how can the Quran be of other than Divine origin?

12. Internal Ocean Waves

Oceans can be stratified, that is, have layers of lower density water above layers of higher density water because of differences in temperature and/or salinity. This occurs, for example, at river outlets where warm brackish water from the river forms a layer above that of the cold salty water of the ocean. In the open seas stratification can occur because of temperature differences due to warming of surface waters by the Sun or due to other factors. When the layer structure is disturbed, internal waves are generated at the boundary between two layers, as illustrated in Figure 4.7.

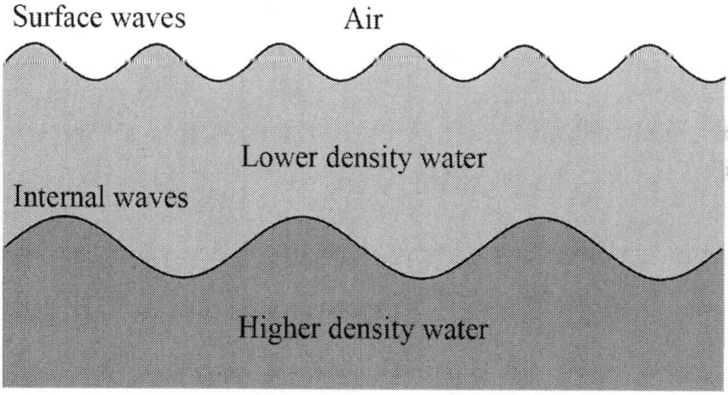

Figure 4.7 Internal waves in water

This is like disturbing the surface of a water body, as when throwing a stone into a pond for example, which generates waves between the adjacent layers of water and air having different densities. In a similar fashion, waves are generated between layers of water of different densities when the layer structure is disturbed. The disturbances that generate these internal waves could be a river outflow, or tidal motion of water over underwater ridges or breaks in the seafloor, or atmospheric disturbances.[68] Internal waves can exceed 50 m in height; their wavelength, that is, the distance between successive crests, can vary between a fraction of a meter to kilometers; and their periods, that is the time interval it takes successive crests to cross a given location, can vary between seconds and hours.

Internal waves typically have much larger amplitudes than surface waves between water and air, because the density differences, and therefore the restoring forces, between the water layers, are much smaller than between water and air.

Internal waves are not felt at the surface but can result in bands of rough, dark waters over the troughs of the internal waves alternating with bands of calm, lighter-colored waters over the crests. These alternating bands were observed since ancient times but their cause was only understood in recent times through measurements of temperature and salinity at various depths, observations from aircraft and satellites, and mathematical and computer modelling.[69]

The Quran states:

> **Or like darkness in a deep sea, covered by waves with waves above them and clouds above them – darknesses, one above the other. When one puts out one's hand, one can hardly see it. He for whom Allāh has not appointed any light has no light.** (24:40)

The verse clearly refers to waves above waves, as in Figure 4.7, with darknesses, one above the other, in layers. And this many centuries before the nature of internal ocean waves was understood based on fluid dynamics. Did the Prophet Muhammad have expert knowledge in oceanography in addition to geology and cosmology? So how can the Quran be of other than Divine origin?

13. Water and Life

Water was a prominent and sacrosanct feature of all ancient myths and beliefs. The Greek philosopher and mathematician, Thales of Miletus, who died in the 6th century BCE, hypothesized that water is the principle and origin of all matter and that matter is alive, containing souls. The Greek philosopher Empedocles, who died in the 5th century BCE, considered water to be one of the four ultimate elements that made all the structures in the world, the other elements being earth, fire, and air.

Many verses in the Quran mention water in several contexts, particularly as water sent down from the sky to revive the earth after its "death" following a dry season, this being one of wondrous Signs of The Almighty. What is of concern here is the direct relation between water and living matter, as revealed by two verses of the Quran:

> **...and (We) made from water every living thing...** (21:30)

> **And Allāh has created every animal from water: among them are those that go upon their bellies, and among them are those that go upon two legs, and among them are those that go upon four. Allāh creates whatsoever He wills. Truly Allāh is Most Capable of everything.** (24:45)

The first statement is part of the verse quoted previously in "Item 4. Origin of the Universe", and includes all living things – animals and plants. This is in accordance with modern scientific knowledge that the cytoplasm, that is, the inside of cells excluding the nucleus, is roughly 80% water by weight. Body organs and parts have a high percentage of water, the brain and kidneys 80-85%, even bone is 20-25% water, and teeth 8-10% water.[70] The extracellular media and blood are all water-based.

The second verse specifically refers to terrestrial animals. The word that has been rendered as animal is *dābbah*, which means an animal that "ambulates on the surface of the earth",[11] as clarified in what follows this word in the second verse. "Creation from water" can refer to water being the basic constituent of every living thing, as in the first statement. But the reference to terrestrial animals can additionally mean that these animals originated in water, since *dābbah* excludes marine animals. The origin in water could imply that terrestrial animals "evolved" from marine animals. It is noteworthy that the verses are carefully worded so as not to be contradicted by scientific discoveries.

The reference in the Quran to water and living things is authoritatively succinct, devoid of superstitious appendages, and consistent with present-day science. The Prophet Muhammad could not have possibly possessed the knowledge to pronounce such statements. This knowledge only became available many centuries later. So how can the Quran be of other than Divine origin?

14. Milk Production

The Quran asserts:

> **Verily, in cattle there is a lesson for you. We give you to drink of what is inside their bodies, from a coming together of the content of their intestines and blood, a milk pure and tasty to the drinkers.** (16:66)

The word *baṭn* can mean "belly" or equally well "the inside, or interior, of anything".[71] It is translated therefore as "inside their bodies". The word *farth* means "contents of intestines".[72] It has been incorrectly translated as "refuse", or "excrement", because these refer to what is discharged outside the body from the contents of the intestines.

But what has blood to do with the contents of the intestines and milk? As explained by Bucaille,[73] the meaning can be understood only with reference to modern physiology. The contents of the intestines are the product of digestion of ingested food. Some of these contents are absorbed through the intestinal wall and transported by blood to the liver, where they undergo some chemical transformations before circulation in the bloodstream to the rest of the body. The mammary glands of the breasts absorb the required constituents from the blood in order to form milk and secrete it. To quote Bucaille: "Here the initial process which sets everything else in motion is the bringing together of the contents of the intestine and blood at the level of the intestinal wall. This very precise concept is the result of discoveries made in the chemistry and physiology of the digestive system. It was totally unknown at the time of the Prophet Muhammad and has been understood only in recent times. The discovery of the circulation of the blood was made by Harvey roughly ten centuries after the Quranic Revelation."[73]

So how can the Quran be of other than Divine origin?

A large number of verses in the Quran is related to physical phenomena.[74] The preceding 14 items are only a small selection, as an extensive discourse on this topic, which can be found in the references cited in this chapter, is well beyond the scope of this book. However, it must be kept in mind, as mentioned earlier, that some of the claims of miraculousness that are found in the literature are rather overzealous and not very convincing. Moreover, as mentioned previously, many verses cannot yet be interpreted in the light of present knowledge.

The following item is not related to physical phenomena; yet it is considered as truly miraculous.

15. Abū Lahab

Abū Lahab, or "the father of flame", was the nickname of a paternal uncle of the Prophet Muhammad, because of his bright-red complexion. Abū Lahab and his wife were such fierce opponents of Islam from the very beginning that a special, short chapter of the Quran was revealed condemning them. The following are its first three verses:

> **May the hands of Abū Lahab perish, and may he perish. His wealth avails him not, nor what he has earned. He will burn in a Fire of blazing flame.** (111:1-3)

The Fire of blazing flame refers to Hell in the Afterlife (see Chapter 5, Section "The Afterlife"). But why are these verses considered miraculous? There were many fierce opponents of Islam, some of whom converted later and became very pious and prominent Muslims. In fact, ʿUmar ibn al-Khaṭṭāb had intended to kill the Prophet Muhammad but had a change of heart after his exposure to Chapter 20 (*Ṭā Hā*). He later became the second Caliph and is considered one of the greatest personalities of Islam. Abū Lahab never converted, although the aforementioned verses were revealed ten years before he died in 624 CE. Had he converted and became a pious Muslim like others, after these verses were revealed, he would surely have avoided Hell, but at the same time he would have inflicted a glaring contradiction in the Quran. For how could a pious Muslim be burned in Hell? No mortal, not even the Prophet Muhammad, could have been absolutely certain that Abū Lahab will never convert to Islam and therefore contradict the Quran. This certainty could only be of Divine origin.[75]

The verses concerning Abū Lahab are also very

significant in another respect. According to the Quran humans have free will, as discussed in the next chapter in the Section "Why Is There Suffering and Evil?". Abū Lahab was free to convert to Islam, as others did, but chose not to. The verses illustrate that whatever choice one makes in exercising free will, The Almighty has prior knowledge of it, hence the certainty that Abū Lahab will never convert.

Numerical Miraculousness

Another manifestation of the miraculousness of the Quran, which was discovered more recently, is the large number of special numerical relations that occur. Only a sample is considered here for illustration purposes.[76,77] Some of these examples are related to the context of the Quranic verses involved. Others are in the form of multiples of some prime number such as 7 or 19. The number 7 has a mystical symbolism in practically all ancient cultures and religions since at least Babylonian times and occurs frequently in many different contexts.[78] It occurs frequently in the Quran although early exegetes were of the opinion that in many instances the number 7 meant plurality, and not a definite number, just like the word *yawm*, in reference to the creation of the universe, means an indefinite time period and not a 24-hour day.[79] The number 19, which also has mystical symbolism, is mentioned in the Quran as well and has special significance, as will be explained later.

1. Consider some global numbers to begin with: the number of chapters (114) and the number of verses (6236) of the Quran. If these are laid side by side, with the smaller unit (verse) on the right and the larger unit (chapter) on the left, bearing in mind that Arabic is written and read from right to left, the

resulting number **1146236** is a multiple of 7. Laying the numbers side by side is equivalent in this case to forming a new 7-digit, decimal number whose value is one million, one-hundred-and-forty-six-thousand and two-hundred-and-thirty-six. If the order of the numerals is reversed, the number **6326411** is also a multiple of 7. If the individual numerals in the numbers 114 and 6236 are added, the sum is **23**, the number of years over which the Quran was revealed. If this number is laid side by side with the number 23 replacing the number of chapters, the result **236236** is a multiple of 7. If the order of the numerals is reversed, the number **632632** is also a multiple of 7. If the number 23 is laid side by side with the number of chapters replacing the number of verses, the resulting number **23114** is a multiple of 7. If the order of the numerals is reversed, the number **41132** is also a multiple of 7. The number of digits of the first number formed (1146236) is 7, the number of digits of the second number formed (236236) is 6, and the number of digits of the third number formed (23114) is 5. If these are written in the order of the number of digits of the first number on the right, the resulting number **567** is a multiple of 7. If the number of the first chapter, (1), is written to the right of the number of the last chapter, (114), the resulting number **1141** is a multiple of 7. The 4 numerals of 1141 also add to 7. All coincidences? Not very likely.

2. Consider an example of some context-related numbers. The reference in the Quran to the development of the embryo is in verse 13 and the first part of verse 14, Chapter 23:

Then we made him a small life-germ in a safe lodging, then we turned the life-germ into a clot, then we turned the clot into a lump, then into bones, then we clothed the bones with flesh, then produced it another creation... (23:13-14)

In Arabic, this passage consists of **23** words and uses **23** letters of the Arabic alphabet of 28 letters (this being a multiple of 7, by the way) and occurs in Chapter **23**. Humans have **23** pairs of chromosomes, which contain the genetic material responsible for the transmission of hereditary characteristics through fertilization of the egg by the sperm in a "safe lodging", which is the fallopian tubes that connect the ovaries to the uterus. Coincidence? Not very likely.

3. In Chapter 18 (The Cave) the Quran narrates the parable of a number of youths who escaped religious persecution by taking refuge in a cave where they were put to sleep for 309 years. For our purposes, the key verb in this narrative that is related to their length of stay is *labithū*, "they remained". The first occurrence of this verb is in verse 12, and the last reference to this same verb is in verse 26. Verse 25 and the first part of verse 26 are:

And they remained in their cave for *three hundred* years, to which were added nine. Say: "Allāh knows best how long *they remained*..." (18:25-26)

If the first occurrence of "they remained" is numbered as word number 1, the last occurrence of this verb in verse 26 (italicized above) is word 310. That is, there are 309 words in Arabic from, and including, the first word "they remained" until the last "they remained" is reached. The actual count can be readily checked in accordance with the rules of counting used.[80] Moreover, the word "three" (italicized above) is number 299, and the word "hundred" (italicized above) is number 300. Following this latter word there are exactly 9 words in Arabic till the passage ends with the last "they remained", which includes the statement "to which were added nine". All coincidences? Not very likely.

4. The following are some numbers pertaining to full verses at the beginnings of chapters:
   i. Only two verses in the Quran begin with the statement: "Verily this Quran…" The first verse (17:9) has 69 Arabic letters. The second verse (10:76) has 45. The sum 114 is the number of chapters in the Quran.
   ii. Exactly seven chapters of the Quran begin with the explicit glorification of Allāh (Chapters 17, 57, 59, 61, 62, 64, and 87).

   Coincidences? Not very likely.

5. The following numerical relations involve the first verse of the Quran:
   i. Chapter 1 (The Opening) of the Quran consists of 7 verses in which 21 Arabic letters are used, a multiple of 7. Its first verse is referred to as the *basmalah*, because it starts with *bi'smi'Llāh*, "In the name of Allāh". It is the most-often cited verse of the Quran: it is repeated in each of the daily prayers and is uttered by pious Muslims, in blessing, before embarking on an important action and even before eating or drinking. The first verse consists of 4 words in Arabic: the

first word, "in the name of" has 3 letters; the second, Allāh has 4 letters; the third, "the Most Compassionate" (*al-Raḥmān*) has 6 letters; and the fourth, "the Ever-Merciful" (*al-Raḥīm*) has 6 letters. If laid side by side, in the order of the letters of the first word on the right, the resulting number **6643** is a multiple of 7. If only the letters of the first and last words are laid side by side, the number **63** is a multiple of 7.

ii. Consider the number of letters in each of the four words of the *basmalah*: **3** in the first word, 4 in the second word, and 6 in each of the third and fourth words. If the number of letters in the second word is added to that in the first word, the sum is **7**. If the number of letters in the third word is added to this sum, the result is **13**. Adding to this the number of letters in the fourth word gives **19**. If these four highlighted numbers are laid side by side, starting with the number of letters in the first word on the right, the resulting number **191373** is a multiple of 7. Now reverse the procedure starting with the number of letters in fourth word, which is **6**, then adding the number of letters in the third word, which gives **12**, then adding to this the number of letters in the second word, which gives **16**, then the number of letters in the first word, which gives **19**. If these four highlighted numbers are laid side by side, in the same order of words as before, the resulting number **6121619** is a multiple of 7×7.

iii. The first word in the *basmalah* (*ʾism*) is repeated in the Quran 14 times in the singular and 8 times in the plural, or a total of 22 times.[81]

The fourth word in the first verse (*al-Raḥīm*) is repeated in the Quran 115 times in various forms.[82] If laid side by side, with the number of repetitions of the first word on the right, the resulting number **11522** is a multiple of 7.

iv. The third word in the first verse (*al-Raḥmān*) is repeated in the Quran 57 times in various forms.[83] As mentioned in Chapter 5, Section "Nature", this is a special name that applies only to The Almighty. The number **57** is a multiple of 19. If 57 is laid side by side, with the repetitions of the fourth word (*al-Raḥīm*) word on the left, in accordance with the ordering of words being followed, the resulting number **11557** is a multiple of 7.

v. The number of repetitions of the name Allāh (the second word) in the Quran is cited as 2699 times in various forms.[84] This number is a prime number, which could be a reference to the uniqueness and Oneness of The Almighty. In Arabic, the word "Allāh" consists of 4 letters in Arabic, three of which are different letters, with the letter "l" repeated twice. If the number of occurrences of any number of these different letters in each of the 4 words of the *basmalah* are laid side by side in the order of the smallest to the left and the largest to the right, the number **0224** is a multiple of 7. If the number of occurrences is ordered in the same order as the words, with the number in the first word on the right and the number in the fourth word on the left,[85] the resulting number **2240** is a multiple of 7.

All coincidences? Not very likely.

6. The following numerical relations involve the words and letters of the first and last verses of the Quran:
   i. The last verse of the Quran (114:6) has 4 words (counting the conjunction *wāw* as a separate letter, according to the counting rule followed), which is the *same number of words as in the first verse*. The first word, "from" has 2 letters; the second, "jinn" has 5 letters; the third, "*wāw*" has 1 letter; and the fourth, "mankind" has 5 letters. If laid side by side, in order of the letters of the first word on the right, the resulting number **5152** is a multiple of 7, just as in the case of the first verse. Moreover, the first and last digits add to 7.
   ii. The 19 letters of the first verse in the Quran (the *basmalah*) consist of 10 different Arabic letters, some of which are repeated in the total of 19. If the number of occurrences of any number of these 10 letters in the 4 words of the *basmalah* are written side by side, with the smallest number of occurrences on the left and the largest number on the right,[86] the resulting 10-digit number **1111122334** is a multiple of 7.
   iii. Similarly, the last verse of the Quran, consisting of 4 words, has 13 letters, 8 of which are different. If the number of occurrences of any number of these 8 letters in the 4 words of the last verse are written side by side, with the smallest number of occurrences on the left and the largest number on the right,[87] the resulting 8-digit number **11111233** is a multiple of 7.

   All coincidences? Not very likely.

7. The following numerical relations involve the

chapter numbers of the first and last verses of the Quran:

i. The last verse of the Quran (114:6) has 4 words and is verse number 6 in the last chapter. The first verse (the *basmalah*) has 4 words and is verse number 1 in the first chapter. If these numbers are laid side by side in the order: (number of words in last verse, verse number, number of words in first verse, verse number) the resulting number **4641** is a multiple of 7.

ii. If the chapter number is added to the right of the verse number in both cases, the resulting 8-digit number **46**_114_**41**_1_ is a multiple of 7.

iii. The last verse contains 13 letters and the first verse 19 letters. If these are added to the left of the number of words, since the letter is a smaller unit than the word, the resulting 12-digit number ***13*****46**_114_***19*****41**_1_ is still a multiple of 7.

iv. If the (number of letters, number of words, verse number, chapter number) are considered alone for the first and last verses, the resulting number is **19411** for the first verse and **1346114** for the last verse. Each of these numbers is a multiple of 7.

All coincidences? Not very likely. It should be noted that the numerical relations in the preceding items 5, 6, and 7 are concerned with only the first and last verses of the Quran, excluding numerical relations involving other verses, particularly those "special" verses that are often repeated in prayers, most of which remain to be discovered!

8. The number 7 is first mentioned in the Quran in (2:29) and last mentioned in (78:12). Chapter 78 is

the 77th chapter starting with Chapter 2, where **77** is a multiple of 7. Similarly, the number of verses from the first verse until the last verse in which 7 occurs is cited[88] as **5649**, a multiple of 7. The verse in which 7 first occurs is preceded in Chapter 2 by **28** verses, a multiple of 7. The verse in which 7 last occurs is also followed in Chapter 78 by 28 verses. Because of grammatical Arabic parsing in the verses concerned, the word 7 is formed by 3 letters (*sīn, bāʾ, ʿyn*) in the verse in which it first occurs and by 4 letters (*sīn, bāʾ, ʿyn, alif*) in the verse in which it last occurs, the total number of letters being 7. All coincidences? Not very likely.

9. The number of chapters of the Quran is **114**, a multiple of 19, and the first verse (the *basmalah*) consists of 19 Arabic letters, as noted previously. The first five verses revealed to the Prophet Muhammad (96:1-5) consist of **76** letters,[89] a multiple of 19. Chapter 96 (The Clot) in which these verses occur consists of 19 verses and 76 words,[89] equal to the number of letters in the first five verses revealed. All coincidences? Not very likely.
   It is noteworthy that the number 19 is explicitly mentioned in the Quran in a verse of its own: **"Over it are nineteen."** (74:30). Most exegetes interpret this verse as an allusion to the number of angels who are the keepers of Hell, although some consider this a reference to the miraculous numerical relations that involve the number 19.[89] In Arabic gematria, whereby each letter is assigned a numerical value,[90] the value of the Divine Name *Wāḥid* (One), is 19. The number 19 consists of the first (nonzero) and the last numerals of the decimal system and is

considered to be a reference to The First and The Last, these being two of The Most Exalted Names of The Almighty (see Chapter 5, Section "Will and Power"). These two names occur in the verse: **"He is the First, and the Last, and the Outward, and the Inward; and He is Knower of all things."** (57:3). This is similar to the Biblical passage: "I am the Alpha and the Omega, the first and the last, the beginning and the end." (Revelation 22:13), where alpha and omega are the first and last letters, respectively, of the classical Greek alphabet.

10. The fifth verse of the first chapter is an important consecration by the pious: **"You (alone) we worship and from You (alone) we seek help."** (1:5) In Arabic, the verse consists of 5 words having the number of letters as: 4(1), 4(2), 1(3), 4(4) and 6(5), where the number of letters in each word is followed by the word number in parentheses. The total number of letters is 19. If the number of letters in each word are ordered side by side, with the number in the first word on the right, following the direction of writing in Arabic from right to left, the resulting number **64144** is a multiple of 19. If the chapter number is written on the right, followed to the left by verse number, then the number of words, and the number of letters, as was done in Item 7.iv., the resulting number is **19551**, which is a multiple of both 19 and 7. Coincidences? Not very likely.

11. The previously mentioned assurance by The Almighty concerning the collection and recitation of the Quran is: **"Surely on Us rests the collecting of it and the reciting of it."** (75:17) In Arabic the

verse consists of **17** letters and **5** words. The verse number is **17** and the chapter number is **75**. The sum of these four numbers is **114**, the number of chapters of the Quran, also a multiple of 19. The number of letter in each word is: 2(1), 5(2), 4(3), 1(4) and 5(5), where the number of letters in each word is followed by the word number in parentheses. If the number of letters in each word are ordered side by side, with the number in the first word on the right, as was done in Item 10., the resulting number **51452** is a multiple of 19. Coincidences? Not very likely.

12. **29** chapters of the Quran begin with special letters (usually referred to as *al-ḥurūf al-muqaṭṭaʿa* (disjoined letters)): a single letter or a group of 2 to 5 letters whose significance or meaning remains enigmatic to this day. Nevertheless:
    i. They form a set of 14 different phrases, without repetition, and they use 14 Arabic letters. The number **14** is a multiple of 7 and the sum of the two fourteens is **28**, the number of letters of the Arabic alphabet. 28 added to 29, the number of chapters, is **57**, which is a multiple of 19.
    ii. The Arabic letter *qāf* (equivalent to the English letter "q") is the first letter of the Arabic word "Quran". It is the special letter at the very beginning of Chapter 50 (*Qāf*) and is also part of the two sets of special letters at the beginning of Chapter 42 (The Counsel). These are the only two occurrences of *qāf* in the special letters. Now *qāf* occurs 57 times in Chapter 50 and 57 times in Chapter 42 when the two *qāf*s in the special letters are included.

57 is a multiple of 19, and the sum of the two 57s is 114, the number of chapters of the Quran. In other words, the special letter *qāf* at the beginning of the chapter makes the total number of *qāf* in the chapter a multiple of 19.

iii. One of the special letter combinations is the two-letter *yā sīn* at the beginning of Chapter 36 (*Yā Sīn*), which is considered "The Heart of the Quran". In this Chapter, *yā* is repeated 237 times and *sīn* is repeated 48 times, including the occurrences in the special letters. The two letters are repeated a total of **285** times, a multiple of 19. The order of this chapter in the sequence of Quranic chapters that begin with special letters is also 19.

All coincidences? Not very likely.

Many more instances of these special numerical relations can be found in the references cited in the first paragraph of this section and more relations continue to be identified. It seems that the Quran has a large intricate web of numerical relations involving letters, verses, and chapters.[91] What has been discovered so far is but the tip of the iceberg. An amazing result applies to the much venerated "Throne Verse" (2:255), which consists of **57** words, a multiple of 19. If the number of occurrences of any number of the 10 different letters of the *basmalah* in each word of the Throne Verse are laid side by side, there results a 57-digit number[92] that is a multiple of 7!

An important aspect of these numerical relations is that they can be readily checked using a number of freely available, online Arabic search tools[93,94] and following well-defined rules of counting.[95] In the preceding Items 1-12 the conjunction *wāw*, equivalent to English "and", has been counted, where applicable, as a separate word. If *wāw* is not considered a separate word but as a letter that is part of the word that follows it, then the numerical relations based on this manner of counting will not hold. Incredibly, though, other numerical relations will then apply. For example, consider the verse in the Quran that poses a challenge to produce the like of it:

> **Say: "Surely if mankind and jinn banded together to bring the like of this Quran, they would not bring the like thereof, even if they supported one another."** (17:88)

If conjunctive *wāw* is counted as a separate word, the verse in Arabic consists of **21** words, which is a multiple of 7. If conjunctive *wāw* is not counted as a separate word, the verse consists of **19** words. Irrespective of how conjunctive *wāw* is counted, the verse has **76** letters, a multiple of 19, and uses **19** letters of the Arabic alphabet. The total 19 + 76 + 19 is 114, the number of chapters in the Quran. Another coincidence? Not very likely. (For the meaning of jinn in the preceding verse see Chapter 7, Section "Virtuous Conduct".)

There can be no doubt that the numerical relations of the Quran could not have occurred by accident but were intended to be discovered at some future time as a recurring miracle that will continue to be manifested with time. What is special about this kind of miracle is that it is completely objective and clear-cut; it does not depend on any linguistic or philosophical interpretations, just simple arithmetic and consistent rules of counting Arabic letters and words.

If one picks a book at random it is entirely possible that a number of numerical relations can be found that occur by chance and not by design. As illustrated in the preceding examples, the types of special numerical relations that are found in the Quran are varied, based on: numbers of letters in words or verses; numbers of words in verses or chapters; numbers obtained by addition, or by positioning as decimal digits; or numbers of letter combinations in some words; or numerical relations that are context-related. The resulting numbers have special significance or are multiples of prime numbers such as 7 or 19. If each individual numerical relation has a probability between 0 and 1 of occurring by chance, the probability of *all* the very large number of these relations occurring by chance is of the order of the product of the individual probabilities and is vanishingly small. Moreover, the totality of the evidence presented in terms of miraculous revelations and numerical relations should be mutually reinforcing. That is, if one is skeptical about some of the evidence, but is convinced of other evidence, this conviction should dispel the doubt about the evidence that might be considered equivocal.

It is possible nowadays, at least in principle, and using supercomputers and appropriate algorithms and programs, to design a meaningful text of the size of the Quran – of about 77,000 words – having any number of desired special numerical relations. But was that possible in the 7th century CE? And produce a book having all the features of the Quran, as summarized in the following concluding section? So how can the Quran be of other than Divine origin?

Where Do We Stand?

The present chapter aimed at providing objective evidence for the existence of The Almighty. Neither a philosophical argument nor an argument based on some abstract conceptions is used. Concrete evidence is sought that, as far as the author is aware, is best provided by the

Quran. Two types of evidence are presented, one focusses on scientific revelations of the Quran, the other on special numerical relations discovered. The presentation had to be brief, by necessity, but sufficiently convincing.

All things considered, there can be no reasonable doubt that the Quran cannot possibly be of human origin, as was concluded by Bucaille in the quotation cited at the beginning of this chapter. It is a book dealing primarily with matters of faith, spirituality, and religious observances, yet it is replete with astoundingly intricate numerical relations while authoritatively touching on many diverse topics – such as cosmology, geology, oceanography, zoology, botany, physiology, psychology, ethics, legislation, and economics – including prophetic references to physical phenomena, which have since been corroborated by science, and all in a captivating style that is linguistically and literarily inimitable (see Chapter 3, Section "Linguistic and Literary Inimitability") and which makes the text easy to remember. In the words of Bruce Lawrence, the Nancy and Jeffrey Marcus Humanities Distinguished Professor Emeritus of Religion, Duke University: "As tangible signs, Qur'anic verses are expressive of an inexhaustible truth, they signify meaning layered with meaning, light upon light, miracle after miracle."[96]

In all honesty, how can the Quran possibly be of other than Divine origin?

Accepting the Divine origin of the Quran is believing in the existence of The Almighty who revealed it to humanity. The "supernatural" in the definition of spirituality presented in Chapter 1 can be unequivocally identified with The Almighty, so that belief in The Almighty is the linchpin of the spirituality advocated in this book. To distinguish this form of spirituality from other forms, it will henceforth be referred to as Spirituality, with a capital “S”.

However, mere belief in the existence of The Almighty is not sufficient for this Spirituality. The Almighty must be accorded a special status in one’s everyday thoughts and acts, as will be elaborated in Chapter 7. To do so meaningfully and in full conviction one must have a fairly good notion about The Almighty. That is the subject of the next chapter.

Chapter 5

What Can Be Said About The Almighty?

Theme: The Almighty is Transcendent, Omnipresent, Omnipotent, and All-Perfect.

The Image of God

Michelangelo's *The Creation of Adam*[1] (Figure 5.1) is a highly acclaimed fresco painting. It is undoubtedly a great work of art, but in its depiction of God as a bearded man in a celestial setting with an outstretched right arm imparting life to Adam, it is untenable from a theological viewpoint. According to Thomas Aquinas, God cannot be decomposed into parts, such as body and soul, nor described in terms of matter or form, and his essence is His Existence, which is not only unknown but unknowable.[2,3] William Lane Craig, the Christian theologian, cites Thomas Aquinas affirming that God is: "...a Personal Creator of the universe, who, sans the universe is timeless, spaceless, beginningless, changeless, necessary, uncaused, and enormously powerful."[4]

Figure 5.1 Michelangelo's The Creation of Adam

The preceding chapter affirmed the Divine origin of the Quran. It is only logical, therefore, in thinking about The Almighty to resort to the Quran as a book of Divine origin to ascertain what it has to say about The Almighty. As a book of faith the Quran is very much concerned with advocating belief in The Almighty, which it had to do in a simple and clear manner that was understandable and convincing to illiterate Bedouin Arabs of the 7th century CE but at the same time convey the profoundness of meaning that is demanded by the nature of the subject. This the Quran achieved, to a varied audience, through impelling, inimitable language and style, through appeal to reason and good judgement, as mentioned in Chapter 4, and directly through many enlightening verses, as will be demonstrated in the present chapter by examples under various headings.

The Arabic word *rabb* often occurs in Quranic verses and is conventionally translated as "Lord", which is almost synonymous with "God" and connotes power and authority. It should be noted, however, that *rabb* not only means "owner" or "master" but also an "orderer", "rectifier", "rearer", "fosterer", "nourisher", or "someone who brings (a thing) to a state of completion by degrees".[5] The nearest in English would be "Nourisher unto perfection".[6] Because these meanings are more relevant to the present discourse, "*Rabb*" with a capital "R" is retained in the translation of Quranic verses.

Essence

A number of verses in the Quran directly relate to the Essence of The Almighty, the most famous is the phrase:

> **...Nothing is like Him...** (42:11)

This is a clear and succinct statement that The Almighty is beyond anything that humans can conceive or imagine or define. In other words, He is absolutely Transcendent. Some Islamic scholars interpret this phrase more strongly: "Nothing is like His likeness", that is, nothing can exist other than Him that might be His likeness.[7]

The famous Light Verse states:

> **Allāh is the light of the heavens and earth. The parable of His Light is a niche, wherein is a lamp. The lamp is in a glass. The glass is as a shining star kindled from a blessed olive tree, neither of the East nor of the West. Its oil would well-nigh shine forth, even if no fire had touched it. Light upon light. Allāh guides unto His Light whomsoever He will, and Allāh sets forth parables for mankind, and Allāh is Knower of all things.** (24:35)

The first sentence and the parable have been the subject of numerous treatises by prominent Islamic scholars in search of their meaning and their spiritual and mystical significance.[7] The interpretation of the first sentence focusses on two of the main characteristics of light: it is visible by itself and makes everything else visible. The sentence thus asserts that The Almighty is the most evident Reality in Himself and also through Whom everything else in the heavens and earth is known. This knowledge derives from His having created the heavens and Earth and from His control and guidance of all that transpires in them. The Light (*al-Nūr*) is one of The Most Exalted Names (see Section "Will and Power" in what follows).

It is intriguing that in near-death experiences (NDEs) (see Chapter 6, Section "Near-death Experience") light is a recurrent theme, whether in The Light, or Beings of

Light, or beings "lit from within".

> **He is The First, and The Last, and The Outward, and The Inward...** (57:3)

The First means that there was nothing before Him. The Last means that He remains after all creation perishes. In other words, The Almighty is timeless. The Outward has been interpreted to mean that He is everywhere, that everything that exists is a manifestation of His Self-Disclosure, and that He is above, or predominating over, everything. The Inward has been interpreted to mean that He is also within all things guiding them and knowing all their hidden aspects. The Almighty is therefore timeless and Omnipresent. After all, He is the creator of space and time. Among the Exalted Names (see Section "Will and Power" in what follows) are the four attributes mentioned in this verse: The First, The Last, The Outward, and The Inward.

Creator and Guide

The greatest Act of The Almighty is the creation of the heavens and Earth, as is often repeated in the Quran in attestation to His Divinity and elaborated in what follows. The following is an exchange between Moses, with his brother Aaron (Harūn), and the Pharaoh of Egypt:

> **He (Pharaoh) said: "Who then is the *Rabb* of you two, O Moses?" He (Moses) said: "Our *Rabb* is the One Who has given everything its form, and further guided (it)."** (20:49-50)

The answer of Moses is very concise, precise, and profound. The Almighty is identified to the Pharaoh by His

Acts of creation and guidance. The following should be noted: (i) In Arabic, the two acts of creation and guidance are separated by *thumma*; this does not always imply a sequence in time[8,9] and is rendered in a translation as "further";[10] the two acts are therefore considered conjoint. (ii) The Acts of creation and guidance are for *everything*, living and nonliving. When only living things are meant, that is expressly stated, as in (21:30) (see Chapter 4, Section "Miraculous Revelations, Item 13. Water and Life"). "Everything" would therefore include all that is found in nature – galaxies, stars, planets, mountains, etc. (iii) This raises the question as to what guidance means in this case. Evidently, when applied to both living and nonliving things, guidance would mean ordaining the laws of nature, for these govern the existence and continuation of everything. All things, living and nonliving, comply with the laws of nature. In ordaining these laws, The Almighty guides and sustains everything He created.

Will and Power

> **He is Allāh, The Creator, The Originator, The Fashioner. His are The Most Exalted Names...And He is The Almighty and The All-Wise.** (59:24)

The meaning of this concise verse is very profound and far-reaching. As The Creator (*al-Khāliq*), He willed and previsioned all creation. He is The Originator (*al-Bāri'*), or maker, of what He creates from its very beginnings and without prior example, and He is The Fashioner (*al-Muṣawwir*) of the form of what He creates. Many exegetes understood this to refer to three stages in the unfolding of creation: the will and prevision, the actual bringing into being, and the endowment with various characteristics.

In the Quran and in the sayings of the Prophet Muhammad, The Almighty is ascribed names – conventionally considered to be 99 Most Exalted Names – that represent Attributes or Qualities of His Essence and which can be perceived in the minds of those who use them, as in supplications, or who contemplate on the Nature of The Almighty. The Most Exalted Names are referred to as a group in this and three other verses of the Quran and individually in many verses. In fact, this verse contains six of The Most Exalted Names: Allāh, The Creator, The Originator, The Fashioner, The Almighty (*al-ʿAzīz*), and The All-Wise (*al-Ḥakīm*).

His Command when He desires anything is only to say to it, "Be!" and it is. (36:82)

Like many verses in the Quran this verse attests to His absolute Will and Power. He can will anything and has the power to do it. His Will is not only absolute but is also supreme, subordinating human will.

Humans cannot will anything except by His Will:

And you cannot will unless Allāh Wills… (76:30), (81:29)

Although the context of this phrase is the will to follow or not follow His Way, it is nevertheless of general applicability. It does not nullify human free will. Humans do have free will, as discussed in the last section of this chapter, but this was granted by the Will of The Almighty, so human free will is subordinated to His Will. This is exemplified by the common, everyday *inshallāh* (Allāh willing), which makes His Will a condition for the occurrence of whatever one wills or wishes to happen.

In any case, whatever action results from the exercise of human free will is known beforehand to The Almighty, for He knows the Unseen (see Section "All-Knowing" in what follows). This was previously mentioned in Chapter 4, Section "Miraculous Revelations, Item 15. Abū Lahab". The beautiful simplicity and coherence of the logic should be noted. If the Will of The Almighty is supreme, then everything is subordinated to His Will, including human free will. And if The Almighty is All-Knowing, then He knows beforehand the choice that a human will make in the exercise of human free will.

Glorification

> **...All that is in the heavens and the Earth glorifies Him...** (59:24)

> **...And there is not a single thing but glorifies Him with His Praise, but you do not understand their glorification...** (17:44)

The reference here is again to everything in the universe, living and nonliving, glorifying Him. Everything glorifies Him by its mere existence, which He brought into being, and by its continuation in this existence through abiding by the laws of nature, which He ordained. Whereas The Almighty guides everything through His ordained laws of nature, everything glorifies Him by being governed by these laws. In addition, all living things glorify Him in being alive and in their everyday activities, such as moving, feeding, etc. which He made possible through His Will, Power, and Design. But we do not understand their way of glorification, for we do not understand the nature of life, nor do we understand the ultimate constitution of matter.

In thinking about glorification, I am reminded of a personal anecdote. As a young child I used to spend a lot of time with a great-aunt who lived with my family. My father was very busy with his medical practice, his academic and administrative responsibilities at the university, and his writing medical textbooks in Arabic. My mother was busy most of the time with household chores. My great-aunt doted on me, which was all the more reason to spend time with her and enjoy the benefits and pleasures of getting spoiled. As I watched birds come to drink from the water fountains in the garden of our house, I couldn't help but notice that they would drink by dipping their beaks in the water then raising their water-filled beaks toward the sky. When I asked my great-aunt why birds do that she replied: "They are glorifying The Creator." Though incomprehensible to a five-year-old, this answer seemed plausible enough at the time in the absence of any alternative explanation. Several years later, I learned from biology at school that most birds lack the ability to suction water into their throats. They drink by filling their beaks with water then raising them upward for water to flow under gravity into their digestive system. Ah! I thought. "This is the correct scientific explanation. The answer of my poor great-aunt reflected her ignorance of biology. One must resort to science for the right answers." Many years later, I studied undergraduate and graduate electrical engineering, physics, and biology. As I read and thought about religion and philosophy, I came to realize that my great-aunt, bless her soul, had it right after all! The birds were indeed glorifying The Almighty in merely being alive, in having the anatomy and physiology that He brought into being, in subsisting on the food and water He made available to them, and in making use of the laws of nature that He ordained, such as water flow under gravity.

Oneness

The Oneness of The Almighty is epitomized by the oft-repeated Chapter 112:

> **Say, "He is Allāh, the One and Only. Allāh, the Eternally Sufficient unto Himself. He begets not; nor was He begotten. And none is Comparable to Him."** (112:1-4)

In the second verse, *al-Ṣamad*, which occurs in the Quran only this once, is applied to The Almighty alone and it is one of The Most Exalted Names. It has no English equivalent. Its theological meaning comprises the concepts of the Primary or Initial Cause of all things and an eternal, self-sufficient, independent Being needed by all but needing none; everything is dependent on Him for its coming into being and its continued existence. The third verse asserts that He was not born nor did He give birth to anyone. The last verse affirms His Transcendence, as previously mentioned under "Essence".

The Oneness of The Almighty is an overriding theme of the Quran. It gives consistency and coherence to the perception of an Almighty Being in a manner that is eminently reasonable and easy to grasp. The Quran itself explains:

> **Were there gods other than Allāh in the heavens and Earth, these would surely have been corrupted...** (21:22)

Having more than one god would result in disorder and chaos, as when one god wishes to do something which another god does not want done. If The Almighty has the supreme Will and is Omnipotent, there cannot be other gods with Him. That would be logically absurd.

> **Truly, Allāh forgives not that any partner be associated with Him, but He forgives what is less than that to whomsoever He pleases. Whosoever associates partners with Allāh has surely committed a most grievous sin.** (4:48)

Associating partners with The Almighty means worshipping someone or something other than Him. It is a grave and unforgivable sin because it negates the very notion of the role that The Almighty should have in governing our thoughts and guiding our actions. Someone or something will then be sharing with, or replacing, Him in this respect. These points are of crucial importance for Spirituality, to be discussed later (see Chapter 7, Section "Virtuous Conduct"). *Al-Wāḥid* (The One) is one of The Most Exalted Names.

All-Knowing

> **...and He is Knower of all things.** (57:3)

> **...And no fruits come forth from their sheaths, nor does any female bear or bring forth, but by His Knowledge...** (41:47)

> **...Not a tiny speck's weight evades Him in the heavens or in the Earth, nor smaller than that, nor larger, but is recorded in a clear book.** (34:3)

> **And with Him are the repositories of the Unseen; none knows them but He. And He knows what is in the land and sea. And there falls not a leaf but that He knows it, nor any grain in the dark recesses of**

the earth, nor anything moist or withered, but is recorded in a clear book. (6:59)

The Almighty is Omniscient, having total knowledge of everything. His knowledge encompasses all that happens in the heavens and Earth, including the most minuscule. He alone has full knowledge of the Unseen, that is everything that is beyond human perception, such as future events, metaphysical matters, and all the inner aspects of everything. Moreover, this knowledge is perspicaciously recorded and is timeless; it is not obliterated with time.

...And they cannot attain to anything whatever of His Knowledge except what He Wills... (2:255)

The Almighty gives access to some of His knowledge according to His Will and to whomsoever He pleases. This would include all scientific discoveries, for example, since scientific knowledge is part of His knowledge. How much of this knowledge will humans ever attain to is contingent on His Will.

We did indeed create the human being, and We know what his innermost-self whispers within him; and We are nearer to him than his jugular vein. (50:16)

...Verily, of His subjects He is All-Versed, All-Seeing. (17:96)

And if you speak openly, verily He knows what is secret and what is more hidden still. (20:7)

...Verily, Allāh is the All-Hearing and the All-Seeing. (40:20)

...And He is with you wherever you may be. And Allāh sees all that you do. (57:4)

The Almighty has created all humans, referred to in the second verse as His subjects (*ʿibādihi*) (literally, his servants or his slaves), irrespective of whether or not they are believers, since they are all subjugated to His Will and Power. He knows them only too well, their innermost selves, nature, intentions, and thoughts. He knows what they "speak openly" and "what is secret", that is, what they keep to themselves, hiding it from others; "what is more hidden still" is what is in their subconscious, that they themselves are not aware of. He is with them wherever they may be, being closer to them than their jugular veins, which is an expression of "the Immanence of God in all of creation, that the Divine Reality is the substrate of every reality."[11] He is All-Seeing and All-Hearing, for nothing escapes Him. He is witness to all their acts, good or bad, which are also recorded. Among The Most Exalted Names are: The All-Knowing (*al-ʿAlīm*), The All-Versed (*al-Khabīr*), The All-Hearing (*al-Samīʿ*), The All-Seeing (*al-Baṣīr*), The Witness (*al-Shāhid*), and The Watcher (*al-Raqīb*).

Self-Sufficient

...truly Allāh is The Self-Sufficient, needing nothing of any of His creation. (3:97)

O mankind! It is you who stand in need of Allāh, and Allāh is The Self-Sufficient, The All-Praiseworthy. (35:15)

Having created the universe by His Will and Power,

The Almighty does not need anything or anyone in the universe. They need Him for continuation and sustenance. All creation needs the laws of nature that He ordained for their existence and continuation. All living creatures are sustained by food chains that He brought into being. Plants are directly or indirectly the ultimate food source for all terrestrial life. Fruit-bearing trees are a stark example of how plants are intended by design to serve as food for other species. A fruit-bearing tree such as an apple tree typically bears at least a hundred apples, each containing many seeds that are enclosed by a thick, edible, and nutritious pulp. Considerable energy, derived mainly from the Sun, is required to make so many apples with so much pulp. Of what use is this pulp to the apple tree? If so many seeds are required to ensure the continuity of apple trees, wouldn't some compact pulp-free enclosure of no nutritional value have been less energy-intensive and most likely requiring less complex processing by the apple tree? Evidently, the pulp was made for some creatures to feed on. Did this happen by accident? With so many varieties of fruit? And so many edible plants? And all having various vitamins, minerals, and phytonutrients?

The Almighty has made it all possible for living and nonliving things through His Will, His Design, and His Power. He has endowed all creatures with what it takes to perform their daily activities. They are all dependent on Him, but He is independent of all.

...And Allāh is The Sustainer of all things. (4:85)

The Sustainer (*al-Muqīt*) is one of The Most Exalted Names.

Two of The Most Exalted Names that occur together and are amongst the most revered are: The Ever-Living (*al-Ḥayy*) and The Self-Subsisting (*al-Qayyūm*). The Ever-Living not only means that He is eternal, but also that He is All-Powerful and able to actualize His Will in accordance with His All-Knowing. The Self-Subsisting means that He subsists through Himself and sustains everything else. Another of His Most Exalted Names is The Self-Sufficient (*al-Ghanī*), which means that He is completely independent of everything else.

Ownership

> **To Him belongs whatsoever is in the heavens and on Earth, and what is in between, and what lies beneath the ground.** (20:6)

> **Surely it is We Who give life and cause to die, and We are the Inheritors.** (15:23)

In several verses of the Quran, it is clearly stated that everything in the universe belongs to The Almighty. When all of creation perishes, everything returns to The Almighty. This is not a claim of property ownership but has profound meaning and implications. Theologically, since everything belongs to The Almighty, one should make important requests, and seek help in consequential matters, only from The Almighty. In actual fact, we have only temporary, illusory ownership of our material possessions. They can be taken from us anytime, one way or another, if He so pleases, and we leave them all behind when we die. Spiritually, this has a profound implication for our view of material possessions (see Chapter 7, Section "Formative Attitudes", subheading "Material Possessions").

That everything belongs to The Almighty is part of

Islamic culture. When street beggars ask for alms, they often plead: "from the wealth of Allāh" as a reminder that the alms are really from The Almighty. Many years ago, a wealthy non-Muslim businessman built a very imposing building that was the first of its kind in an Arab capital. He had inscribed in stone above the entrance: "The ownership is to Allāh", which shows that this notion was commonly held in a Muslim society, even by a non-Muslim. Later, someone cynically scribbled underneath this statement: "But the rent goes to (Name of the businessman)."

The ownership of The Almighty to what is beneath the ground is of course a reference to what may lie there as buried treasure or natural resources. The famous Biblical verse: "Blessed are the meek, for they shall inherit the earth" (Matthew 5:5), was reportedly interpreted in jest by an oil tycoon as excluding petroleum and mineral rights, because petroleum and minerals are beneath the ground. Many centuries before this oil tycoon, the Quran preempted such an interpretation; what is beneath the ground also belongs to The Almighty, as stated at the end of the aforementioned verse (20:6).

Owner of the Kingdom (*mālik al-mulk*) and The Inheritor (*al-Wārith*) are two of The Most Exalted Names.

Nature

The Divine Nature is expressed by The Most Exalted Names. The following is a selection of the Names that are to be emphasized for our purposes:

The Most Compassionate (al-Raḥmān), The Ever-Merciful (al-Raḥīm)

These two Names are mentioned in the first verse of the Quran, the *basmalah* (see Chapter 4, Section "Numerical Miraculousness, Item 5.i.") immediately following the name Allāh, which attests to their cardinal importance. Both Names derive from the noun *raḥmah*, which is usually translated as mercy and sometimes as tenderness. *Raḥmah* combines mercy with love and connotes being kind, gracious, gentle, forgiving, compassionate, and benevolent through charitable acts of kindness to relieve the suffering. The difference between the two derivations of *raḥmah* is one of emphasis. The first derivation (*al-Raḥmān*) signifies intensity and extent of the quality, the second its constant repetition. *Al-Raḥmān* "is said to be one of the Divine Names that can only apply to God (The Almighty), for it is one of the Names by which existence itself is made manifest, a universal blessing or mercy (*raḥmah*) that cannot be attributed to anyone other than God...It thus differs from The Merciful (*al-Raḥīm*), which is said to pertain to a more particular form of Divine Mercy and by which human beings may also be described."[12] Because of this, *al-Raḥmān* is rendered as The Most Compassionate, rather than The Most Merciful to emphasize this uniqueness. These two Names are frequently repeated in the Quran, often in combination with other Names such as The Most Gracious (*al-Ra'ūf*), as in:

> **...And that Allāh is Most Gracious, Ever-Merciful.** (24:20)

The mercy of The Almighty is all-embracing:

> **...and My Mercy encompasses all things...** (7:156)

The All-Forgiving (al-ghaffār), The Ever-Forgiving (al-ghafūr)

These Names are also of great importance in the Quran.

Both names are derived from the same root of forgiveness, the first emphasizes intensity and extent, whereas the second emphasizes constant repetition, as in the preceding Names. The Ever-Forgiving is combined with The Ever-Merciful in many verses, as in:

> **And whoever does evil or wrongs himself, and then seeks forgiveness of Allāh, will find Allāh The Ever-Forgiving, The Ever-Merciful.** (4:110)

The Ever-Forgiving is sometimes combined with The All-Forbearing (*al-Ḥalīm*), which is another of The Most Exalted Names, as in:

> **...And Allāh is The Ever-Forgiving, The All-Forbearing.** (2:225)

The one unforgivable sin is ascribing partners to Him, as mentioned previously in Section "Oneness".

The Relenting (al-Tawwāb)

The Almighty forgives those who repent and ask for His Forgiveness. This is a reflection of His mercy, so The Relenting is combined with The Ever-Merciful in many verses, as in:

> **Know they not that Allāh accepts repentance from His subjects, and receives the alms, and that Allāh is The Relenting, The Ever-Merciful?** (9:104)

The Responsive (al-Mujīb)

The Almighty responds to supplications and answers those who call on him, as in:

> **...I answer the prayer of the supplicant when he calls on me. So let them respond to Me and believe in Me, that they may be led aright.** (2:186)

> **And your *Rabb* has said: "Call upon Me and I shall respond to you"...** (40:60)

These verses and many others emphasize the direct relation between The Almighty and humans, which is highly important from a spiritual point of view, as discussed in Chapter 7. In any spirituality that centers around a Divine Being, such as the Spirituality advocated in this book, a person should have recourse to the Divine Being anytime, anywhere. There should be no intermediary, nor a special place, nor a particular posture or activity required between a person and the Divine Being.

The All-Loving (al-Wadūd)

> **And seek forgiveness from your *Rabb*; then turn unto Him in repentance. Truly my *Rabb* is The Ever-Merciful, The All-Loving.** (11:90)

> **And He is The Ever-Forgiving, The All-Loving.** (85:14)

Love is the gateway to all goodness and a foundation of spirituality. The Almighty's Love of His subjects is very special and encompassing. The aforementioned qualities expressed by The Most Exalted Names such as The Most Compassionate, The Ever-Merciful, The Most Gracious, The All-Forgiving, The Ever-Forgiving, The All-Forbearing, The Relenting, and The Responsive are all manifestations of His Love.

What is special about His Love is that it transcends all other kinds of love in not being based on any form of need from anyone or anything, for He is The Self-Sufficient. Even a mother's love, which is the most selfless kind of human love, is based on an innate drive, which He instilled, and which fulfills for the mother, consciously or subconsciously, a need for self-fulfillment, for a special role and purpose in upbringing the dependent and needy youngsters, and in the likely expectation of a reciprocation in being taken care of in old age. His Love, on the other hand, is the purest form of love, above all need.

Someone might interject at this point to pose the question that if The Almighty is All-Loving of His subjects, possesses all the noble qualities expressed by The Most Exalted Names, and is Omnipotent, then why does He allow suffering and evil in this world? This question is addressed in the last section of the present chapter.

The All-Wise (al-Ḥakīm)

The All-Wise is one of The Most Exalted Names. It occurs in the Quran 93 times at the ends of verses, 47 times in association with The Most Exalted Name, The All-Mighty (*al-ʿAzīz*), and 35 times in association with The Most Exalted Name, The All-Knowing (*al-ʿAlīm*). Examples are:

> **But if you falter after receiving the clear-cut message, then know that Allāh is All-Mighty, All-Wise.** (2:209)

> **And whoever commits a sin, commits it only against himself, and Allāh is All-Knowing, All-Wise.** (4:111)

Wisdom at the human level is the ability to discern what is

the right decision or course of action in a given situation. It is based on good knowledge of the various aspects of a given situation, on experience gained about the outcomes of similar situations, and on good evaluation and judgement. It involves having a wide perspective, being open-minded, unbiased, understanding, and compassionate, as well as upholding values, particularly fairness and justice. There can be no wisdom without knowledge, as a wise decision cannot be made without adequate knowledge of various aspects of a given situation. Power without wisdom can be tyrannical, as the exercise of power can be misplaced in the absence of wisdom. In the end human wisdom is imperfect because humans are limited in all the aforementioned respects and can never be certain about the outcome of the decision or course of action in a given situation.

The Wisdom of The Almighty is unlimited. Having created the universe, He is All-Knowing of everything that takes place in it. There is perfect wisdom behind everything He does, although as humans, we may not understand that wisdom because of our very limited knowledge and perspective. Moreover, He is The Most Compassionate, The Ever-Merciful, and The All-Loving, so all His dispensations will do perfect justice in the big picture that only He is fully aware of, as He is All-Knowing of the consequences. Note that wisdom, as a moderator and guide, comes after power in the first verse whereas knowledge, as a prerequisite, comes before wisdom in the second verse.

The All-Just (al-ʿĀdil)

Allāh bears witness that there is no god but He, as do the angels and the possessors of knowledge.

Upholder of justice. There is no god but He, the All-Mighty, the All-Wise. (3:18)

As The Most Compassionate, The Ever-Merciful, The All-Knowing, The All-Wise, and The All-Loving, The Almighty cannot be but perfectly just in everything He does. The All-Just is one of The Most Exalted Names. But His criteria for justice may not be understandable to humans in many cases because of their limited knowledge and perspective. Justice is strongly commanded in all human actions and relations, as in the following verse:

Allāh commands doing justice, doing-good (to others), and giving to kinsfolk, and He forbids indecency, abomination, and aggression: He admonishes you so that you may take heed. (16:90)

This verse and other similar verses are of great importance from the practical aspects of Spirituality and are discussed in Chapter 7, Section "Virtuous Conduct".

Disbelievers and Quasi-Believers

Let us review at this stage the discussion in this and the preceding Chapter 4. The latter chapter was chiefly concerned with presenting objective evidence for the existence of The Almighty based on miraculous verses of the Quran and on numerical relations of letters and words. The existence of The Almighty could also be argued on theological grounds,[13] on philosophical grounds,[14] or by invoking a universal morality.[15] The approach of Chapter 4 is more objective, concrete, and incontrovertible. One might argue about the interpretation of some of the verses or the occurrence by chance of a few numerical relations, but to reject *all* of them, and there are many not mentioned in Chapter 4 for the sake of brevity, as coincidental is utterly absurd and completely irrational, as emphasized at the end of Chapter 4.

Following the belief in the Existence of The Almighty, one has to know about Him in order to submit to His Will and Serve Him. What exactly this means in practical terms is considered at length in Chapter 7. In essence, this means Serving Him in earnest and having Him the sole guide and purpose in our everyday thoughts and acts. The present chapter aimed at conveying some idea of the indescribable Greatness, Majesty, and Glory of The Almighty. But it is impossible to do justice in this regard. After all He is Transcendent, beyond human perception and imagination. What was emphasized earlier in this chapter is that He is The One and Only, The Creator of everything and its Guide and Caretaker, not bound by space or time, the All-Knowing, the real Owner of everything in the universe, The Willer of all things that are, The Doer of whatever He Wills, The Most Compassionate, The Ever-Merciful, The All-Forgiving, The Ever-Forgiving, The Relenting, The Responsive, The All-Loving, The All-Wise, and the All-Just. The Almighty is maximally perfect. His are The Most Exalted Names, for He possesses all the perfect attributes to the highest degree possible. Upon contemplating all this, the mental image that emerges is truly overwhelming and overpowering, beyond human imagination and comprehension. So what would be the reaction to such a revelation about The Almighty?

Those who have come to believe in the existence of The Almighty and who truly understand the implications of this revelation about Him will choose to submit to His Will. Those who do so are the true believers who would embrace the Spirituality advocated in this book. Others may react in some form of denial. Some of these deniers may be confirmed atheists who adamantly deny the existence of The Almighty despite all evidence, such as that presented in the preceding chapter. For some psychological reasons, of which they might or might not be aware, these deniers have an impenetrable barrier to any belief in a supernatural deity. They are irredeemable disbelievers.

Nevertheless, what is probably a majority, would fall in between believers and disbelievers. These may not deny the existence of The Almighty but may be somewhat skeptical about it, which makes them agnostic in this respect, or they may profess belief in His Existence but have not come to terms with the full implications of believing in His Existence and submitting to His Will. This category between believers and disbelievers will be referred to as quasi-believers.

Quasi-believers may have some notion of The Almighty in a rather abstract manner at the back of their minds, without meaningfully involving Him in their everyday thoughts and acts. They may occasionally remember The Almighty if they come across His Name, or they may utter His Name on some occasions as a matter of habit, or they may even pray regularly. Other than that, The Almighty is absent from their everyday thoughts and actions. These quasi-believers simply get on with their lives guided by whatever considerations they deem appropriate and that best suit their interests, aspirations, and the short-term or long-term goals they have set in life. They may abide by moral principles and core values to varying extents, their commitment to these principles and values being tempered at times and to various degrees by being practical or pragmatic. They pursue success and happiness according to the measures they have set for themselves or that are prevalent in their milieu. These measures generally revolve around: one's earnings (without much regard as to how earned and for what purpose), the ostentatiousness of one's lifestyle (without much regard as to its intrinsic value and meaning), and the advancement in one's career, profession, or occupation (without much regard as to how this advancement is attained). Although they have a rather vague belief in the existence of The Almighty, the quasi-believers have not submitted to His Will in any true and profound sense either because of inadequate comprehension, complacency, or arrogance.

Some quasi-believers find it difficult to grasp the implications of His Qualities and Attributes and to accept the notions of His absolute Will and Power and His being All-Versed and All-Knowing about all that transpires and will transpire in the universe. Not being able to comprehend is no excuse for denial. Anyone early in the 18th century, for example, would have been quite incredulous if told that it will be possible in the future to store the contents of hundreds of thousands of pages of information on a thin chip of material just several millimeters across, or that it would be possible to almost instantly "hear" and "see" someone else on the other side of the globe. This person would reasonably argue that such feats are quite impossible. Yet, we take these matter-of-factly today. So how can we deny The Creator, The Originator, and The Fashioner qualities or attributes that seem implausible to us in this day and age and with our limited knowledge and mental capacity? The infiniteness and the perfectness of The Almighty are beyond human perception and comprehension. They simply have to be accepted, not on blind faith but, rather, in the light of incontrovertible evidence, contemplation, and reason as well as the immense practical benefits that accrue and which are elaborated in Chapter 7.

The complacency of other quasi-believers is mainly due to a regrettable, confused ordering of life's goals and priorities. These quasi-believers are too preoccupied with their worldly pursuits to give much attention or consideration to anything else, particularly to something nonmaterialistic or spiritual. Such pursuits are considered an untoward distraction and a waste of time. This complacency of some quasi-believers is to their own detriment, at the expense of their peace of mind and self-fulfillment, as will become clear from Chapter 7.

Still other quasi-believers persist in their ways out of arrogance. One form of arrogance is in feeling intellectually superior. These quasi-believers may be highly cultured, well-informed, and very knowledgeable. They pride themselves on their keen ability to apply analytical thinking, reasoning, and judgement to their discourse and conduct of their affairs. They may be quite accomplished and distinguished in their careers. They place a premium on their intellectual prowess and independence. Consciously or subconsciously, they believe that their intellect encompasses everything so that nothing can exist outside its grasp. They consider their intellect the ultimate arbiter of everything. Although they may grudgingly accept the existence of some supernatural deity, this is as far as they are willing to go. Any submission to a higher will is considered to be intellectually debasing and therefore unacceptable. Such an attitude is utterly misguided. First, as mentioned in Chapter 2, the human mind is inherently of limited capacity. No matter how powerful is the human intellect, and no matter how great are its accomplishments, they pale in comparison with the great mysteries of the universe – how it all came about, how it is sustained, the nature and origin of life, the wonders of our being, our consciousness, even our intellect that is in fact being abused by such an attitude. All this calls for intellectual humility, not arrogance. Second, in being preoccupied with basking in the glory of their intellect and applying it in the conduct of their daily affairs, these quasi-believers are avoiding confrontation with the ultimate question: what is the meaning and purpose of our existence? This is considered at length in Chapter 7 in the light of Spirituality. Suffice to say here is that these quasi-believers are woefully forsaking the self-fulfillment that is central to the meaning and purpose of life.

Another form of arrogance comes from those quasi-believers who wield power and authority, because of their wealth, or status, or position. These quasi-believers may be so preoccupied with pursuing their worldly interests or exercising their influence that they become oblivious to any nonmaterialistic, let alone spiritual, considerations. Moreover, any submission to a higher will seems rather demeaning and unwarranted in view of all that is accessible to them. Such an attitude is pitifully delusional. Sooner or later, a moment of truth is upon them, on their deathbed if not earlier.

What disbelievers and quasi-believers seem to forget is that although they think they can keep The Almighty out of their minds and their lives, they are nevertheless subject to His Will and Power, like everything else, whether they like it or not, or whether they care to admit it or not. All their thoughts and all their actions are known to Him, as He is All-Versed and All-Knowing. Their persistence in their ways is subject to His Will and Wisdom. They are completely unaware of what He has in store for them. In the light of all this, do their ways make sense?

It is noteworthy that the Quran recognizes in various instances the obstinate and quarrelsome stance of humans when it comes to believing in The Almighty and submitting to His Will:

> **Does not the human being see that We have created him from a small life-germ? Then Lo! he is an open disputant.** (36:77)

> **...And the human being is more than anything contentious.** (18:54)

This human characteristic is of course the result of human free will and intellectual capacity that were endowed by The Almighty as part of the trial for humans in this worldly life. But disbelievers and quasi-believers choose to be contentious and dispute His Presence and Will. Needless to say, they do that at their own peril and are bound to suffer the consequences, if not in this life then in the Afterlife (see Chapter 6, Section "The Afterlife").

Why Is There Suffering and Evil?

The following question is often asked: "If The Almighty has the power to do anything, and since He is The Most Compassionate and The Ever-Merciful, then why does He allow suffering and evil in the world?" At face value, this seems to be a legitimate question, but in fact, it is based on false premises. Such a question will never cross the mind of a true believer, because for such a believer The Almighty is also All-Wise and All-Just. Since the true believer has fully submitted to the Will of The Almighty, then the true believer will never question His Wisdom and Justice. The question, therefore, is one that is posed by disbelievers and quasi-believers. It is to these that the rebuttal should be directed.

It should be recognized that any judgement passed

by humans on any issue is inevitably subject to the constraints of: (i) limited knowledge and perspective, and (ii) human values on which the judgement is based. Both of these constraints do not apply to The Almighty, for He is All-Knowing and has the ultimate overall picture. He knows everything pertaining to any matter; we don't. Moreover, the considerations that The Almighty bases His decisions on do not have to be the same as those of humans, for He is All-Wise, All-Just and Ever Merciful to all, whereas humans base their decisions and judgement on a limited set of considerations and are subject to their own biases, prejudices, value systems, and the vagaries of human nature. The eminent Islamic scholar, al-Ghazzālī, who lived in the 11th and 12th centuries CE, provides a beautiful allegory,[16] which although he applied in a somewhat different context, is nevertheless very befitting for your purposes. Paraphrasing al-Ghazzālī, we are like ants on a piece of writing; we can see the lines, curves, and dots of what is written, but we do not understand their meaning, nor can we see the writer. Ultimately, therefore, whatever occurs in this world is part of His Wisdom and Justice, which may not be comprehensible to humans. The question, therefore, as to why does The Almighty allow suffering and evil in the world is completely misplaced to begin with. Nevertheless, several issues concerning suffering and evil will be addressed in what follows.

The Quran asserts that if The Almighty so desires He could make all people believers:

> **Had your *Rabb* so willed, all on earth, every single one, would have believed...** (10:99)

But if everyone on earth is a believer and a doer of good, what would be the meaning of life? The meaning and purpose of life are discussed at length in Chapter 7. Essentially, The Almighty endowed humans with free will so they may or may not choose to submit to His Will. Either choice has its consequences, as the following verses proclaim:

> **...Say (O Prophet): "All is from Allāh...Whatever good befalls you comes from Allāh; whatever evil befalls you comes from your own self."** (4:78-79)

> **Truly Allāh commits not so much as a mote's weight of wrong: if there is a good deed, He will multiply it and grant from Himself a great reward.** (4:40)

> **And whatever misfortune befalls you is because of that which your hands have earned; and He pardons much.** (42:30)

These verses clarify some very important points: (i) The Almighty is the ultimate source of all that happens; all good and evil that befall humans are in accordance with His Will. This is only logical considering that He has absolute Will and Power. (ii) The Almighty does not do wrong. He is perfect in every way and is the source of all goodness. (iii) He is Most Beneficent, multiplies the rewards of good deeds, and pardons much of the bad that is committed. But what misfortune befalls those who do not submit to His Will is a consequence of their own actions. There can be no doubt that such persons can do much evil and cause much suffering. They will undoubtedly suffer the consequences of their actions, if not in this life, then in the Afterlife.

A most important point is that this life is a test by The Almighty as to which human beings will be the most righteous in their conduct:

> **He Who created death and life that He may test you as to which of you is most righteous in deed, and He is The Almighty, The Ever-Forgiving.** (67:2)

> **...And We try you with evil and with good, as a test...** (21:35)

The test is in both good fortune and misfortune. The good fortune may be in good health, wealth, and stature. The test is whether or not one will be grateful to The Almighty for what He has provided, will do good unto others, and becomes a true believer. The misfortune could be in sickness, poverty, fear of what may come, loss of lives of family and friends, or other sufferings. The test is for being patient and having full trust in the Wisdom, Justice, and Mercy of The Almighty:

> **And surely We shall try you with something of fear and hunger, and loss of wealth, lives, and produce; and give glad tidings to those who endure with patience – those when affliction befalls them, say: "Truly we belong to Allāh, and to Him we shall return."** (2:155-156)

That life is a test for humans also answers the somewhat simple-minded question that is sometimes posed in various contexts and in a form such as: "If this is what The Almighty meant, then why didn't He say so plainly and simply?" The answer may well be that in His Will, Design, and Wisdom He created humans to be "the most contentious of beings" (see (18:54), Section "Disbelievers and Quasi-Believers" in the preceding). But contentiousness over an issue sets apart the sincere and well-meaning from the devious and malevolent. And that is part and parcel of the tests that humans are subjected to. Similarly, the different interpretations of Quranic text are part of this test, for which all will be accountable.

In summary, humans have been endowed with free will so that they may choose whether or not to submit to His Will. The choices that humans make in the exercise of their free will: (i) are by way of trial for them, (ii) will have consequences for them, if not in this life then in the Afterlife, and (iii) are known beforehand to The Almighty.

Another important point is that, for true believers, suffering also serves as a form of spiritual purification and advancement, for it is a reminder and an inducement to some hard thinking about life's priorities, about what is truly important and what is vain and superfluous. However, the suffering is never beyond what one can bear:

> **Allāh tasks no self beyond its capacity...** (2:286)

Moreover, because of limited human knowledge and perspective, we may think that something is bad for us, when in fact it is good, and conversely:

> **...But it may be that you hate a thing though it be good for you, and it may be that you love a thing though it be evil for you. Allāh knows, and you know not.** (2:216)

It is also important to keep in mind that suffering in this world, no matter how painful and distressing, is but temporary. By His Will, believers who suffer are rewarded, if not in this life, then in the Afterlife, which is what matters. The reward in the Afterlife is everlasting and most gratifying, as discussed in Chapter 7. Worldly life is but a fleeting moment on an eternal scale. Any suffering, no matter how severe and painful to the sufferer, can in no way even remotely compare to what transpires in the Afterlife, whether in punishment or reward.

To illustrate how limited knowledge can lead to misjudgment, the Quran narrates the tale of Prophet Moses and the Khiḍr, a holy man to whom The Almighty has given special knowledge. Prophet Moses sought his company to learn from him:

> **Moses said to him: "May I follow you so you can teach me some of the right guidance you have been taught?" The man said: "You will not be able to bear with me patiently. How could you be patient in matters beyond your knowledge?" Moses said: "Allāh willing, you will find me patient, and I will not disobey any of your orders." The man said: "If you follow me, then do not ask me about anything until I make mention of it to you." So they set out. Once aboard a boat, he made a hole in it. Moses said: "Did you make a hole in it to drown its passengers? You have done a dreadful thing." The man said: "Did I not tell you that you will never be able to have patience with me?" Moses said: "Forgive me for forgetting, and do not be hard on me for what I did." So they journeyed on until they met a boy, and the man slew him. Moses said: "Have you killed an innocent person who has not killed anyone? You have done a horrible thing." The man said: "Did I not tell you that you will never be able to have patience with me?" Moses said: "If I ever question you about anything after this, then do not keep me in your company, for by then I would have given you**

> **enough of an excuse." So they journeyed on until they came to the inhabitants of a town; they asked them for food, but the inhabitants refused them hospitality. Then they came upon a wall about to collapse, and the man restored it. Moses said: "If you wished, you could have taken payment for it." The man said: "This is the parting between you and me. I will tell you the explanation of what you could not bear with patience. As for the boat, it belonged to some needy people who toiled on the water. So I intended to mar it, because there was a king coming after them who was seizing every boat by force. As for the boy, his parents were believers, and we feared he would overburden them with his rebellion and disbelief. So we intended that their *Rabb* will grant them in his place one of greater purity and closer in mercy. As for the wall, it belonged to two orphan boys in the town, and beneath it was a treasure that belonged to them. Their father was a righteous man, so your *Rabb* intended that they attain their maturity and retrieve their treasure as a mercy from your *Rabb*. And I did not do this of my own accord. This is the explanation of what you could not bear with patience."** (18:66-82)

The three actions in this narration were, on the face of it, gratuitous (the restoration of the wall), malicious (the marring of the boat), and evil (the killing of the boy). Yet, they served a higher purpose of goodness which even Prophet Moses could not comprehend because of his lack of full knowledge.

What all the foregoing boils down to is that in the face of suffering and evil we must refrain from passing judgement based on our own perceived values and limited knowledge and perspective. By the Will and Wisdom of The Almighty worldly life is a test, and suffering and evil are part of it as well as a form of spiritual purification. We should have full trust in the Wisdom, Justice, and Mercy of The Almighty. After all, we have to trust others at one time or other. In our upbringing we implicitly trust our parents in knowing what is best for us, and we submit to their will. We trust doctors with our health because of their knowledge and experience. We trust surgeons with life-threatening operations because of their skill and expertise. As law-abiding citizens, we trust the authorities with our security and general welfare. So why not trust the Creator of the universe in His infinite Wisdom, Justice, and Mercy and submit to His Will? Indeed, humans are the most contentious of beings and oftentimes irrational to boot!

Chapter 6

Is Death the End?

Theme: Death is not the end. It heralds the beginning of what has no end.

Facing Death

Death is said to be the great equalizer. All living things have a finite life span and will die, from one-celled bacteria, to the lowliest insects, to the most powerful, influential, distinguished, and accomplished humans. Humans are believed to have become aware of their mortality some 150,000 years ago, which required a sense of the identity of the individual, alive or dead, and the realization of dying at a future time. So how did humans come to face this most inevitable of ends? Naturally, death evokes anxiety and fear, which leads to attempts to circumvent it somehow. An early and quite revealing account of facing death is portrayed by the famous classic, *The Epic of Gilgamesh.*

The Epic of Gilgamesh[1,2]

Gilgamesh was a king of the Sumerian city-state of Uruk, who ruled sometime between 2800 and 2500 BCE and who became the hero of future legends and myths. The Epic took a unified and cohesive form many years later, around 1700 BCE, as revealed by recovered clay tablets. Several additions and modifications were later made to the Epic; the latest version commonly discussed is known as the Standard Babylonian 12-tablet version, dating to about 700 BCE.

The following relates the part of the Epic that is most

relevant for our purposes. Gilgamesh was two-thirds god (from his goddess mother) and one-third human (from his king father), which made him, therefore, superhuman in stature. As king, he tyrannized his people with his excesses, causing them to complain to the deities, who created Enkidu, the wild man, as a counterpart. When Gilgamesh and Enkidu encounter one another, they fight furiously, but recognizing that they are equals, they strike up a deep friendship. In search of fame and adventure, they journeyed together to the Cedar Forest of Mount Lebanon to slay its guardian, the fearsome demi-god Humbaba, which they were able to do with the help of the Sun god. After they returned to Uruk, the goddess Ishtar, impressed by Gilgamesh's exploits, enjoins him to become her husband, but Gilgamesh rebuffs her because of her betrayal of earlier lovers. Enraged, Ishtar succeeds in sending down the Bull of Heaven to kill Gilgamesh. Although the Bull wreaked havoc in Uruk, Gilgamesh and Enkidu were able to slay the beast. Now the deities decided that Enkidu must die for the sacrileges of their two heroes, Humbaba and the Bull of Heaven. Enkidu fell ill for twelve days then died. Gilgamesh was devastated with grief. He refused to believe that Enkidu had died, until a maggot dropped from the corpse's nostril. He mourned the loss of his dearest companion with great ritual and offerings to the gods of the netherworld – the realm of the dead. Realizing that he will also die like Enkidu, Gilgamesh genuinely fears death for the first time. He forsakes his formal obligations and roams the wild, disheveled in animal skins, grieving for his lost friend and in search of Uta-napishti, the human being granted immortality by the gods, in the hope of gaining an eternal life for himself. He arrives at the seaside tavern of Siduri, the innkeeper, who tries to dissuade him from his quest, warning him of the dangers involved. Nevertheless, she directs him to Uta-napishti, who explains that his immortality was a reward for his building a strong boat and surviving the great deluge that the gods had set to destroy mankind, and that the granting of immortality to a human will not be repeated by the gods. After he failed a test to beat sleep by remaining awake for six days and seven nights Gilgamesh despaired of conquering death and was convinced by Uta-napishti to accept his mortality and his role as king. Gilgamesh returns to Uruk and revels in his great past achievement of building the impressive walls of the city.

What concerns us here is how Gilgamesh faced the death of his dearest friend and companion. First, Gilgamesh refused to accept Enkidu's death and clung to his corpse:

> ...my friend Enkidu, whom I loved so dear
> who with me went through every danger:
> *the doom of mortals* overtook him.
> Six days I wept for him and seven nights.
> I did not surrender his body for burial,
> until a maggot dropped from his nostril.[3]

Second, Gilgamesh must have been horrified by seeing a maggot drop from the corpse's nostril, a sign of the impending decay of the human body after death. Third, he realized that he would meet the same fate, which stirred in him a fear of death:

> Then I was afraid *that* I *too would die*,
> I grew fearful of death, and so wander the wild.
> What became of my friend Enkidu *was too much* to bear,
> ...my friend Enkidu, whom I loved, has turned to clay.

Shall I not be like him, and also lie down,
never to rise again, through all eternity?[3]

Fourth, Gilgamesh sought to avoid death by becoming immortal, but eventually had to accept his mortal destiny. What Gilgamesh went through illustrates the attitude of many people toward death: ignoring death, fearing death as a horrifying and inevitable end, and seeking ways to circumvent it somehow. Even today, there are people who make arrangements for their corpses to be preserved at a very low temperature, in the hope that future medical advances would allow their resurrection.

Thinking About Death

Some ignore death by simply trying not to think about it. This is particularly true at a younger age, when death seems far off into the future and one is busy with daily pursuits. With advancing age, or when facing a serious health crisis, most people cannot avoid thinking about death. This can lead to anxiety and depression, particularly in older people as they experience the waning of their physical powers and mental faculties.

With some people, anxiety about death turns to fear of death, as felt by Gilgamesh. A morbid fear of death can be psycho-pathological, referred to as thanatophobia. Some people fear death simply because they do not want to stop living. They want to continue to enjoy the perks, pleasures, and privileges of their lives; they do not want to leave their loved ones or their circle of friends; they may have something unfinished to attend to. Some people fear death as an ignominious and horrifying end: as ashes in an urn, or as a corpse in a grave, slowly decomposed by bacteria and fed on by worms. We can imagine the mighty Gilgamesh horrified by seeing a maggot drop from Enkidu's nostril and realizing that the same fate might befall him one day. This, in fact, is an odd incongruence in human-centered philosophies of life, such as humanism, discussed in Chapter 1. Such philosophies, implicitly or explicitly, extol the worth of the human being, and rightly so. Humans are truly wondrous beings endowed with a marvelous physiology, incredibly complex electro-biochemical bodily processes, exquisite senses, and amazing manual dexterity. Human mental activity is no less astonishing, involving unfathomable consciousness, vivid imagination, incisive intellectual powers and enthralling creativity, whether in the arts or in the sciences, engineering, and technology. Yet, all this simply faces a debasing physical end? Like human, like dog, or like rat, as mentioned earlier? How much more worthy of human stature is the belief in an afterlife in some form or other.

Not many contemplate death and its profound meaning. Thinking about death brings to the fore the meaning and purpose of life. As British author, Stephen Batchelor, points out: "In taking life for granted, we likewise fail to notice it. (To the extent that we get bored and long for something exciting to happen.) By meditating on death, we paradoxically become conscious of life."[4] If we are going to die, and that is the end of it all, why were we born in the first place? Is it just a matter of continuation of the species? Or is it just a matter of chance? So we might just as well enjoy what we can out of living, amass as much wealth as we can, and achieve what we can in our endeavors? What does it all mean? Thinking about death might also make one look back on one's life. What have I achieved? What do I want to achieve? What should I have done or not done? And, Why? Given a second chance, what would I have done differently? All this can be very empowering and can have a hugely positive impact if it makes one realize what is really important in life and how one should henceforth chart one's life. Thinking about death and its possible imminence might also make one realize the urgency of some matters, such as an undertaking, or finishing some task, or making amends for some wrongdoing to an associate, a friend, or a loved one, before it is too late.

Some of those facing a terminal illness learn to cope with the wait before an impending death despite the pain and suffering that they may be experiencing, and which to some is the real cause of the fear of death, more than death itself. They reconcile themselves to the inevitable and take matters rather philosophically. They might make plans for their families after their departure, as in wills. They might learn to make the best of their circumstances, by finding meaning in small things, savoring their favorite acts, reaching out to their loved ones in tender farewell, and living out their last moments in accordance with their cherished values and desires. A person near death may relish the touch of treasured memorabilia, or the sight of a bird hopping on the windowsill, or the taste of a forbidden delicacy or a favorite drink, or even the puff of a last smoke.

On the other hand, to the true believers in The Almighty and the Afterlife, as discussed later, death is the end of the trial of life. As true believers they would have lived their life virtuously, as elaborated in Chapter 7. Having submitted to His Will, they have cruised through life serenely and are even more serene at the moment of death – a moment at which they embark on the life that matters, an eternal life of peace and bliss in the embrace of The All-Loving, The Most Compassionate, and The Ever-Merciful. The following verses are attributed to the fourth Caliph and cousin of the Prophet Muhammad, al-Imam ʿAlī ibn abī Ṭālib:

> Your mother gave birth to you, son of Adam, crying while people around you were laughing with pleasure. Hence, perform your daily acts (to the satisfaction of Allāh) so that when they cry on the day of your death, you will be rejoicing in laughter.[5]

Evidently, this is a very different view of death. A similar attitude to death is expressed by Khālid ibn al-Walīd, the famous Islamic commander who referred to his army in his address to kings of Persia as "...people who love death as much as you love life"[6] and in an address to provincial governors of Persia as "...people who love death as much as you love drinking wine."[6]

The view of death by the pious is that it is just a transition between a worldly life of finite duration that is but a test for humans and a life of eternal bliss for those who understood the nature of this test and have done well in it. The fate of the physical body is of no concern.

Near-death Experience

A confrontation with death can result in a near-death experience (NDE) – a profound, subjective experience reported by some people, usually upon a close encounter with death, as in a suicide attempt; or as a result of serious injury in military combat, or in an accident such as a car collision, drowning, or falling from a height; or during a life-threatening medical condition, such as cardiac arrest, major surgery, or complications of childbirth. It is estimated that NDEs occur in 10% to 20% of people who come close to death. Reported experiences share common features, such as:

- Overwhelmingly positive and intense feelings ranging from incredible peace and tranquility to joy and ecstasy

- Out-of-body-experience (OBE) with a sense of detachment or dissociation from the body
- Moving through darkness or a dark tunnel
- Seeing a beautiful bright light and feeling surrounded by it
- Enhanced visual and auditory perception
- Feeling of oneness and interconnectedness with the universe

These features are well illustrated by the following vivid narrative of someone who underwent a 12-hour surgery for the removal of a nerve tissue tumor (neuroma):

> …I floated up to the ceiling where I looked down and saw the medical team dressed in green gowns and caps working seriously over a body. As I observed the process I realized that was the body I had just left. I had no attachment to it whatsoever. Also I had no form; I was like a mist. The next recollection was floating without effort through a dark tunnel to a beautiful yellow-white light. I had no thought of choosing to go there. It just seemed to naturally draw me to it. I saw no other Beings in the tunnel. In The Light there was only pure beautiful Light. No forms, no boundaries, nothing but beautiful white light. The feeling of peace in the light was nothing like I have ever experienced. There was no such thing as time and space. I refer to me as "I," but I felt no separation…I knew all there was and I had all knowledge…
>
> At some point three Beings of Light, (as I called them), came to me…
>
> There is no form on The Other Side, at least not the State of Being where I was, therefore there are no mouths or

> ears – all communication is telepathic. The Beings told me I must return to my body. In that indescribable state of peace, I did not want to return to my body and told them so. They said I must return, that my mission, my purpose on earth was not yet finished. I had no choice. In hindsight I appeared to be like a wisp of smoke or mist that re-entered the body at the crown of my head. The next thing I recall is the doctor slapping my face, calling my name. I was back in my body. I opened my eyes to see family and friends standing around me. While in the Light as a Being of Light myself I was told and shown many things yet do not recall them except as time goes by wisdom and recognition come to me. I sense from what I was told and shown on the Other Side.[7]

The core NDE is remarkably consistent and independent of distinguishing characteristics such as culture, religious belief, or age. There are, nevertheless, individual differences. Some near-death experiencers (NDErs), for example, report being united with deceased loved ones who appear in the form of beings "lit from within". Others see a flash review of their lives. Other differences seem to be related to the individual's beliefs, life experiences, or culture. The Being of Light, so bright and beautiful, radiating such indescribable warmth, peace, love, and joy, may be associated with God, Jesus, Buddha, or even a celebrity who had inspired the individual with much awe and reverence. Japanese NDErs might report seeing beautiful flowers and long dark rivers. Such differences are ascribed to different personal interpretations. NDErs struggle hard to express in words what they have experienced. In doing so, they inevitably resort to familiar images from their own repertoire of experiences.

So what are NDEs? Are they dreams, or hallucinations

triggered by physiological events associated with death, or are they a transcendental entry into "another dimension of being"?[8] NDEs have been the subject of serious study by numerous investigators, resulting in voluminous literature in books and articles on the subject. The International Association for Near-Death Studies (IANDS) was established under this name in 1981 to foster research into NDEs and to promote various related activities. The Association has been publishing since 1988 a quarterly peer-reviewed *Journal of Near-Death Studies*. Because episodes that have some commonalities with NDEs can occur under different circumstances, such as deep meditation, profound grief, influence of psychedelic drugs, or some mystical experiences, and because people can have many kinds of experiences when facing death, it was necessary to have some standardized criteria for NDEs. Psychiatrist Bruce Greyson, a founder of IANDS, developed a 16-item scale, which has since become known as the Greyson NDE Scale,[9] and which is used to quantify the intensity of the main component features of the NDE. A minimum score would then identify the experience as an NDE.

NDEs are not like dreams. Dreams are associated with characteristic brain activity commonly referred to as rapid eye movement (REM) brain activity. It was suggested that NDEs were due to REM intrusions into normal wakeful consciousness, which often occurs. However, several objections were raised to this hypothesis:[10] (i) The rate of REM intrusions in NDErs was found to be no higher than in random samples of the general population who did not have NDEs; (ii) REM brain activity in NDErs was found to be actually lower than in other people; (iii) NDEs can occur under general anesthesia, which suppresses REM brain activity; and (iv) comparison of NDE, real, and imagined memories has revealed that the pattern of brain wave activity for the recall of NDE memories was typical of memories of real events and differed from that for memories of imagined events.[11] The study further concluded that "NDE memories were similar to real memories in terms of detail richness, self-referential, and emotional information", and that NDE memories are stored as episodic memories of events experienced in a peculiar state of consciousness.[11]

NDEs are not hallucinations, as evidenced by the following considerations: (i) The findings of the study referred to in item (iv) of the preceding paragraph, since imagined memories include memories of hallucinations. (ii) A more recent study found a positive correlation between the total score of the Greyson NDE scale and the total score of the Memory Characteristics Questionnaire (MCQ), which is a measure of phenomenological characteristics of memories. In particular, a strong association was found between the NDE's intensity and sensory details, importance to the person concerned, and how often one thought or talked about the memory in question.[12] (iii) Marked differences between hallucinations and NDEs in nature, aftereffects, and how they are viewed by those experiencing them: "Hallucinations are usually illogical, fleeting, bizarre, and/or distorted, whereas the vast majority of NDEs are logical, orderly, clear, and comprehensible. People tend to forget their hallucinations, whereas most NDEs remain vivid for decades. Furthermore, NDEs often lead to profound and permanent transformations in personality, attitudes, beliefs and values, something that is never seen following hallucinations. People looking back on hallucinations typically recognize them as unreal, as fantasies, whereas, people often describe their NDEs as 'more real than real'."[13] Furthermore, people who have experienced both hallucinations and an NDE describe them as being quite different.[14]

Hallucinatory experiences that share some common features with NDEs can be induced by psychedelic drugs such as psilocybin, LSD (lysergic acid diethylamide), ketamine, and DMT (dimethyltryptamine),[15] which also produce effects that do not appear in NDEs. However, this does not mean that NDEs are hallucinations. As has been pointed out by Dr. Sam Parnia, "the notion that a hallucinatory experience occurring in response to one stimulus, implies that another human experience in response to another stimulus (with or without possible shared features) is also hallucinatory, is neither consistent with the scientific principles governing the determination of reality, nor cause and effect."[16] By way of example, "It is incorrect to assume that since hallucinogenic agents can bring about the sensation of love, then other experiences involving love (such as a mother's love for her child) are also hallucinatory. Similarly, one cannot assume that a person's love is real or hallucinatory based on the underlying neurobiological correlates of love (e.g. dopamine, oxytocin and vasopressin) as these are similar irrespective of whether love is experienced in response to hallucinogenic or a real trigger."[16] One final point is that hallucinations produced by drugs may be of the living or the deceased, but those of NDEs are almost always of the deceased.[17]

NDEs are not explained by abnormal states of the brain due to: (i) malfunctioning, such as epileptic seizures, or abnormal activity in various parts of the brain,[18] nor (ii) the release of chemicals to help cope with the stress of death, such as endorphins, serotonin, or adrenaline,[19] nor (iii) the effects of various physiological factors that come into play when death is imminent, such as oxygen deficiency (hypoxia) or increased levels of carbon dioxide (hypercarbia).[16,20] It should be noted that "brain malfunctions generally produce clouded thinking, irritability, fear, belligerence, and idiosyncratic visions, quite unlike the exceptionally clear thinking, peacefulness, calmness, and predictable content generally seen in NDEs."[17] Moreover, many physiological parameters are closely monitored and controlled during surgery, when many NDEs are experienced. In correlating brain activity with perceptions, it must be borne in mind that all perceptions are associated with some activity in the brain, but this does not mean that this activity is the cause of the perception. It may well be that the brain activity simply reflects the perception.

NDEs are not explained as a psychological defense mechanism in reaction to trauma. Although some psychological models may have features that are similar to those of NDEs these similarities are superficial and inconsistent with other features of the NDE.[17] For example, in the depersonalization model, one can have a sense of detachment from the physical body in the face of extreme stress, as in an NDE. However, one loses one's sense of identity in depersonalization, but not in an NDE. In the dissociation model, the sense of self becomes detached from body sensations. In a measure of dissociation, NDErs showed a degree of dissociation "typical of a general response to trauma, but not typical of mental illness."[21] The same is true of the post-traumatic stress disorder (PTSD), which leads to vivid dreams of a traumatic event and efforts to block out reminders of it. Again, it was found that NDErs "had more features of PTSD, but far fewer than the amount required for a diagnosis of PTSD. Unlike people who have PTSD, those who had NDEs tended to have dreams and flashbacks of the brush with death, but no attempts to avoid reminders of it…That…is not typical of a mental disorder."[22]

Some NDErs undergo a life-changing transformation:[23] loss of the fear of death, more spirituality and a feeling of being loved and valued by some higher power, less materialism, a general feeling of peace and tranquility in their lives, higher self-esteem and better self-understanding, a heightened sense of purpose and appreciation of life, a greater compassion for others and a sense of connection to them, an enhanced concern for the environment, and a desire to learn. These positive changes are long-lasting and do not fade away. In fact, "Positive changes were more apparent at 8 years than at 2 years of follow-up."[24] The life-changing transformation of NDErs is not only in values, attitudes, and feelings, but could be in lifestyles as well, resulting in a change of career and occupation. However, the aftereffects of NDEs are not always positive.[25] Some feel depression, anger, or regret for having to return to their lives after the bliss and peace of the NDE. Not surprisingly, the transformation of NDErs affects their family and friends as well, and not always for the better, leading to divorce sometimes because of difficulty in adjusting to the transformation. To be sure, not all NDEs are pleasant. For some reason about 8% of NDEs are unpleasant involving frightening sounds and encounters that seem like hell rather than the heaven reported by most NDErs.[26] A smaller percentage still of NDErs report neither pleasant nor unpleasant experiences, they only encounter a featureless void.

So what does all this mean? NDEs remain essentially anecdotal recounts that cannot be objectively verified. But no single neurophysiological or psychological explanation has been able to account for all features of NDEs; it may well be that NDEs involve more than one mechanism. Nevertheless, there are two striking features of NDEs that are relevant for our purposes and which will be pursued further: (i) the apparently paranormal nature of some features of NDEs, and (ii) implications of some reported features of NDEs. Before proceeding further, it is helpful to elaborate somewhat on some physiological aspects of death.

When is Death?

A dead body, or corpse, is unmistakable. It shows no signs of life; there is no respiration, no heartbeat, no movement of any kind, and the color is deathly pale. What has become problematic, however, is when exactly can a person be pronounced dead? The uncertainty has arisen with advances in medical technology that allow a brain-dead person to be kept alive on a mechanical ventilator with the heart beating, blood circulating, and vital organs, other than the brain, still functioning. Depending on factors such as age and extent of injury to parts of the body other than the brain, patients may be kept in this state for days, months, or even years. The question of whether or not such a patient can be considered dead is clearly of ethical, legal, and practical importance. Under these circumstances, could the decision be made by doctors or family to stop the life-sustaining procedures, resulting in irrevocable death? Could the terms of the patient's will be executed and estate transferred? Could a person who might have caused the injury be prosecuted for homicide? If the patient has willed the donation of organs upon death, can these organs be removed immediately upon the stoppage of life-sustaining procedures at a time when they are in a healthy state of perfusion with oxygen and before they start deteriorating? To appreciate the meaning of death in this context, it is necessary to consider some physiological background.

Under normal conditions, the circulating blood keeps the cells of the body alive by supplying them with oxygen and nutrients while removing metabolic waste products including carbon dioxide. In the lungs, the carbon dioxide in the blood is exchanged for fresh oxygen inhaled from the air through breathing. The carbon dioxide is exhaled into the surrounding air and the fresh oxygen is carried back by the blood to the tissues and organs of the body. The pumping action of the heart keeps the blood circulating to the lungs as well as to all tissues and organs of the body, including the heart itself. Inhalation is initiated in a part of the brain referred to as the brainstem, which automatically controls the rate and depth of breathing in accordance with body needs. Thus, when we physically exert ourselves, we breathe faster and deeper. Although the rate and depth of breathing is also under voluntary control, one cannot voluntarily stop breathing. If any of these three vital processes of breathing, heartbeat, and circulation is severely disrupted, death ensues. Circulation may be interrupted locally by a clot in the arteries supplying part of an organ, such as the heart or the brain, with oxygenated blood. If the loss of oxygen is prolonged enough the affected cells will die. This precipitates a heart attack in the case of the heart or a stroke in the case of the brain. A stroke in the brain can also result from rupturing of blood vessels, which deprives brain cells of oxygen. Damage or injury to the brainstem will cause cessation of breathing. The heartbeat is also controlled by the brainstem, but the heart can beat on its own at a reduced rate, which might keep the body alive but might not pump enough blood to the brain to prevent loss of consciousness. Under certain conditions, a disruption of the heart's rhythm might cause the heart to stop beating altogether – a state referred to as cardiac arrest. The disruption of the heart's rhythm may be due to a heart attack or other conditions such as too low or too high a concentration of potassium ions in the blood or due to heart failure resulting from severe weakening of the heart muscle.

Cardiac arrest is referred to as clinical death. The brain

is the most sensitive organ to loss of oxygen. Loss of consciousness may be experienced within a few seconds of cardiac arrest, brain damage sets in within a few minutes, as will be elaborated later, and generally, the person will die after about 10 minutes or so from irreversible cessation of heartbeat and breathing. This is the most commonly applied criterion of death and is referred to as circulatory death or death by cardiopulmonary criteria. However, normal body functions can be restored following cardiac arrest by quick application of certain measures, such as defibrillation (which uses electric shocks to restart the heartbeat) or cardiopulmonary resuscitation (CPR).

What about brain death? Anatomically, the brain may be divided into three parts (Figure 6.1):

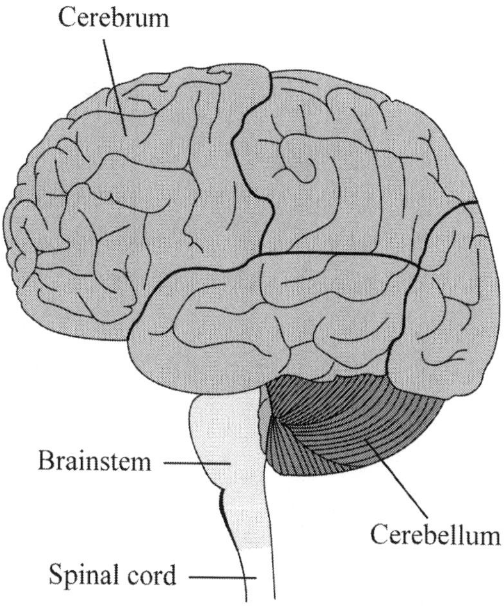

Figure 6.1 Divisions of the brain

(i) the cerebrum, also known as the higher brain, comprising the outer cortical layer – the cerebral cortex –

and immediately underlying structures, (ii) the cerebellum, or little brain, behind the cerebrum, and (iii) the previously mentioned brainstem, also known as the lower brain, located between the cerebrum and the spinal cord. Activity in the cerebrum, is associated with the mental activities discussed in Chapter 1, namely, feelings, cognition, consciousness, and spirituality. On the other hand, the brainstem, is concerned with the control and regulation of involuntary and vegetative activities, such as respiration, heart rate, blood pressure, swallowing, and sleep-wake cycles. The brainstem serves as the main pathway for sensory inputs to the cerebrum and plays a central role in states of consciousness such as awareness and alertness.

When the brain is deprived of oxygen, the cerebrum and cerebellum are irreversibly damaged in 2 to 4 minutes. The brainstem, however, can hold for another 10 to 15 minutes. In what is known as a persistent vegetative state the higher brain ceases to function while the lower brain maintains its normal activity. The patient is able to breathe spontaneously, and brainstem reflexes and sleep-wake cycles are present. The patient is "awake but unaware".[27] If the brainstem also dies, and a mechanical ventilator is applied soon enough, breathing is restored artificially, the heart may be resuscitated, so that respiration, circulation, blood pressure, and body temperature are maintained. The patient is comatose and is fed intravenously or through a feeding tube. As mentioned previously this state can persist for days, months, or even years.

When all functions of the entire brain are lost, the patient is pronounced brain dead. Clinically, brain death is ascertained by a number of tests. The absence of electrical activity in the cerebral cortex is indicated by the lack of electrical signals recorded by electrodes on the scalp; these recordings are referred to as the electroencephalogram

(EEG). The cessation of brainstem functions is indicated by the absence of spontaneous breathing and brainstem reflexes such as the pupillary reflex (movement of the pupils when light is shined on the eye) or a pain reflex elicited by pressing a thumb into the indentation above the eye, near the nose.

In many countries, legal death is considered to be the irreversible cessation of either respiratory and circulatory functions, or all functions of the entire brain. It should be noted, however, that even if a person is officially pronounced dead by competent medical authorities, some tissues can survive for a while without any blood circulation. For example, the spinal cord can survive for at least 30 minutes, skin and bone for up to 12 hours. Pronouncement of death of the person does not mean that all the cells in the body have died.

Paranormal Experiences

Studies of survivors of cardiac arrest have been particularly relevant to the investigation of NDEs in that:[28] (i) they are prospective rather than retrospective in nature since survivors can be interviewed within days of the experience, thereby greatly reducing the potential of memory distortion; (ii) they allow correlation with objective physiological and pharmacological measurements; and (iii) they provide the opportunity to verify seemingly paranormal aspects of some NDE features.

Some famous cases of these seemingly paranormal aspects have been reported by serious investigators and have been published in reputable scientific journals (such as the *Lancet* and *Progress in Brain Research* cited later). Naturally, the paranormal aspects have been challenged by other investigators who remain unconvinced and who believe that non-paranormal explanations have not been completely ruled out.[28] Even then, "There can be little doubt, however, that the OBE component of the NDE still provides the best opportunity to seriously challenge conventional views of the relationship between consciousness and the brain."[28] Some examples of these seemingly paranormal accounts will be cited next, to give an idea of what is being talked about, followed in the next section by some implications of these components of the NDEs to the mind brain problem in the opinion of proponents of a non-physical aspect of NDEs.

The first case is that of Pam Reynolds, a 35-year-old who in 1991 underwent a complex surgical procedure for removing a large aneurysm in an artery in her brainstem.[28] (An arterial aneurism is an abnormal, blood-filled sac formed by ballooning of an artery at the location of a weakness in the wall of the artery.) Her body temperature was lowered to 16°C, her heartbeat and breathing stopped, and blood drained from her head. She was fully anesthetized and had small molded speakers inserted in her ears that were used to emit loud 100-dB clicks so that auditory evoked potentials recorded from the brainstem could be used to monitor her level of consciousness throughout the operation. After recovery from the operation, she recounted an NDE with an OBE in which she observed the surgical procedure from above the neurosurgeon's shoulder and described very well the surgical instruments used and the conversation between the neurosurgeon and the nurses. She mentioned seeing deceased relatives who looked after her and helped her return to her body. She also reported on the music that was playing in the operating theater.

The second case was reported by a Dutch coronary-care-unit nurse about an ambulance bringing a 44-year-old cyanotic, comatose man who had been found in a meadow by passers-by about an hour earlier.[24] CPR and defibrillation were applied. When the patient was to be intubated, she removed his upper dentures and put them in the crash cart. After about an hour and a half the man had sufficient heart rhythm and blood pressure, but was still intubated, ventilated, and comatose, when he was transferred to the intensive care unit for continuation of artificial respiration. After more than a week, he was transferred back to the cardiac ward, with his dentures still missing. When he sees the nurse he says, "that nurse knows where my dentures are," and he goes on to describe how she took them out of his mouth and put them in a sliding drawer underneath the cart. He further explained that he had an OBE in which he was observing the doctors and nurses from above, and described correctly and in detail the small room where he was resuscitated and the appearances of those present. He also expressed his apprehension at the time that they would stop his CPR as they were in fact quite negative about his prognosis due to his very poor medical condition. The authors of the paper pose the question as to how can a clear consciousness outside one's body be experienced during clinical death when the brain is "no longer functioning and the EEG is flat."[24]

The third case is that of Al Sullivan, a 56-year-old truck driver who had a heart attack and had to undergo an emergency quadruple coronary bypass surgery during which he had an NDE, with an OBE, which he later recounted to the psychiatrist mentioned previously, Dr. Bruce Greyson.[29] During the operation his eyes were taped shut – something often done to keep the eyes from drying out while the patient is anesthetized for a long period. He reported an OBE during which he viewed his chest held open by metal clamps and could see his heart in his chest cavity. At the time that assistant surgeons were stripping a piece of vein out of his leg to be used for the bypass graft, when he was fully anesthetized, he reported seeing the surgeon having his palms on his (the surgeon's) chest and wiggling his elbows "as if he was trying to fly". As this behavior of a surgeon was too bizarre and unheard of, Dr. Greyson obtained a written permission to talk to the surgeon concerned. It turned out that this surgeon, after scrubbing his hands and donning sterile gloves, and in order to avoid any risk of contamination to his hands, was in the habit of placing his hands on his chest, against his sterile gown, and would use elbow movements in instructing his team to do various things. Al also reported seeing his mother, who had died years earlier when he was seven, and the warmth, joy, love, and peace felt in the encounter. At one point his mother drifted toward the surgeon and placed his hand on the left side of Al's heart. The surgeon then made "a sweeping motion as if to rid the area of a flying insect". Following Al Sullivan's account, Dr. Greyson, a Distinguished Life Fellow of the American Psychiatric Association, recounts in his afore-cited book other cases of anesthetized patients being operated on and being able to accurately describe events in a manner that was puzzling to explain.

There are also intriguing accounts of visual perceptions by NDErs who are blind from birth. This does not mean that they are able to see what they report on in the same way that sighted people do. According to the main investigator of such cases, Dr. Kenneth Ring, Professor Emeritus of Psychology at the University of Connecticut, "the form of knowing reported by the blind during their NDEs, which he (Dr. Ring) refers to as 'mindsight', is beyond conventional scientific explanation and is in fact the same form of transcendent knowing that is reported by the sighted during NDEs."[30]

Implications of Some NDE Features

Some investigators have raised a number of thought-provoking questions concerning NDEs, not the least being the relation between mind and brain and the nature of consciousness. The idea that the mind is simply "what the brain does,"[31] that is, the mind is just the product of physical events in the brain, is seriously challenged. As mentioned in Chapter 2 under "Nature of Science", it is like saying that in an orchestra musical instruments produce music. Well, they do, but someone has "to decide what sound to make and to make the instrument produce that sound."[32] NDErs report clearer than ever thoughts and perceptions from outside their bodies, while brain function is at least severely impaired. Does this mean that the mind and brain are separate entities that can sometimes act independently of one another? Dualists beginning with Descartes in the 17th century CE have claimed that the mind and brain are two separate entities. What then is the relationship between mind and brain? If the mind and brain are separate entities, where and how does the mind exist? Does the mind continue after death?

Consciousness during an NDE seems to differ from consciousness in the normal state in several respects. First, the consciousness of NDErs reporting an out-of-body-experience is from a perspective outside the body, with a sense of detachment from the body. Second, NDErs often report much clearer and faster thinking and more vivid sensations involving sounds and colors not normally experienced. Third, as illustrated by the aforementioned narrative of the three beings of light, there is a feeling of being outside of space and time, a sense of all-knowledge and of oneness with the universe, also known as the unitive experience. It would seem that consciousness during an NDE is at a higher level than consciousness in the normal state. This seems to accord with suggestions since many years ago that the mind belongs to a greater realm and that the brain acts as a filter that focusses and limits the mind and consciousness to what is important and relevant for our survival and daily activities.[33] It is interesting in this regard that neuroimaging studies on the effects of psychedelic drugs, which can "reliably induce spiritual experiences that are effectively indistinguishable from spontaneously-occurring spiritual experiences,"[34] have shown that the state induced by these drugs is that of higher entropy in the brain, that is, a higher degree of randomness, or disorder, manifested as less synchrony in the electrical activity of neurons of the brain.[34] It has been argued "that this entropy-suppressing function of the human brain serves to promote realism, foresight, careful reflection and an ability to recognize and overcome wishful and paranoid fantasies. Equally, however, it could be seen as exerting a limiting or narrowing influence on consciousness."[34] As physician Larry Dossey put it more starkly: "We are conscious not because of the brain but in spite of it."[35]

An intriguing feature of NDEs is the life review reported by many NDErs, in which they see a kind of a flash presentation of their lives in exquisite detail. In the words of one experiencer: "My life review was absolutely, positively, everything basically from the first breath of life right through the accident. It was that panoramic view. It was everything…Everything was more accurate than could possibly be perceived in the reality of the original event…I watched the mowing of the lawn from straight above, anywhere from several hundred to a couple of thousand feet, as though I were a camera. I watched all of that…I could have counted the mosquitoes."[36] In the life review one sees events that have long been forgotten, and one experiences not only one's feelings at the time of events but also those of others who were involved. How can a clinically dead or severely impaired brain recollect and reconstruct all these memories at such high speed and in such detail? Where are all these memories stored? Even if the brain retains some activity during an NDE, what about the deceased who are reported by many NDErs to interact with them? The deceased might tell the NDErs something these didn't know. So the deceased appear to have consciousness and memory although they have been dead for a long time. Their bodies have decomposed, yet their consciousness and memory are preserved. How can that be?

The foregoing is of course largely speculative in the absence of convincing evidence that NDEs are real. But then no convincing evidence has been forthcoming that NDEs are not real. Naturally, the spiritual or transcendental explanation of NDEs is that they are very real and that they provide evidence of an immaterial mind or soul departing upon death from the physical body to an afterlife that also exists. This explanation is further corroborated by the paranormal nature of some NDEs whereby NDErs can see or hear things that are inaccessible to the senses of their physical bodies.

Maverick Views from Biology and Physics

It is of interest to consider two maverick views from biology and physics that have some bearing on our discussion.

Rupert Sheldrake, mentioned in Chapter 2 under "What Present-Day Science Does Not Know", developed and extended the idea of morphogenetic fields first proposed in the 1920s by embryologists as a hypothesis to explain some features of morphogenesis that were referred to in Chapter 2. Sheldrake defines a morphic unit quite generally as a unit of material form such as an atom, molecule, cell, plant, animal, galaxy, or as a unit of some organized behavior such an element of culture or a pattern of instinctive activity.[37] This means that morphic units are in general organized as hierarchies of constituent units.[38] A sugar crystal, for example, is a morphic unit composed of sugar molecules (also morphic units), which are made up of carbon, hydrogen, and oxygen atoms (morphic units), which are composed of subatomic particles, with all these smaller and smaller components being morphic units. Similarly, an animal has a hierarchical arrangement of organs, composed of tissues, made up of cells, consisting of organelles such as nuclei and mitochondria, which are in turn composed of organic molecules, and so on, with the constituents of each level in this hierarchy being morphic units.

A morphic unit has within and around it a morphic field "that organizes its characteristic structure and pattern of activity."[37] Morphic fields are varied in nature; they could be morphogenetic, behavioral, social, cultural, or mental fields. The morphic field of a given morphic unit organizes its constituent parts. Thus, the morphic field of an organ organizes the constituent tissues of the organ, and the morphic field of a tissue organizes the cells that compose the tissue, and so on.[39] The morphic field also organizes the pattern of activity of its associated morphic unit through what Sheldrake calls morphic resonance, defined as the influence of previous patterns of activity on subsequent similar patterns of activity organized by morphic fields. This influence is not diminished by distance nor time from the past to the present. Morphic fields are thus "shaped and stabilized by morphic resonance from previous similar morphic units, which were under the influence of fields of the same kind. They consequently contain a kind of cumulative memory and tend to become increasingly habitual."[37] New patterns of activity in response to situations not encountered before will affect the morphic field and would be beneficial to other morphic units through morphic resonance. The greater degree of similarity between morphic units, the greater the influence of morphic resonance. "In general, morphic units closely resemble themselves in the past and are subject to self-resonance from their own past states."[37] Thus, morphic units have self-resonance with their own morphic fields as well as resonance with the morphic field with which similar morphic units resonate.

Sheldrake attempts to explain many phenomena associated with living organisms in terms of morphic resonance. Thus, animal and human memory is due to morphic resonance and is in the morphic field; that is why all attempts to locate memory in the brain have failed so far. Instinctive behavior of animals is influenced by genes but is not genetically programmed; "its characteristic patterns are organized by morphic fields inherited by morphic resonance from past members of the same species."[40] Sheldrake illustrates the beneficial effects through morphic resonance by the results of a well-documented series of experiments conducted in three continents over a span of more than thirty years on maze learning by rats.[41] These experiments were started in 1920 by Harvard psychologist William McDougall to test if learned behavior can be passed on to offspring. McDougall used a maze in the form of a T-shaped water tank from which the rats could escape by climbing up one of two gangway exits, one of which was illuminated, the other kept dark. The rat's natural inclination was to swim to the illuminated exit, but if they did, they would receive an electric shock on the way out. The dark exit was safe. On the next trial, the previously dark exit was illuminated and the other exit made dark. The rats had to learn that the dark exit was always the safer. The first generation of rats made an average of 165 errors before learning to take the dark exit. Subsequent generations learned more quickly, so that the thirtieth generation took only twenty errors to learn the maze. McDougall showed that the improvement was not due to selective breeding of bright rats, for even if he selected the dullest rats as parents for the next generation, there was still a progressive increase in the rate of learning. He interpreted these results in terms of modification of the rats' genes, in accordance with the controversial postulate of the French naturalist Jean-Baptiste Lamarck, who lived in the 18th and 19th centuries CE, that acquired traits could be transmitted to offspring.

One of McDougall's critics, the Scottish researcher Francis Crew, set out to disprove McDougall's results. To his surprise, his rats in Scotland, with no genetic relation to McDougall's in the United States, started up where McDougall's rats left off, averaging only twenty-five errors, and some doing it right the first time without an electric shock. Following this, an Australian researcher, Wilfred Agar, and his colleagues also found out that the first generation of rats they tested, and which again were from a completely separate genetic line from those of McDougall, learned far quicker than McDougall's earlier generation of rats. They tested fifty subsequent generations over a period of twenty years, confirming an increase in the rate of learning in successive generations. Significantly, they found similar improvements in control rats that were not descended from trained parents, which showed that the improvements were not genetically transmitted. Sheldrake explains these results by hypothesizing that the learning by rats in any given generation was fed back into their morphic field and affected the learning in subsequent generations through morphic resonance. Many other examples of invoking morphic fields in morphogenesis and other phenomena are given by Sheldrake in his afore-cited book.

Although the nature of morphic fields and morphic resonance is unexplained, and the hypothesis may well be untenable and will be superseded by something else in the future, it has been presented here not by way of support or endorsement but because it constitutes a paradigm shift in the following respects: (i) Contrary to conventional materialistic theory, the behavior and activity of an organism is not completely determined by information that is contained entirely within the organism. Thus, a genome does not seem to contain the blueprint or instructions that guide morphogenesis; outside influences, of some form or other, seem to be involved in some way. (ii) Tied to this, is the notion of wholeness and connectedness outside the limits of space and time to what is beyond the individual. (iii) All attempts to identify how memory is stored in the brain have failed so far, which casts some doubt about the framework within which memory is conventionally considered. (iv) The idea that the brain acts as some tuning and processing device. The analogy of the brain to a television (TV) set is illustrative. A person who is unfamiliar with broadcasting and the generation, propagation, and reception of electromagnetic waves (like someone suddenly resurrected from a past era) would reasonably assume that what is seen on a TV screen is generated in the TV set itself. This view is supported by the fact that any tinkering with the components of the TV set will generally affect the image on the screen or might obliterate it altogether. But in fact the TV set is just tuning to an outside signal and is merely processing this signal into a form that can be perceived by the viewer. Similarly, brains may be tuning to something external and are merely processing or filtering this "something".

It is noteworthy that points (i)-(iv) of the preceding paragraph correlate with some features and implications of NDEs. Thus: (i) In an OBE, NDErs report clear perceptions from outside their physical bodies, which implies that these perceptions do not depend on processes inside their bodies, particularly with normal brain function severely impaired during an NDE. (ii) Morphic fields extend through space and time, providing a wholeness and connectedness reminiscent of the oneness and interconnectedness with the universe that is experienced in an NDE. (iii) As mentioned previously, NDEs imply that memories are carried outside the brain, just as memory is assumed to be in the morphic field. (iv) Also, as previously mentioned, NDEs imply that the brain somehow limits consciousness, acting as some kind of filter, in the same way as the brain is assumed to tune to the morphic field and somehow process the information coming from this field.

A maverick view from physics is David Bohm's interpretation of quantum mechanics, referred to in Chapter 2. Bohm is considered as one of the most brilliant theoretical physicists of his generation – the generation that followed that of Einstein and Bohr. Bohm postulates that quantum particles are acted on by a quantum force derived from a quantum potential that acts at the subquantum level, not to drive the particles, but to guide their motion.[42] The quantum potential pervades all space, like gravity, but unlike gravity and other fields, such as electric or magnetic fields, its influence does not diminish with distance. The guidance provided by the quantum potential is analogous to that provided by radar signals to a ship on automatic pilot. The radar signals do not drive the ship but guide its motion in accordance with the information they contain about the environment. The quantum potential experienced by the particle depends on the instantaneous positions of all the particles that the particle in question has ever interacted with and on the positions of all particles that these particles have ever interacted with. The influence of the quantum potential is instantaneous, extending, in principle, over the whole universe and over all time that has passed. In this way, the motion of "each particle is guided not by its own 'private' information, but rather, by a 'pool' of information belonging to the whole system,"[43] much like a ballet dance in which the ballet dancers are moving in accordance with a score, which constitutes a common pool of information that guides each of the dancers.

In Bohm's view, there is therefore a universal connectedness in which everything is part of an unbroken whole that is the deeper level of reality. This level of reality is what Bohm calls the implicate, or enfolded, order, whereas the level of reality in which particles appear to be separate is the explicate, or unfolded, order. The fundamental reality is a quantum interconnectedness of the whole universe, a wholeness that is undiminished by space and time. Thus, the tangible reality of everyday life, the explicate order, is like a holographic image (see Chapter 2, Section "What Present-Day Science Does Not Know"). But underlying this image is a deeper level of reality, that of the interference pattern, which is the implicate order. The image is enfolded throughout the interference pattern and can be seen as the holographic image under appropriate conditions. Because of the nonlocality of the encoding, each part of the interference pattern contains information about the whole image. Since a hologram involves a static image, whereas the implicate order is basically dynamic, Bohm calls this order a holomovement. Hence, "All things found in the unfolded explicate order emerge from the holomovement in which they are enfolded as potentialities, and ultimately they fall back into it. They endure only for some time, and while they last, their existence is sustained in a constant process of unfoldment and re-enfoldment, which gives rise to the relatively stable and independent forms in which they appear in the explicate order."[43] Thus, each moment is a projection of the whole – the implicate order – onto the explicate order. But that moment is then injected back, generally with some differences, into the whole. The next moment would then involve, in part, a re-projection of that injection, and so on. As for future events, the implicate order in the present may anticipate these events in some cases, since there is a tendency for a certain content in the past to be followed by a related content in the future.[44]

Bohm further believes that consciousness is part of the implicate order, along with living and nonliving matter.[45] According to Bohm, "...nature is much more than what appears at the surface...it could equally well be called Idealism, Spirit, Consciousness. The separation of the two – matter and spirit – is an abstraction...The ground is always one."[46] Bohm goes further and speculates on how his theory can be extended to encompass parapsychological phenomena such as psychokinesis (the production or control of motion, especially of remote and inanimate objects, by the exercise of psychic powers) and telepathy (communicating by the exchange of thoughts, without involving the senses).[43]

Bohm's ideas are not yet sufficiently developed, in that much of the mathematics, such as that of enfolding and unfolding between the implicate and explicate orders, has not been formulated. But Bohm's ideas point in the direction in which quite a number of investigators foresee the future of science, namely a unified treatise that brings together nonliving matter, living matter, and consciousness (see the views of Linde and Chalmers, Chapter 2, under "Scientific Theories Are Fragmented"). Nevertheless, Bohm's ideas remain controversial, being accepted by some physicists, wholly or partly, and rejected by others.[47] Bohm died in 1992.

Clearly, there is some commonality between the views of Bohm and Sheldrake.[44,46] Bohm considers the implicate order to be more general than morphic fields and can provide an explanation for them and for morphic resonance. Both the implicate order and morphic fields have a wholeness that is undiminished by space and time. Both have a cumulative memory: morphic fields inherently have memory. In the case of the implicate order, the projection at any given moment from the implicate order of what was re-injected into this order in previous moments is a kind of memory. Both the morphic field and the implicate order evolve with time. Each member of a morphic unit is influenced by the morphic field but in turn contributes to it, which can modify the morphic field in some way. In a similar manner, re-injections into the implicate order can modify it in some way.

Death and The Afterlife in the Quran

After having discussed how people view death, and the NDEs of some who have had a close encounter with death, we turn our attention to what the Quran says in considerable detail about death and the hereafter. The Quranic view of the hereafter is referred to in this book as the Afterlife, with a capital "A".

Self and Spirit

The Quran uses the word *nafs* in what can be understood to mean the conscious self, which as discussed in Chapter 1 is what defines every human being as a unique individual.

Nafs in this sense is the essence of conscious being and occurs in the Quran in the singular, masculine or feminine, and plural. As such, *nafs* is also used in the Quran to refer to person or persons. The Quran also speaks of the Self of The Almighty:

> **And when Allāh said, "O Jesus son of Mary! Did you say to people, 'Take me and my mother as two gods instead of Allāh?'" He said, "Glory be to You! It is not for me to utter that to which I have no right. Had I said it, You would surely have known it. You know what is in my self and I know not what is in Your Self. Truly, it is You Who are the All-Knower of the Unseen."** (5:116)

In the case of Jesus, the self is his human self, whereas in the case of The Almighty, His Self is His Essence.

The word *rūḥ*, in referring to humans in the Quran, is understood to mean the essence of life, or spirit. When the Prophet Muhammad was asked by some about the spirit, he later received the revelation:

> **And they ask you about the spirit. Say: "The spirit is at the command of my *Rabb*, and you have been given but little knowledge."** (17:85)

In giving life to man, The Almighty speaks of:

> **...breathed into him of My Spirit...** (15:29), (38:72)

This essence or nature of life is indeed a big mystery still, as mentioned in Chapter 2. Elsewhere in the Quran, The Spirit is understood to refer to Archangel Gabriel, the messenger through whom the Quran was revealed to the

Prophet Muhammad.

Although *rūḥ* is invariably translated as spirit, *nafs* is also almost invariably translated as soul, although "soul" in English, according to the Cambridge English Dictionary is: "the spiritual part of a person that some people believe continues to exist in some form after their body has died, or the part of a person that is not physical and experiences deep feelings and emotions."[48] The first part of this dictionary entry is more like the spirit, whereas the second part is more like the conscious self. Because of this dual meaning of the word "soul", *nafs* is translated as self in Quranic verses quoted in this book.

The body-self-spirit has been compared to a car. The material parts of the car are analogous to the human body. The ignited fuel (or the charge in the batteries in the case of an electric car) that "brings the car to life" and makes it move is analogous to the spirit. To be useful, the car must be acted on in a purposeful manner – moved forward or backward, turned right or left, accelerated or decelerated, or driven to some destination. The driving agency, which may be a human driver or some form of autonomous or remote control, is analogous to the conscious self.[49] Thus, *rūḥ*, or spirit, is the essence of life, whereas *nafs*, or self, is the essence of conscious being that defines every human as a unique individual.

Death and Its Aftermath

Three verses in the Quran begin with the following statement:

> **Every self shall taste death...** (3:185), (21:35), (29:57)

On the face of it, this statement, as understood by most exegetes, is a truism in that all human beings will die.

Indeed, **"...Everything will perish but He..."** (28:88). The Almighty is the only Eternal. The eminent Islamic scholar of the 12th century CE, *al-Rāzī*, interprets the foregoing statement more precisely and profoundly.[50] He argues that the taster must exist during the act of tasting and understands the statement to mean that the self tastes the death of the body. He concludes from this and other verses that the self is different from the body and does not die with the death of the body.

The Quran makes a parallel between death and sleep:

> **Allāh takes selves at the moment of their death, and those who die not, during their sleep. He withholds those for whom He has decreed death, and sends forth the others till a term appointed. Truly in that are signs for a people who reflect.** (39:42)

The first verb in this verse is *tawaffā*, which can mean "to cause to die" or "to take, or receive, fully, or wholly."[51] The verb that is commonly used in the Quran to refer to causing death of a person is *yumīt*, as in: **"He gives life and causes death, and to Him you shall return"** (10:56). The verse says that The Almighty takes the self at the time of death of a person as well as when the person goes to sleep. If the person is not to die in sleep, The Almighty "sends forth" the self upon awakening, but for a certain length of time until the person is due to die. "Sending forth" is interpreted by some as meaning "returning to the body."[50] In sleep, one loses consciousness temporarily and at least partially but is still alive, in the presence of all vital signs. In Arabic lore sleep is referred to as the "littler death", and death as the "greater sleep".

The following verse refers to the time of death.

> **...And if only you could see when the wrongdoers are in the throes of death while the angels stretch forth their hands saying "Yield up your selves! This day you shall be requited with a humiliating punishment for having spoken untruth against Allāh, and for showing arrogance against His revelations."** (6:93)

The wrongdoers try to resist "yielding up their selves" at the moment of death because they glimpse what awaits them in pain and suffering. On the other hand, the righteous receive the good tidings of the Paradise that awaits them:

> **Gardens of Eden will they enter, underneath which rivers flow, wherein they will have whatever they desire. Thus does Allāh recompense the righteous, those whose lives the angels take while they are virtuous, saying, "Peace be upon you! Enter Paradise for what you used to do."** (16:31-32)

The peace they feel at the time of death is reminiscent of what many NDErs report feeling. Other features of NDEs are suggestive of references in the Quran: First, NDErs report the ability to see things that are not normally seen, such as "beings of light" or colors not seen before. The Quran says:

> **...Now We have removed from you your cover; so today your sight is piercing.** (50:22)

The interpretation is that: "At the moment of death, the veils that cover one's perceptions in this life are lifted and one sees the reality of creation and of one's own condition."[52]

Second, is the report by some 26% of NDErs of a border

or point of no return.[53] The Quran states:

> **...And behind them is a barrier till the Day they are resurrected.** (23:100)

The word *barzakh*, conventionally translated as barrier, means a "thing that makes a separation between two things" and also "the period, or state, from the day of death to the Day of Resurrection."[54] The verse is understood to refer to a no return to the life of this world.

Third, some 64% of NDErs report a sense of timelessness, of time losing its meaning.[53] Several verses of the Quran refer to a radical change after death in the experience of time. For example:

> **...It shall be for them, on the day when they see that which they are promised, as though they had tarried naught but an hour of a day...** (46:35)

Thus, the time between death and resurrection would seem but an hour, although by earthly time it may be indefinitely long.

The Afterlife

Although many verses in the Quran describe in some detail the end of time, resurrection, and judgement, the following verses from the revered Chapter 36, *Yā Sīn*, are very succinct:

> **And they say, "When will this promise come to pass, if you are truthful?" They await naught but a single cry that will seize them while they dispute among themselves, and then they can make no bequest, nor return to their kin. And the trumpet will be blown.**

> **Then, behold, they will rush forth from their graves unto their *Rabb*. They will say, "Oh, woe unto us! Who has raised us from our place of sleep? This is that which the Most Compassionate did promise; and the message bearers spoke true." There shall be but a single cry. Then, behold, they will all be arraigned before Us! This day no self will be wronged in the least, and you will not be requited, save for that what you used to do.** (36:48-54)

The first verse has disbelievers mock the Prophet Muhammad about not knowing the timing of the Hour (*al-sāʿah*), that is, the end of time, and the Day of Resurrection, about which he warned them. Only The Almighty knows the timing of these events, as is explicitly stated in other verses. But the Hour comes suddenly while they contend with their worldly affairs, so they have no time to make bequests nor return to their families. Sometime after the end of time the trumpet is blown – a metaphor for gathering people together for a momentous purpose. This is the Day of Resurrection, the raising of the dead.

Thus, at a time known only to The Almighty, comes the Hour, or the end of time, which is terrifyingly described in some verses as a time when people then alive become like scattered moths and the mountains like carded wool (101:4-5), seas boil over (81:6), and the Sun and Moon are brought together (75:9). From the time life on Earth ends till the Day of Resurrection is the *barzakh*, or the "trial of the grave". During this period, which seems "like an hour", consciousness is heightened, and every self will experience a taste of what is to come, Heaven or Hell. Resurrection is in some physical body form, after which comes the reckoning and judgement by The Almighty, when everyone is confronted with one's deeds in this life.

The reckoning is the moment of truth for everyone, when every person faces the stark reality of one's life conduct and the true nature and value of one's deeds in this world. The loneliness and forlornness of that Day are devastating, with every person being preoccupied with one's self:

> **The Day when a man flees from his brother, his mother and his father, and his spouse and his children. For every man that Day will have enough concern to make him heedless of others.** (80:34-37)

On that Day there can be no denial of what one has done:

> **On that Day We shall seal their mouths. Their hands will speak to Us, and their feet will bear witness to that which they used to earn.** (36:65)

On the Day of Reckoning the disbelievers will be dumbfounded, unable to speak in their own defense. But their body parts will speak of the misdeeds they have committed. The reckoning is just, based on the preponderance of good deeds:

> **And the judging on that Day will be just. So as for those whose good deeds are heavy, it is they are the successful. And as for those whose good deeds are light, it is they who have ruined their selves by having treated Our signs wrongfully.** (7:8-9)

The state of the believers will be in sharp contrast to that of the disbelievers:

> **Some faces that Day will be radiant, laughing, and rejoicing. While faces that Day will be covered with**

dust, overlaid with gloom. Those are the disbelievers, the dissolute. (80:38-42)

Heaven and Hell

The Quran vividly portrays the bliss of Heaven and the suffering in Hell in terms that could be readily apprehended by illiterate Bedouin Arabs of the 7th century CE and which will have maximum impact on them. However, these portrayals have a deeper meaning and significance beyond their literal interpretation. Thus:

No self knows what blissful delights are kept hidden for them as a reward for what they used to do. (32:17)

This verse, along with other verses and sayings of the Prophet Muhammad, would indicate that the settings of Heaven, with the descriptions of gardens and rivers, and the rewards for the righteous are beyond human imagination; what is portrayed in the Quran is allegorical. Nevertheless, those in Heaven and Hell are not disembodied spirits, they have some physical form and sensory perceptions. Those in Heaven can taste the delights of what they are offered to eat and drink, and those in Hell can also taste things and feel the physical pain. In Heaven, good and virtuous speech prevails:

They hear no idle talk therein, nor incitement to sin, only exchanging greetings of "Peace be upon you! Peace be upon you!" (56:25-26)

There is no sorrow or fatigue:

And they will say, "Praise be to Allāh, Who has dispelled grief from us. Truly our *Rabb* is Ever-Forgiving, Multiplier of reward, Who, by His Grace,

> **has installed us in the mansion of eternity, wherein no toil nor weariness shall touch us."** (35:34-35)

Nevertheless, several verses affirm that the greatest reward is in fact spiritual, as in:

> **Allāh said, "This is the day wherein the truthful shall benefit from their truthfulness. For them shall be gardens beneath which rivers flow, abiding therein forever. Allāh is content with them, and they are content with Him. That is the great triumph."** (5:119)

Contentment from The Almighty and feeling His Pleasure with what they, the righteous, used to do in this world is the supreme bliss of Heaven. Al-Rāzī refers to this state of mutual contentment as one of the wondrous secrets that cannot be expressed in words.[50]

The experience of Heaven and Hell is in degrees commensurate with the righteousness of those who go to Heaven and the unrighteousness of those who go to Hell, but is contingent above all on His Will, Grace, Mercy, and Judgement. Importantly, existence in Heaven is not quiescent rest and enjoyment; it is permeated by the desire and endeavor for ceaseless spiritual advancement, and a plea to The Almighty:

> **...Our *Rabb*, perfect our light for us and grant us forgiveness. Truly You are All-Powerful over all things.** (66:8)

That there is room for advancement is spoken of in verses such as:

> **But as for those who reverence their *Rabb*, they will have lofty abodes above which are lofty abodes, and beneath which rivers flow. That is Allāh's Promise; Allāh never fails to fulfil His Promise.** (39:20)

Lofty abodes being above other lofty abodes does not signify a spatial configuration, for space and time lose their meaning in the hereafter. "Lofty" is to be understood as "exalted state" and "above" as referring to a "more exalted state". Similarly, "beneath which rivers flow" is to be understood as a reference to some kind of sustaining flow rather than a physical location of rivers.

The descriptions of torments of Hell are truly blood-curdling. The food of those in Hell is *zaqqūm*, described as:

> **Truly it is a tree that emerges in the depths of Hell. Its spathes are as the heads of *shayāṭīn*. They will eat from it and fill their bellies therewith. Then on top of it they will have a brew of a boiling liquid. Then their return shall be unto Hellfire.** (37:64-68)

In Arabic, *zaqqūm* is "a certain tree having small leaves, stinking and bitter."[55] *Shayāṭīn* is plural of *shayṭān*, which means devil in respect of foulness and ugliness, or "a certain species of serpents having a mane of foul aspect."[56]

The following verse is a terrifying portrayal of continuing pain:

> **Those who disbelieve Our revelations, We shall surely cause them to burn in a Fire. As often as their skins are consumed, We shall replace them with other skins, that they may taste the punishment. Truly Allāh is Almighty, All-Wise.** (4:56)

In this world, pain caused by external physical stimuli is mediated by receptors in the skin. In keeping with the allegorical nature of Quranic descriptions of Heaven and Hell, no one can imagine what is the body form of the occupants of Hell, nor their type of skin, nor the nature of its blazing "Fire". But what the preceding verse emphasizes, in a highly impressive way, is that the pain felt in Hell is incessant. This is further reinforced by not being dead or alive in Hell:

> **Verily, whosoever comes unto his *Rabb* guilty, surely his shall be Hell, wherein he neither dies nor lives.** (20:74)

For dying means the cessation of torment, whereas being alive implies at least the possibility of some reprieve.

On the other hand, some verses clearly indicate that the torment in Hell is not everlasting but is contingent on the Will of The Almighty:

> **...The Fire is your abode, to abide therein, except as Allāh wills. Truly your *Rabb* is All-Wise, All-Knowing.** (6:128)

> **As for those who are wretched, they shall be in the Fire, wherein there shall be for them groaning and wailing, abiding therein for so long as the heavens and the earth endure, save as your *Rabb* wills. Surely your *Rabb* does whatsoever He wills.** (11:106-107)

Other verses can be understood to mean that torment in Hell is eternal, although "eternal" might signify an indefinite period of unspecified end, except as The Almighty wills. As emphasized in Chapter 5, The Almighty is All-

Powerful, is able to actualize His Will in any way He pleases, and is Most-Compassionate and Most-Merciful, and as corroborated by some well-authenticated sayings of the Prophet Muhammad, it is the opinion of some prominent Islamic scholars that the torment in Hell is not everlasting.[57,58]

> **...I will inflict My torment on whomever I will, and My Mercy encompasses all things...** (7:156)

This is in keeping with the overarching Quranic ethos of the Mercy of The Almighty. In line with this view, The Almighty has given humans free will and has sent them revelations to guide them in the righteous path, which is in fact the path for their continued advancement, as elaborated in the following chapter. Righteous believers are destined for heaven, where they continue their spiritual advancement. Disbelievers, on the other hand, choose to ignore these revelations and pursue their base, worldly desires despite all the Signs of The Almighty in themselves and around them, if only they reflect and reason. For this persistent transgression throughout their lives, they are destined for Hell, where they are tormented. But in the Mercy of The Almighty, this torment is not vengeance or punishment for the sake of punishment but a means for their spiritual purification, which is the ultimate purpose of their suffering and pain.

We started out this chapter with an overview of how people confront death with a gamut of feelings from morbid fear, to anxiety, to philosophical resignation, to joyful anticipation. In a closer encounter with death, some people experience a near-death-experience that to some is the portent of an afterlife. The chapter ended with a brief account of the Quranic portrayal of the Afterlife and its significance. If one comes to believe in the Existence of The Almighty and in His revelations in the Quran, as presented in the preceding chapter, then one must also believe in the Afterlife of the Quran. Believing in the Afterlife as a consequence of one's conduct in this life should engender a profound sense of vigilance in this life.

After consolidating belief in the Afterlife, what remains is to consider what the advocated Spirituality means for oneself, for one's relationships to others, and for the conduct of one's daily affairs. That is the subject of our concluding chapter.

Chapter 7

What Does It All Mean?

Theme: Spirituality is the foundation for ever-fulfilling self-development, which gives meaning and purpose to life.

In a nutshell, the meaning of life is self-development, focusing principally on the spiritual, psychological, moral, and intellectual aspects of personality and character. It will be argued that Spirituality is the indispensable foundation for this ever-fulfilling self-development. For what purpose is this self-development? It is ultimately to attain eternal bliss in the Afterlife, contingent on the Will, Grace, Mercy, and Judgement of The Almighty, which gives purpose to our worldly life. But how do we cultivate this Spirituality? What does it mean in practical terms, in our daily thoughts and conduct? What would be its benefits to individuals and to societies? These are the questions that are addressed in this concluding chapter. Spirituality is first discussed in practical terms, followed by self-development.

On The Human Condition

Why were we born? Is there a meaning and purpose to our lives? Are we born with a disposition for good or evil? Do we have free will or is our life predestined? Is there a moral code we should abide by and why? These are existential questions that have engaged philosophers, theologians, and thinkers throughout history, with widely divergent views expressed. What concerns us here is their relevance to Spirituality. As the Quran has provided the incontrovertible evidence for the existence of The Almighty, it behooves us to consider some major themes of the Quran on key aspects of the human condition.

On the nature of the human self the Quran states:

> **And the self and the One Who fashioned it. So He instilled within it its iniquity and its *taqwā*. He is indeed successful who makes it thrive. And he indeed is a failure who stunts it.** (91:7-10)

These verses are very profound in meaning and encapsulate in a few words the crux of the human condition. The first verse is in the form of an oath by The Almighty that affirms His creation of the human self in a supremely exalted form. The conscious self is indeed a most wonderful creation that provides the substrate of all human mental activities, as mentioned in Chapter 1, with their capacity for dazzling intellectual achievements, sublime spirituality, stunning creativity, profound feelings, and enchanting appreciation of beauty in all its manifestations. The second verse declares very clearly that the human self has the propensity for wickedness and unrighteousness as well as for *taqwā*. This word, usually translated as "piety", "reverence", or "conscientiousness", is derived from a root verb that means "to preserve or guard oneself exceedingly".[1] It is used extensively in the Quran in the sense of guarding oneself from committing evil or sinful acts and is considered to be a central moral virtue. It is realized through believing in The Almighty and submitting to His Will, as elaborated later. The third verse spells out the practical objective: *It is to make the self thrive, that is, to grow and flourish.* In other words, it is self-development that is the practical objective that gives meaning to our lives and which provides a measure for real success in life. It is not in considering as ends in themselves the accumulation of wealth, or the attainment of positions of power and influence, or the relentless pursuit of worldly goals, no matter how seemingly lofty. All these endeavors need not be shunned, as long as: (i) they are pursued lawfully and righteously, (ii) their true worth is recognized, and (iii) they do not distract from genuine self-development but rather contribute to it in meaningful ways. On the other hand, the fourth verse states that the stunting of self-development, which could be through passive neglect or willful commission of evil acts, is the mark of failure in life.

The Quran recognizes three states of the self along the path of its development:

> **...Surely the self is wont to command evil, save whom my *Rabb* may show mercy. Truly my *Rabb* is Ever-Forgiving, Ever-Merciful.** (12:53)

At the base level the self is likely to command evil acts. Why? Because this is usually the path of least resistance, that of short-term, immediate but transitory gratification, which many would find alluring and irresistible. Not everyone treads this path. Those who seek and receive His Mercy are spared this predicament. Of those who transgress some may experience the self-reproach of the second state:

> **And I do swear by the blaming self.** (75:2)

The blaming self is the stirring of a conscience in resistance to the transgression committed. Some people may choose to ignore these stirrings and continue in their ways. Others may heed them and make a course correction.

The sublime state of the self that one should strive for is the serene self:

> **O serene self! Return to your *Rabb*, well pleased with Him and well-pleasing to Him. So enter among My servants. And enter My Garden.** (89:27-30)

The serene self is at peace with itself and the world. It is transparent, having nothing to hide. It has shed all vestiges of vain and mundane desires, is free from all trepidation and fear of any mortal or any worldly outcome, harbors no ill feelings towards anyone, is compassionate to all, and is preoccupied with benevolent and virtuous acts. It has certainty as to what is right and what is wrong, profound knowledge of what is paramount and worthy and what is not, and perspicacious wisdom concerning the right decisions to make, and courses of action to take, in any given situation. It experiences sublime spirituality submitting to The Will of The Almighty and Serving Him. The second verse affirms that the serene self feels content with what it has achieved by Mercy of The Almighty and has pleased Him with its achievement. The last two verses speak of the ultimate reward: Heaven in company of the righteous. This sets the real purpose and objective of self-development: the eternal bliss in Heaven, contingent on the Will, Grace, Mercy, and Judgement of The Almighty.

To sum up, the human self is a miraculous creation endowed with an innate disposition for good or evil. Our everyday thoughts and conduct have a direct bearing on the development of this self. Evil-doing or simply benign neglect, as is most often the case, stunts this self-development and demeans our humanness. Choosing the righteous course of self-development and diligently following this course is ever-fulfilling and is what gives meaning to our lives. The ultimate purpose and goal of this self-development is the serene self in this world, which is a requisite for eternal bliss in the Afterlife.

Spirituality provides the solid foundation for this continuing and ever-fulfilling self-development. It is the principal element of this grand edifice of self-development. But how is this Spirituality cultivated in practical terms? This will be pursued in what follows, focusing on five key components: (i) beliefs, as the embrace of some underlying, or foundational, convictions, (ii) feelings engendered by these beliefs, (iii) occupying thoughts, as sustained remembrance of The Almighty, predicated on these beliefs and feelings, (iv) attitudes, as dispositions emanating from the aforementioned beliefs, feelings, and thoughts, and (v) conduct, as a behavioral manifestation or embodiment of all the preceding. Figure 7.1 depicts the five building blocks for the advocated Spirituality.

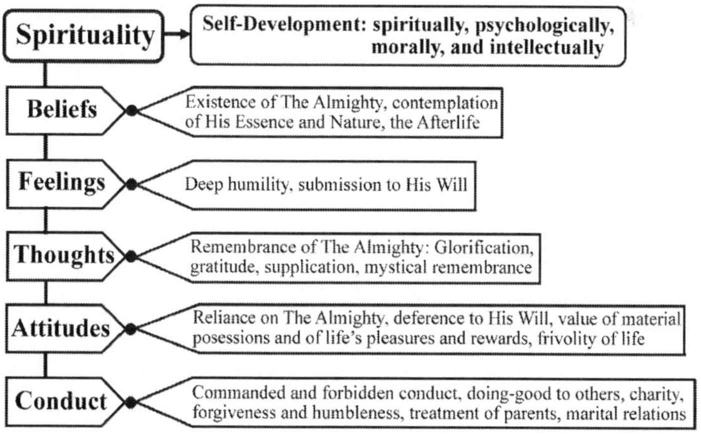

Figure 7.1 Spirituality: its outcome and building blocks

Foundational Beliefs

Existence of The Almighty

The mainstay of the advocated Spirituality is first and foremost the firm belief in the Existence of The Almighty. The unequivocal evidence for His Existence was presented in Chapter 4 based on the revelations of the Quran. Fifteen miraculous verses were presented together with indisputable numerical relations of letters and words, as examples of evidence for the Divine origin of the Quran. Anyone who approaches the totality of this evidence with an open mind and searches in earnest for explanations cannot but arrive at this conclusion. Brushing all this evidence aside can only be ascribed to a stubbornly irrational denial of an evident Truth, that of the Existence of The Almighty, the Creator of the universe and the Guide and Sustainer of everything in it.

Contemplation of His Essence and Nature

Some people may have a mental image of God that they find disturbing and hard to accept, like that of a bearded, sullen old man somewhere high up in the sky surrounded by cherubic angels. They may believe that He created the heavens and Earth in six weekdays, resting on the seventh, and then retired, letting nature take care of itself. The Quranic view of the Nature of The Almighty, as presented in Chapter 5, is that it is beyond human comprehension. Some would find this hard to accept: how can one believe in what one cannot understand or picture in one's mind? This is really a naïve and conceited view shrouded with a veneer of fake sophistication and intellectualism. It presupposes that our mind is able to understand everything there is to understand about the universe. Problem is, there is no realistic basis whatsoever for this able-to-understand-it-all syndrome. Those who entertain such a view should abandon it (not for God's sake, as the saying goes) but for their own sake, for the sake of their self-development as conscious human beings and not just higher animals.

What was presented in Chapter 5 about the Nature of The Almighty is that He is Transcendent, beyond human perception and imagination. He is The One and Only, The Creator of everything, its Guide and Sustainer, not bound by space or time, the real Owner of everything in the universe, the All-Knowing, The Willer of all things that are, The Doer of whatever He Wills, The Most Compassionate, The Ever-Merciful, The All-Forgiving, The Ever-Forgiving, The Relenting, The Responsive, The All-Loving, The All-Wise, and the All-Just. The Almighty is maximally perfect. His are The Most Exalted Names, for He possesses all the perfect Attributes to the highest degree possible.

The Afterlife

Belief in the Afterlife follows inexorably from the belief in the existence of The Almighty and in the truth of His Quranic revelations. If we have been given the freedom of choice over our acts and behavior, then it is only fair and reasonable that we should bear responsibility for these choices and be held accountable for their consequences for ourselves and others. Life is therefore a test for each and every one of us whether or not one has made the right choices that are conducive to the development of the self in every way, mainly spiritually, psychologically, morally, and intellectually. The Quran states:

> **He Who created death and life that He may test you as to which of you is most righteous in deed, and He**

is The Almighty, The Ever-Forgiving. (67:2)

The test may involve some misfortune or good fortune, as explained in Chapter 5, Section "Why Is There Suffering and Evil?". Based on His judgement, there is reward or punishment in this life and in the Afterlife. Moreover, to believe in the Afterlife is to believe in something that is more sublime than the material body and that outlasts it after it degenerates with death to feed bacteria and worms.

Engendered Feelings

Deep Humility

The mental image of The Almighty that emerges from the preceding is truly overwhelming and overpowering, beyond human imagination and comprehension. This should engender a feeling of deep humility. For who is the most powerful and glorified human being compared to His indescribable Greatness, Majesty, and Glory? No matter the self-delusion, everyone is utterly helpless and powerless against His Will, whether one realizes it or not, or cares to admit it or not. Just think of our pitiful weakness against debilitating disease, calamities that might befall us all of a sudden, without any anticipation or preparedness, or the inexorable ravages of aging. Everyone will face the consequences of their actions if not in this life then in the Afterlife. On the Day of Judgement, everyone will face their Creator alone, without bodyguards, companions, or any of the trappings of wealth and power in this world. To brush all this aside and cling to an illusory belief of one's grandeur, superiority, and invincibility is the height of conceit, arrogance, and ignorance of the realities of our existence.

Submission to His Will

Recognizing our insignificance and powerlessness with respect to The Almighty, and in deep humility, the inescapable choice for our successful self-fulfillment is to submit to His Will. As a matter of fact, all living and nonliving entities have submitted to His Will in complying with the laws of nature that He ordained. This includes all entities governed by the four fundamental forces – gravity, electromagnetism, the weak nuclear force, and the strong nuclear force – or by the biochemical-electrical reactions and interactions underlying the physiology of all living cells, tissues, organs, and systems, or by instinctive animal behavior and reflexes; all have submitted to His Will. In other words, His Reality permeates every reality. It is human free will, which He created by His Will and Design, that has given humans a leash to make life choices, by way of trying them, and for which they are accountable. Whether they recognize it or not, all human beings are subject to His Will.[2] This is attested in the following verses:

> **And you do not will but that Allāh Wills. Truly Allāh is All-Knowing, All-Wise.** (76:30)

> **And you do not will but that Allāh, *Rabb* of the worlds, Wills.** (81:29)

In other words, it is futile not to submit to His Will. On the other hand, it behooves everyone to submit to His Will, for their own sake and immense benefit.

The foregoing are the foundational beliefs of the advocated Spirituality and the feelings they engender. How does one put them into practice? That is considered in what follows.

Occupying Thoughts – Remembrance of The Almighty

Spirituality entails that The Almighty should always be on our minds, consciously or subconsciously, as a means of truly experiencing Him in our daily lives. The Quran affirms:

> **...Indeed prayer deters (one) from indecency and abomination, but the remembrance of Allāh is surely greater...** (29:45)

Remembrance of The Almighty as part and parcel of our daily thoughts and as a companion and guide of our daily acts is surely of greater spiritual and psychological benefit than remembering Him only in prayer and then forgetting Him the rest of the time.

The following paragraphs present some of the ways for making Him an integral part of our everyday thoughts. In thinking of Him or entreating Him, He can be thought of as The Almighty or by any other hallowed name one might choose.

Glorification

One cannot but glorify The Almighty if one ponders His indescribable Greatness, Majesty, and Glory as well as the marvels of His Creation. He is The One and Only, has absolute and uncontested power over everything in the universe, and everything in the universe belongs to Him. He is the only Eternal, who remains after everything else perishes.

Look around you and observe the beauty and wonders of His Creation: the awesome, boundless universe of twinkling stars in the darkness of a cloudless night, the immense oceans girdling our planet, the lovely landscapes of majestic mountains, magnificent forests, sparkling brooks, and bubbling springs; water playfully cascading over glistening rocks in a scenic waterfall; the magnificence of a rainbow arching in the sky; the magic of a full moon over a shimmering lake or scintillating desert dunes; the glory of the Sun rising majestically while casting an enchanting, life-giving glow; or spectacularly setting beyond the horizon amidst soft rays painting cloud patches with a mottled glow and a silver lining.

Witness the power and fury of nature: the deafening claps of thunder and the blinding flashes of lightning of a severe thunderstorm, the torrential rains and howling winds of a hurricane, the mighty waves of a tempestuous ocean, the incandescent fury of an erupting volcano, and the terrifying ground-shaking of an earthquake.

Behold the beauty and incredible variety of flora and fauna around you: the lovely forms and colors of roses and flowers, the lush green of grass and foliage, the marvelous changing colors of trees in the spring and autumn, the gorgeous shapes and colors of butterfly wings, the splendid plumage of birds and their captivating singing, the grace and elegance of swans in flight or floating around the lily-padded waters of an idyllic pond.

And the wonder of wonders remains the human being, having incredible physiology, mystifying consciousness, and capacity for amazing mental feats ranging from sublime spirituality, to dazzling scientific discoveries and philosophical discourse, to splendid achievements in engineering and technology, to stunning creativity in the arts, whether it's literature, poetry, music, painting, or sculpture.

Recurrent glorification of The Almighty in our thoughts cannot but inspire awe, engender humility, and arouse an intense desire to seek His Mercy and submit to His Will.

Gratitude

We have so much to be thankful for that thoughts of sincere and profound gratitude to The Almighty cannot be but a microcosm of our indebtedness to Him.

He privileged us with being born to this world and blessed us with a conscious self that we can nurture and develop along a path of serenity that opens up to an enormity of eternal bliss, contingent on His Grace and Mercy. He endowed us with exquisite senses to see vibrant colors, hear entrancing melodies, smell intoxicating fragrances, taste savory food or drink, and caress a loved one. He gifted us with intense feelings to appreciate beauty in all its forms, whether in scenic landscapes, elating music, beautiful artwork, or inspiring poetry, and to experience the exhilaration of pure love, intimate friendship, and good company.

If all this is not enough to thank Him for, we should thank Him for good health. The processes underlying the functioning of our bodies are so intricate that it is a wonder malfunctions are not the norm. Every time we wake up in the morning feeling refreshed and healthy, can move without discomfort or pain, and with our sanity intact, we have a lot to be thankful for.

We should thank Him for our daily provisions, for the drink that quenches our thirst and for the food that sustains our frail bodies, not only formally by saying grace when assembled for a sumptuous family meal, but just as much when snacking in a picnic, or nibbling at a sandwich as we scurry to a destination.

We should be most thankful when we feel content with what we have, what He bestowed on us through His Mercy, Grace, and Wisdom: a comfortable life, the security of a shelter, the warmth of a home, and the reciprocal affection with those around us.

As one progresses in Spirituality, one would find oneself making at times a sudden, unexpected decision, out of nowhere, concerning a matter at hand, consequential or minor, and which turns out to be the right, beneficial decision. Or one may experience fortunate occurrences in some everyday events, which one would normally ascribe to good luck. Such decisions and occurrences would be but a small example of His Guidance and loving Care, for which one should feel immense gratitude.

How can any feeling human be indifferent to all this, which is but a sample of what to be thankful for? Would not feeling and expressing this gratitude be the epitome of callous ungratefulness? Then again, it is important to keep in mind that gratitude to The Almighty should never be just occasional or opportune, but should be an intrinsic and sustained component of our daily thoughts, consciously or unconsciously.

Supplication

Humbly, earnestly and piously appealing to The Almighty in supplication is one of the most sublime ways of experiencing closeness to Him. The Quran proclaims:

> **And your *Rabb* has said: "Call upon Me and I shall respond to you"...** (40:60)

The Almighty enjoins us to supplicate to Him directly (see also (2:186), Chapter 5, Section "Nature"). No intermediary of any kind is needed, for He is The Responsive and is nearer to every person **"...than his jugular vein"** (50:16), which indicates that He "is the nearest and closest Reality to the human being."[3] (See also Chapter 5, Section "All-Knowing".) To supplicate to The Almighty, one need not be in any special place, for

He is Omnipresent, everywhere, not bound by space; **"... And He is with you wheresoever you may be..."** (57:4). He can be supplicated anytime, even in the stillness of the darkness of night, for **"...He neither slumbers nor sleeps..."** (2:255). Supplication does not require any special posture, the supplicant could be standing, sitting, walking, or lying down. But the supplication must be in deep humility, with utmost reverence, and with profound earnestness. The supplication need not have any special wording or format; it is, in essence, a personalized appeal that expresses what one hopes or yearns for.

The supplication might plead for His Mercy (for the meaning of mercy, see Chapter 5, Section "Nature"), which may be accorded by The Almighty through His Love, Graciousness, Kindness, Compassion and Benevolence, bearing in mind that He is The Most Compassionate, The Ever-Merciful. We need His Mercy for not trying us beyond what we can bear and for alleviating any afflictions that might befall us.

The supplication might plead for forgiveness for any transgressions committed and for accepting repentance for these acts. These could be malevolent acts or deviations from righteousness done unwittingly or uncontrollably under the influence of a self that is "wont to commanding evil" (see (12:53) under "On the Human Condition" above). Such pleas would be in the fervent hope of being accepted, for He is The All-Forgiving and The Relenting (see Chapter 5, Section "Nature"), and would in themselves provide considerable comfort and relief in getting them off one's chest.

The supplication might be for the cessation or alleviation of some distress, be it an ailment, some misfortune, or some anxiety or depression. Or the supplication might be for guidance in following a righteous path, or for some good fortune, in whatever way one might hope for.

In all cases, supplication is an exalted expression of personalized, devoted attachment to The Almighty, while feeling His closeness, and recognizing our humbleness in His most revered Presence.

Mystical Remembrance

Beyond glorification, gratitude, and supplication, Remembrance of The Almighty can take some mystical, that is, spiritually symbolic, forms. This is particularly the case with further development of Spirituality. The Almighty might be solemnly invoked when embarking on any non-trivial task in the hope that He would intercede for a favorable outcome. When faced with having to make a decision on a matter of grave consequences, one would seek some indication or sign from Him as to which decision to make. Devout believers are firmly convinced of the reality of these interventions and communications.

Naturally, a good part of our daily thoughts are concerned with ongoing activities or future plans or other purposeful thinking. Oftentimes, however, our mind is just idling, not engaged with anything in particular, but merely flitting from one idle thought to another, or fantasizing with some fanciful or wishful thinking. With conscious and determined effort one can replace such idle thinking with Remembrance of The Almighty by silent repetition of His Name, or of some formal or personalized phrase focused on Him. This can be greatly beneficial in inducing a soothing, restful calmness and in bringing one closer to The Almighty. Remembrance of The Almighty should be always in the background of our thoughts no matter what we happen to be consciously thinking about. Remembrance of The Almighty can be particularly fulfilling as one drifts into sleep at the end of the day while completely entrusting Him with one's fate and surrendering oneself to His Care.

All in all, Remembrance of The Almighty is an expression of acute awareness of His perpetual and compelling Presence as well as our humbling and earnest need for it. It can engender intense contentment. What could be more comforting and more rewarding than a pervasive feeling of being cared for, guarded, and guided by He Who is The Most Compassionate, The Ever-Merciful, The All-Loving, The All-Knowing, The All-Wise, and The Omnipotent? What more can one wish for? And what on earth (both idiomatically and literally) can substitute for such a feeling? Certainly, no fleeting, superficial gratification in whatsoever form and by whatsoever means.

Remembrance founded on steadfast beliefs and earnest feelings will inspire some potent attitudes that shape one's worldview, as discussed next.

Formative Attitudes

The following are some Spirituality-induced attitudes that would direct one's conduct of life's affairs. Their psychological and sociological impact is considered later.

Reliance on The Almighty

Such a reliance reflects one's confidence and trust in His Wisdom and Mercy, which one should always have, particularly when doing something that has an uncertain outcome that is cause for some anxiety. One should unquestionably leave the outcome to Him, for He is All-Knowing, All-Wise, and All-Just.

Reliance should never be construed as indolent dependence. One should never just stand by, without trying one's best in a given situation, and think one could simply relegate the doing to The Almighty. That is most abhorrent and is not what humans were created for. The Almighty has endowed us with will and abilities and expects us to make the effort, leaving the outcome to His Judgement and Wisdom.

Making the effort is poignantly epitomized in the Quranic parable of The Virgin Mary in labor:

> **And the pangs of childbirth drove her to the trunk of a palm tree. She said, "Oh, would that I had died before this and had become a thing forgotten, utterly forgotten!" Thereupon a voice called out to her from beneath her, "Grieve not! Your *Rabb* has provided a stream beneath you. And shake the trunk of the palm tree toward you, it will drop fresh ripe dates upon you."** (19:23-25)

The Virgin Mary – the only woman mentioned by name in the Quran – was in severe distress while giving birth to Jesus, the Messenger of Allāh who was blessed with performing miracles ((3:49) and (5:110)). The Almighty did not simply have the dates drop upon her to provide her with nourishment. She was asked to shake the trunk of the palm tree, hard as that is and feeble as her effort might be, in order to have the dates drop on her.

The need to make the effort is also emphasized in the following verses:

> **And that a human being has only that for which he makes the effort, And that his effort will be seen.** (53:39-40)

Evidently, in coping with any given situation, one should always strive to do one's best, seeking the help and guidance of The Almighty, but leave the outcome to Him. Reliance on The Almighty relieves one from trepidation and anxiety as to what might transpire and what the outcome might be.

The Quran, in many verses, enjoins believers to put their trust in The Almighty as in:

> **If Allāh helps you, none can defeat you. But if He denies you help, then who else can help you? So in Allāh let the believers put their reliance.** (3:160)

The Arabic word *tawakkul* is usually translated as "trust". In the present context, "reliance" is deemed more appropriate as it implies both confidence and trust.

Deference to His Will

One must invariably defer to The Will of The Almighty in all matters and accept with deep reverence whatever He has decreed for one. Again, it cannot be overemphasized that this is no excuse for complacency and inaction. One should always exert oneself in worldly affairs to the best of one's abilities and judgement, righteously and honorably, but in the end resign oneself to whatever The Almighty has destined for one.

Deference to His Will applies to all facets of our lives including health, occupation, family, and circumstances in general. If one is afflicted with a serious health condition and after seeking the best medical advice and therapy attainable, one should not succumb to depression or despair but accept one's condition and entreat The Almighty for full healing, alleviation of distress, and the strength to cope with it.

If a loved one passes away, it is only human to grieve over the loss. But one should accept this as the unavoidable end of all mortals, and that The Almighty gives and He takes away. One should plead for consolation for the grieving and His Mercy for the deceased.

The roots of any stress or conflict in personal relations, whether at work, within the family, or with others, should be addressed with wisdom, understanding, compassion, and with all appropriate, admissible, and acceptable means at one's disposal. Whatever the end result, one should accept it with dignity, honor, and without remorse or vindictiveness.

When one is powerless against misfortune and adversity, after having done one's best to counter them righteously and sincerely, one should arm oneself with patience and fortitude in deference to His Will and not question or contest it. For He is All-Knowing, All-Wise, and the affliction may well be a test of one's devotion and trust in Him or a means of spiritual purification. If one is not justly rewarded in this life, which is but a blink on the eternal scale, then one should have absolute certainty of a just requital in the Afterlife by the All-Just, The Most Compassionate, and The Ever-Merciful. The Quran assures:

> **...Truly, those who endure with patience shall be rewarded without measure.** (39:10)

> **And surely We shall try you with something of fear and hunger, and loss of wealth, lives, and produce; and give glad tidings to those who endure with patience – those who, when affliction befalls them, say: "Truly we belong to Allāh, and to Him we shall return."** (2:155-156)

The parable of the Prophet Job is recounted in *The Book*

of Job of the Old Testament, and he is mentioned in the New Testament, *Epistle of James* (James 5:11). In the Quran, the parable is alluded to in verses (21:83-84) and (38:41-44) as an example of patience and forbearance in the face of adversity by way of trial by The Almighty. In Arabic lore, the patience of Job is legendary.

Material Possessions

Accumulation of wealth and material possessions should never be an end in itself, but only means for a dignified and comfortable life as well as a means for self-development and Serving The Almighty. For this, the benefactors will be richly rewarded (see Section "Virtuous Conduct", subheading "Charity").

As mentioned previously (Chapter 5, Section "Ownership"), everything in the universe belongs to The Almighty, and we have only temporary custody of our material possessions. All the money in the bank, the jewelry in safes, the luxurious apartments, the sprawling estates, the elegant villas, the expensive cars, yachts, and private airplanes, are only for transitory ownership and enjoyment and will all be left behind when one dies. This should place material possessions in their true perspective and reveal their real worth.

It should be borne in mind that The Almighty also tests humans with abundance of wealth to see if they spend it righteously in His Service (see also Chapter 5, Section "Why Is There Suffering and Evil?" (21:35)):

> **Your wealth and your children are but a trial. It is Allāh with Whom is the greatest reward.** (64:15)

It should be noted that the reference to children in this and in other verses that follow signifies manpower and influence.[4] Moreover, abundance of wealth could be cause for torment and a form of chastisement:

> **So do not be impressed by their wealth or their children; Allāh only desires to chastise them with these things in this life and that their spirits may depart while they are still disbelievers.** (9:55)

The amassing of wealth can exact a heavy toll, in the strenuous effort and the stress of the relentless pursuit of wealth – not to mention the deviousness, the unscrupulousness, and the callousness that might be involved. The toll can also be in the persistent anxiety of the diminution or loss of wealth, and in the distraction entailed by all this from righteous and liberating conduct:

> **O you who believe! Let not your wealth nor your children distract you from remembrance of Allāh. Those who do so, they are the losers.** (63:9)

Ostentatious flaunting of wealth is particularly detestable, in view of the needs of the impoverished and destitute, those who lack proper food, adequate shelter, and the bare necessities of dignified living.

Placing material possessions in their proper perspective leads to renouncing a materialistic way of life that embraces excessive consumption and avaricious consumerism.

Life's Pleasures and Rewards

Embracing Spirituality by no means implies foregoing life's pleasures and rewards. The Almighty has gifted us with senses and feelings for enjoying the good things in life:

O believers! Do not forbid the good things which Allāh has made lawful for you, and do not transgress. Indeed, Allāh does not love transgressors. (5:87)

What is to be enjoyed is bound by the limits of what is lawful and moral. Stepping outside these limits becomes transgression.

Transgression can be instigated by craving and greed. To crave for wealth, power, status, or pleasures is to become enslaved by this craving. Craving is incessant, fueled by greed, so it's never satiated. This means that what is craved cannot be really enjoyed, because no matter how much is attained, one is desperate for more. Craving becomes an all-consuming, unscrupulous drive that can overstep all moral and ethical bounds. In Buddhism, self-centered craving is considered the underlying source of anguish.[5]

On the other hand, true enjoyment of life's pleasures and rewards derives joy from what pleasures become available, without transgression, without yearning, without making their pursuit a central objective, and without regret and sorrow when they cease.

Even without craving, excessive indulgence in pleasures is not only unseemly but can be downright harmful. A familiar case in point is overeating. But with the right perspective and determined effort one can savor a favorite food with just a morsel or a small portion rather than gorge with one mouthful after another.

In all cases, when one is enjoying life's pleasures and rewards, lawfully and morally, one should never forget gratitude to The Almighty for making available the good things in life and for enabling their enjoyment, in the hope that He may continue to bless us with His Favors.

Frivolity of Life

The Quran states:

> **Know that this worldly life is no more than play, amusement, pageantry, mutual boasting, and competition in wealth and children. This is like rain that causes plants to grow, to the delight of the planters. But later the plants dry up and you see them wither, then they are reduced to chaff. And in the Hereafter there will be either severe punishment or forgiveness and pleasure of Allāh, whereas the worldly life is no more than vain enjoyment.** (57:20)

The verse describes the reality of mundane life in this world as commonly experienced by most people: frivolous, showy, and boastful of wealth, power, status, titles, and fruits of other worldly pursuits. What one reaps from all this is enjoyment of delusions and illusions. Although one may enjoy life's pleasures and rewards, lawfully and within the limits of righteousness and morality, one should not be deceived by appearances and outward glamor and should always bear in mind that mundane pursuits and self-centered goals and achievements are by their very nature frivolous, superficial, and devoid of real significance. Moreover, our worldly existence and everything we experience in it is transient and subject to unforeseen and unpredictable change. Nothing worldly is everlasting: neither riches, nor grandeur, nor status, nor good health. They will all come to an end sometime, if not during our lifetime, then with death. *And what does not last cannot be counted on*, to paraphrase the great Muslim scholar, mystic, and philosopher, Ibn ʿArabī who lived in the 12th and 13th centuries CE and who wrote a famous book entitled, in English translation, *Treatise on What Cannot Be Counted On.*[6] What really counts is eternal bliss in the Afterlife which can only be granted by the Will, Grace, and Mercy of an All-Just Almighty. The advocated Spirituality firmly anchors one in the face of the vagaries of life and does not let one flail helplessly and uncontrollably between joy and sadness, hope and despair, or elation and depression.

As one advances in Spirituality, one would feel a sense of detachment from the commotion and tumult of mundane life, a detachment that is a precursor of a soothing tranquility. The Quran exhorts us:

> **That you neither grieve over what you have missed nor exult over what He has granted you. For Allāh does not love any vainglorious boaster.** (57:23)

A consequence of this sense of tranquil detachment and the recognition of the frivolity of our mundane existence is the banishment of envy and its nefarious, corrosive influence on the psyche, as discussed later. For how can one covet the worldly possessions and attainments of others when one is cognizant of their true worth?

Another consequence of the recognition of this frivolity, fortified by reliance on The Almighty, is the deep conviction that as long as one is doing what is right and just, one would fear nothing and no one, no matter how influential or authoritative.

Virtuous Conduct

The beliefs, feelings, thoughts, and attitudes affirmed in the preceding sections, important as they are by themselves, remain woefully insufficient and would have little meaning if they do not translate to proper conduct. A profound and comprehensive description of this conduct is: *Serving The Almighty*. As this might seem vague and incomprehensible at first sight, it will be expounded in this section.

The Quran states:

> **I did not create jinn and humankind, save to Serve Me. I wish no livelihood from them; nor do I wish them to feed Me. Indeed, Allāh is The Supreme Sustainer, the Possessor of unbreakable might.** (51:56-58)

The first sentence is a most definitive and absolute assertion that the purpose of creation of jinn and humans is to Serve The Almighty. The jinn referred to in the first verse, and in many other verses of the Quran, often in conjunction with humans, are beings created by The Almighty from a "smokeless flame of fire" (55:15), which is interpreted by some as "pure energy". They are mysterious beings who "as psychic beings, unseen to most human beings, occupy an intermediate state between the material realm of our physical experiences and the angelic and spiritual realms. Nonetheless, they are also on the earth, and according to some, occupied the earth before human beings."[7] The jinn do not concern us here; they remain, nevertheless, one of the mysteries of the Quran.

The verb at the end of the first verse is usually translated "to worship Me" but has also been translated more correctly as "to Serve Me",[4,8] since the noun *ʿabd*, meaning male slave or servant,[9] is derived from the same root verb (see also Chapter 5, Section "All-Knowing"). "Worship", as commonly understood, connotes acts of prayer, or more generally, adoration and idolization, which, nevertheless, is by itself essentially passive in nature. Service, on the other hand, is an active undertaking. That serving is the intended meaning is corroborated by the second and third verses; slaves and servants do provide their masters with some service required and needed by the master. The Almighty, however, does not wish or need any services for Himself. Then, what does Serving Him mean?

The purpose of creation is mentioned in another verse:

> **And had your *Rabb* so willed, He certainly would have made mankind one community. But they cease not to differ, save those upon whom thy *Rabb* has Mercy – and for this He created them…** (11:118-119)

The first of these two verses affirms that had The Almighty willed, He would have made all mankind a single community of one persuasion and set of beliefs. Yet through His Design and Wisdom, humans have been given some free will so as to choose between Serving Him or not, and in order to test their devotion to Him if they decide to Serve Him, as explained in Chapter 5, Section "Why Is There Suffering and Evil?". As a result of this freedom of choice, humans will not cease to differ because many would pursue their own selfish desires and follow a path of human unworthiness, except for those who seek, and are accorded, His Mercy. Receiving His Mercy as a result of believing in Him, knowing about Him, relying on Him, submitting to His Will, and following His dictates would lead to eternal bliss in the Afterlife. And that is the purpose of human creation and the meaning of Serving Him. Thus, to Serve The Almighty is to receive His Mercy, like the servant who serves his master to please him and earn his beneficial treatment. Since The Almighty does not need this service nor does He benefit from it, the benefits of Serving Him are therefore directed at the servant and for his own good.[10] The benefits accrued by Serving Him are those of "inner-development",[11] that is, development of the self. According to Fazlur Rahman, the Harold H. Swift Distinguished Service Professor of Islamic Thought, University of Chicago, "...the purpose of man is to 'serve' God, i.e., to develop his higher potentialities in accordance with the 'command' (*amr*) of God, through choice..."[12] Again, this refers to self-development through Serving The Almighty.

The question that comes to mind, then, is how would one Serve The Almighty? It is through conduct that embodies the beliefs, feelings, thoughts, and attitudes discussed in the preceding sections. Beliefs, thoughts, feelings, and attitudes are all inner states that are woefully inadequate if they are not manifested outwardly through deeds, words, and treatment of others. The required conduct is frequently described in the Quran by variations on the word *iḥsān*, which derives from a root that means "beautiful". *Iḥsān* denotes doing what is good and beautiful, outwardly, and having good and beautiful morals and character, inwardly, both being manifestations of continued awareness of The Almighty and sensing His closeness through the previously discussed beliefs, thoughts, feelings, and attitudes. Henceforth, the phrase "doing good" is to be understood as referring to *iḥsān*, as doing what is good and beautiful not only in deeds but also in words and in all manner of dealing with others. To emphasize this reference to *iḥsān*, the verb form "do" or "doing" will be hyphenated with the word "good". A related meaning of *iḥsān* is to do a "beautiful job" in whatever one is working on.

The Quran stresses in several verses that good deeds are richly rewarded, as in:

> **Whoever comes with doing-good will be rewarded tenfold. But whoever comes with a bad deed will be**

> **punished for only one. None will be wronged.** (6:160)

The reference to a tenfold increase is considered to be only symbolic of a large recompense for doing-good, whereas the punishment for bad deeds is not multiplied. The Almighty is Most Beneficent for doing-good but is only All-Just for bad deeds.

Serving The Almighty precludes serving any other master:

> **And your *Rabb* has decreed that you serve none but Him...** (17:23)

Serving another master means according someone or something, other than The Almighty, a central role in our lives, commanding our attention, devotion, and loyalty, and governing our behavior. This can be our own selfish egos, pursuit of wealth, power, and status, or other worldly causes and desires. In actual fact, polytheism is still pervasive in modern society but in forms other than those of ancient times, as mentioned in Chapter 3, Section "Resort to Rational Thinking".

In what follows, we focus on some specific forms of conduct that are accorded special significance in the Quran, as exemplars of Serving The Almighty.

Commanded and Forbidden Conduct

The Quran asserts:

> **Allāh commands doing justice, doing-good (to others), and giving to kinsfolk, and He forbids indecency, abomination, and aggression: He admonishes you so that you may take heed.** (16:90)

The verse broadly defines what is righteous conduct and what is not. Justice means: fairness, equitability, and rectitude as well as avoidance of prejudice, discrimination, and arbitrariness. The same root verb in Arabic also means "to make straight, or even, or right"[13] and to take "the middle or moderate course in all things".[13] Doing-good to others was just explained as *iḥsān* and will be elaborated in the next item. The word *faḥshā'*, translated here as indecency, refers to what is against standards of morality or propriety, especially in sexual matters. The word *munkar*, translated as "evil", "wickedness", or "abomination", is interpreted as "deeds that any person of sound intellect and rational faculties could not fail to recognize as inherently wrong."[2] The word *baghi*, rendered as aggression, means "acting wrongfully, injuriously, or tyrannically", particularly as a result of envy, or "exceeding the due bounds, or just limits, in any way".[14] It is interpreted to refer to acts "that indulge human pride and ambition and entail gross injustice".[2] Envy, arrogance, self-conceit, and oppression are much abhorred.

Doing-Good to Others

The Quran exhorts:

> **Serve Allāh, and associate nothing with him, and do-good to parents, to kinsfolk, to orphans, to the needy, to the neighbor from among your own people, to the neighbor who is a stranger, to the companion by your side, to the wayfarer, and to those whom your right hands possess. Truly, Allāh does not love any vainglorious boaster.** (4:36)

Doing-good to parents is emphasized, as elaborated later, as well as to relatives, in recognition of the importance of the extended family. Orphans, generally considered to be minors who have lost their fathers, their primary providers and protectors,[15] are mentioned often in the Quran as targets for special sympathy, care, and charity (see the next item). Doing-good should also be accorded to: (i) neighbors, whether or not they are from one's people or are alien, that is, strangers from different societies or cultures, (ii) companions by one's side, who could be fellow travelers or coworkers or someone by one's side someplace,[16] which practically includes everyone with whom one might come in contact, and (iii) "those whom your right hands possess", or "you rightfully possess", generally refers to slaves, particularly female slaves. In this context, the reference to "those whom your right hands possess" has been interpreted as all those one has been entrusted to take care of, including animals.[8] By wayfarer is generally meant any person who for any reason is unable to return home,[17] and who would most likely be in need of material help, whether financially or in food and shelter.

It may be noted in passing that the Quran did not abolish slavery, which was widespread among Arabs in the 7th century CE. Abolishing slavery outright would have had grave economic and social consequences, not the least for the slaves themselves. Instead, the Quran mandated doing-good to slaves, which included freeing them, and made this freeing an atonement for transgressions such as unintentional killing of a believer (4:92), or the breaking of an oath (5:89), or for retracting certain types of verbal divorce (58:3), or as a form of obligatory charity (9:60), or for not sincerely and diligently following the righteous path (90:13). It has also been pointed out that slavery persists in modern societies albeit in different forms such as dire poverty and need, hunger, injustice, oppression, exploitation, crushing debt, and humiliation in different ways. Deeds that relieve from these adversities are tantamount to "freeing from slavery".[18]

Charity

Alms-giving is particularly praiseworthy and is often mentioned in the Quran. A pious believer is one:

> **...who gives wealth, despite cherishing it, to kinsfolk, orphans, the needy, the wayfarer, and to those who ask...** (2:177)

Relatives, orphans, and the needy are mentioned both here and in the preceding verse (4:36) on "Doing-Good to Others". In fact, the Quran asserts that those who ask and the needy have a rightful share of the wealth of the pious:

> **And in their wealth there was a rightful share for those who ask and for the needy.** (51:19)

The rightful share would seem all the more reasonable and logical bearing in mind that the universe and all that is in it belongs to The Almighty (see Chapter 5, Section "Ownership").

On charity, the Quran says:

> **O believers do not make your charity worthless by reminders of your generosity or by offending the recipients, like one who spends his wealth in order to flaunt it before people but believes neither in Allāh nor in the Last Day. His parable is that of a hard barren rock covered with a little soil; a heavy rain falls, leaving it just a bare stone. Such people will not gain any reward that they thought they had earned. Allāh does not guide the disbelievers. The parable of**

those who spend their wealth to seek the pleasure of Allāh and to strengthen their selves is like a garden on a high and fertile ground: when heavy rain falls on it, it yields twice its normal produce; and if no downpour falls, a light rain is sufficient. And Allāh is All-Seeing of what you do. (2:264-265)

These verses mention three conditions for good charity: (i) the alms-givers should not remind of their generosity, (ii) they should not offend the recipients, as for example, by being uncouth to them or by embarrassing them in any way, and (iii) the alms should not be for show-off. The verses stress a point that is very relevant to our Spirituality. Those who do not believe in The Almighty and in the Afterlife would give alms for show-off and would not benefit inwardly from the alms, that is, spiritually and psychologically. On the other hand, those who do believe give alms seeking the pleasure of The Almighty and would be "strengthening their selves", that is, developing their selves in the process. They will reap spiritual and psychological benefits, as is made clear in the following verse:

Those who spend their wealth for the sake of Allāh, and do not follow up what they have spent by reminders of their generosity or by offending the recipients, shall have their reward with their *Rabb*, and no fear shall befall them, nor shall they grieve. (2:262)

The spiritual and psychological benefits are spelled out: they have nothing to fear and they will not feel grief. These benefits are again spelled out in the following verse:

Those who spend their wealth in charity day and

> **night, secretly and openly, shall have their reward with their *Rabb*, and no fear shall befall them, nor shall they grieve.** (2:274)

Spending by day and night signifies frequent and continuous giving. Secret giving is especially worthy as it implies the giver is not seeking any worldly recognition, only the pleasure of The Almighty. Open giving, without show-off, is also acknowledged as it would encourage others to give.

Forgiveness and Humbleness

The Quran refers to the pious as:

> **Those who donate in prosperity and adversity, restrain their anger, and pardon others. And Allāh loves those who do-good.** (3:134)

The verse is a general injunction for alms-giving and for doing-good, emphasizing the love of The Almighty of those who do-good. Its special significance is in its explicit mention of controlling the feeling of anger and of pardoning others. Anger is a destructive and corrosive feeling that hurts the angry and those against whom it is directed, without serving any useful purpose. The verse urges not only restraining anger but also pardoning others and not holding grudges against them.

The sage Luqmān counselled his son thus:

> **And do not turn your face away from people in contempt nor walk pridefully upon the earth. Surely, Allāh does not love any self-conceited boaster. And let your walk be modest and keep your voice low...** (31:18-19)

The emphasis in these verses is on humbleness and against conceit in one's demeanor, as in swaggering. In addressing people, one should keep one's voice low and not turn one's face away in scorn. Conceit and boastfulness are condemned.

Both forgiveness and humbleness are attributes of those who are at peace with themselves, are compassionate and considerate towards others, harbor no ill feelings, and are Serving The Almighty.

Treatment of Parents

The Quran stresses the good treatment of parents as part of doing-good:

> **And your *Rabb* has decreed that you serve none but Him, and do-good to parents. If either or both reach old age with you, do not express annoyance or complaints to them nor chide them and address them graciously. And lower to them the wing of humility out of mercy, and say: "My *Rabb* have mercy on them, as they reared me when I was little."** (17:23-24)

The phrase "do-good to parents" is repeated four times in the Quran emphasizing respect and love towards parents in deference to their role in bringing up children with loving care, providing for them, protecting them, and guiding them. These verses specifically refer to the caring in turn of parents in their old age when living with a son or daughter. As parents age, they become infirm and sometimes overly sensitive. The parents should be treated with considerateness, patience, and understanding of their needs and dependencies. They should not be chided and one should plead with The Almighty to bless them with

His Mercy.

It is most unfortunate that modernization has led to deterioration of family values and the weakening of family ties almost to the breaking point. Youngsters are encouraged to leave the family nest at an early age under the guise of independence, living their own lives, and other expressions of excessive individualism. Obligations towards the nuclear or the extended family are scorned instead of providing an indispensable social and psychological safety net.

Marital Relations

The following verse is often quoted on the occasion of marriage in Muslim societies:

> **And among His Signs is that He created for you, from among your selves, spouses that you may dwell in tranquility with them, and He has instilled love and mercy between you; verily, in that are signs for those who reflect.** (30:21)

The nature of marital relations is considered as one of the signs or wonders of The Almighty, and that this can be understood upon reflection, or deep thinking, which means that there is much more to this verse than meets the eye. The first part of the verse defines in fact the ideal marriage. It is addressed to both men and women, so that women are created from the selves of men and men are created from the selves of women.[2] The verse also emphasizes the state of "dwelling in tranquility", which can only happen when there is little or no conflict between husband and wife, that is, when there is much harmony between them. But that can only happen when they have a great deal in common, in terms of outlook, desires, likes and dislikes, with nothing to hide from one another; in other words, when their conscious selves are so alike. This is the meaning of creating spouses "for you, from among your selves," for when one self is created from another, figuratively speaking, the two selves have the potential of being much alike and hence achieving harmony and tranquility. The ideal in marriage is for the two spouses to strive to become in perfect harmony. This is not easy; it requires much determined effort by the two spouses in order to relinquish selfish interests, subdue their egos, give in to one another on various matters, and merge their selves together so as to achieve an ideal union in every sense of the word. And all this is between two persons who were at one time more or less complete strangers. That is indeed a great sign.

The second part of the verse adds to the state of tranquility, the feelings that The Almighty has instilled and which should normally govern the conduct of spouses toward one another, namely, love and mercy. As explained in Chapter 5, Section "Nature", the Arabic word that is translated as mercy has a broader meaning that includes being kind, gracious, gentle, forgiving, compassionate, and benevolent. Love and mercy are indeed the feelings that should normally be harbored between husband and wife, who are sharing their lives together in common destiny and who would bring forth into this world a new generation of human beings and nurture them with loving care.

What about guidance to children? How should that be given? Children learn mostly through observation and by example rather than verbally through exhortation, preaching, and lecturing. The best guidance for children is to observe their parents treating one another with love and mercy and their own parents in turn with love, respect, patience, and understanding, while doing-good to these parents and to those they deal with, including righteous and moral conduct.

To sum up, The Almighty is served, not only by following His dictates, like an obedient servant, but also through virtuous conduct that embodies the previously discussed beliefs, feelings, thoughts, and attitudes. A seemingly virtuous conduct that does not so embody would not have an inward reflection that develops the self. It would be like an empty shell, devoid of any real worth, which brings us back to the central role of self-development.

Psychological Impact

Clearly, the five components of Spirituality – beliefs, feelings, thoughts, attitudes, and conduct – have a tremendous psychological impact which is examined in what follows.

Conquering Negative Feelings

"Envy is the ulcer of the soul" according to Socrates. Envy arouses feelings of malice towards those envied, wishing them harm so as to deprive them of what is envied or to negate it somehow. These malicious desires could drive the envier to inflict harm directly or indirectly; they could also make the envier feel guilty over them, if the envied ones are relatives, friends, or associates. Envy is also directed inwards, making the envier feel inferior or inadequate, having failed somehow, or at least having been the victim of bad luck and circumstances. The result is self-pity and self-depreciation, which can have a very negative impact on one's outlook, behavior, and performance. The envier may experience anger and hostility about everything and everyone, anxiety, and depression.

With Spirituality, there is no cause for envy. For

one thing, the yardstick for measuring success is quite different: It is self-development under the Grace and Mercy of The Almighty. It is not success in worldly matters as ends in themselves. It is not how much money those envied are making, or their lifestyles, or their social status, or popularity, or their position in the organization, or their achievements. If all these are conducive to self-development of those envied, under the Grace and Mercy of The Almighty, then good for them. One would feel happy for them and be motivated for more self-development. If, on the other hand, worldly gains and successes are stunting self-development, one would feel sorry for them instead of envying them. These worldly gains and successes would be just frivolities; they could be chastisement or could cause torment, anguish, and damnation in the Afterlife, as mentioned earlier under "Material Possessions". That is certainly no reason for envy.

Another detrimental negative feeling is anger at someone for saying or doing something that upsets one to the point of responding in anger by saying or doing something in return that will hurt the other person. Expressing anger is automatically accompanied by a physiological fight-or-flight stress response, which can be physically harmful, as explained later. In terms of results, lashing out in anger is generally counterproductive and does not lead to positive outcomes. The anger suspends reason and good judgement, which may result in saying or doing hurtful things that one would regret later. Anger arouses resentment and mistrust, gravely damaging personal relations. It can also provoke the other party to do hurtful things in return.

With Spirituality, one would naturally be considerate, understanding, and gracious towards others, hence much less likely to respond in anger even when provoked.

One would try to resolve the matter at hand, coolly and rationally with persuasive argument, and would forgive the other party for any hurt they may have caused.

Alleviation of Anxiety and Stress

Anxiety and stress are the banes of modern life. Although the stress response is beneficial for coping with short-term threats, as it mobilizes the body for action to cope with the threat, chronic stress is very harmful physically, psychologically and mentally. It disturbs: (i) the immune system, increasing susceptibility to disease and cancer, (ii) the cardiovascular system, increasing the risk for various types of heart abnormalities and disease, heart attacks, and stroke, as well as raising blood pressure, which itself can do harm to various organs and tissues, (iii) the digestive system, leading to indigestion and various digestive disorders, and (iv) sleep, resulting in insomnia and preventing a sound, restful, and restoring sleep. It can cause tense muscles and persistent headaches and pains. It adversely affects cognition, memory, ability to focus, and judgement. It induces irritability, worry and anxiety, forgetfulness, and inattention, low self-esteem, seclusion, depression, and in extreme cases can lead to some mental disorders.

In everyday life, anxiety and stress can be felt in many ways. One may wake up in the morning with an intense feeling of dread, of nothing in particular, just a strong apprehension weighing heavily on one's chest about what the day might bring. The same feeling might be triggered anytime by a seemingly trivial incident or event. A common cause of anxiety and stress is related to some activity or task, such as a job application, some type of contest or examination, or some undertaking. The anxiety and stress felt is not so much caused by the activity or task itself, onerous as that might be, but by the uncertainty about the outcome and its consequences.

Spirituality is a potent antidote to anxiety and stress. When one relies on The Almighty with absolute trust in His Love, Compassion, Wisdom, and Justice, has submitted to His Will, and with full acceptance of whatever He ordains, then *ipso facto* that leaves no room whatsoever for apprehension about what tomorrow might bring or what the outcome of an activity or task might turn out to be. That weightiness in the chest is never experienced, nor the tossing in bed in the middle of the night in insomnia or restless sleep.

Spirituality can also overcome some mild phobias and obsessive or compulsive behavior that are not associated with a serious underlying mental disorder. Reliance on The Almighty and seeking His help and Guidance would go a long way towards alleviating such aberrations.

Fostering Positive Feelings and Attitudes

With Spirituality one would enjoy the comfort, contentment, security, and peace of so many positive feelings and attitudes. One would feel tolerance, understanding, and compassion towards all, and wish them all well, without harboring any ill feelings toward anyone, even those who may wish to offend, antagonize or even hurt one. Such persons would be treated with magnanimity, their malicious intents or acts forgiven, with the wish that they be relieved from the maliciousness that must be gnawing at their psyche and anguishing them.

One would derive considerable pleasure and satisfaction from even small, everyday good deeds, such as giving to the poor and needy, putting a happy smile on the innocent face of a child, helping someone in distress, being kind to animals, or being gracious to a complete stranger. In fact, one would seek such acts, if they don't come one's way, for the sake of the pleasure and satisfaction they give.

Being mindful of the frivolity of worldly life and the real, intrinsic value of worldly possessions and pursuits, one would always strive to do one's best without engaging in the rat race nor getting embroiled in dog-eat-dog competition.

One would not succumb to the mindless materialism of a consumer-centered society, revolving around an ostentatious lifestyle that ranks making money as a primary objective, then spending it on things that one does not really need, such as fancy clothing, accessories, and the trappings of consumerism and ostentatious living.

In doing what is right and just, and opposing all forms of injustice, oppression, corruption, and exploitation, one would fear nothing and no one, for one is fortified by what Spirituality dictates in the Service of The Almighty.

With Spirituality, one would never experience a sense of self-depreciation or unworthiness, for one would be deeply cognizant of the sublimeness of the human conscious self and would be preoccupied with continuing development of one's self.

Experiencing The Joy of Living

With Spirituality, one would experience the true joy of living. With life's meaning and purpose in sharp focus, one is relieved of the sense of emptiness that plagues sometimes and drives one, consciously or unconsciously, to mitigate it by all sorts of cravings and petty distractions, which offer but temporary relief, usually at the expense of harmful long-term consequences, and leave unanswered the deep, underlying question as to the meaning and purpose of our existence.

One would enjoy the pleasures that life has to offer,

lawfully and morally, without craving, with moderation and without excessive indulgence or anxiety about the ending of these pleasures. This is because the enjoyment is simply for its own sake and not as an escape from some underlying sense of emptiness, deprivation, or worthlessness of it all.

With Spirituality, one would consider life as but a game, with its ups and downs, to be played as best as one can, without losing sight of its ultimate meaning and purpose and without any attendant fear or trepidation. Life's challenges become stepping stones on the path of self-development, rather than stumbling blocks that one might trip over. Whatever comes, one would take in one's stride, not regretting what was lost, nor overjoying at what was gained.

With Spirituality, one would really feel the joy of human bonds, particularly when strengthened by acts of benevolence and doing-good in the Service of The Almighty: the intimacy with one's immediate family, the closeness of true friendship, and the empathy towards others.

With Spirituality, one would look around and see the beauty of what surrounds us and what often goes unnoticed: captivating landscapes, waves lapping over a seashore and playfully frothing over the rocks, trees tenderly bending over a sleepy lake or a placid stream, a gentle breeze swaying foliage back and forth in a heavenly dance, the blueness of a cloudless sky, the spell of a full moon, the fragrance of roses in full bloom, and the happy, excited carefree chirping of birds. One would simply feel the immense joy at what the Grace of The Almighty has empowered us to witness.

No less enthralling is the enjoyment of what humans have been privileged by The Almighty to create: enchanting music, exhilarating prose and poetry, gorgeous paintings and sculpture, inspiring discourse, and awesome feats of science, engineering, and technology.

Spiritual Elation

The core of the advocated Spirituality, as defined in Chapter 1, is the sense of connection to the supernatural, identified in Chapter 4 as The Almighty. The spiritual aspect of the psychological impact of Spirituality is therefore in the sense of connectedness or closeness to The Almighty that one would feel. This is mainly reflected in the "Remembrance of The Almighty", as discussed previously. The more The Almighty is remembered in one's everyday thoughts and acts the closer to Him would one feel.

One would be thinking of The Almighty in glorifying Him for the wonder and beauty of His Creation, manifested all around us, in gratitude for His innumerable favors that He has bestowed, in supplication when pleading for His Mercy and His forgiveness for any transgressions committed, and in the mystical remembrance referred to earlier. As mentioned previously, the mere confession for these transgressions, or getting them off one's chest, is a big relief that is much reinforced by the extinguishing of the guilt feeling, in the fervent hope that The All-forgiving and The Relenting will accept one's sincere repentance. The more He is remembered in these ways, and in other personalized ways that one can think of, the more one would feel His closeness.

The feeling of closeness to The Almighty engenders intense joy, peace, and tranquility in the belief that one is being accorded His Mercy, Grace, and Care. One would feel detached from the mundane concerns and events of everyday life, and insulated from their effects and consequences. With advance in Spirituality one would experience at times that mystical feeling of exhilaration, unbounded goodness, and oneness with the universe, attended by a wonderful physical sensation of expansion, dilation, or lightness in one's chest that is the exact opposite of the weightiness or contraction in the chest that one might feel when distressed or depressed. One might wholly surrender oneself to The Almighty in the mysterious stillness of the darkness of night, feeling His Presence permeate and infuse one's whole being, body and soul, elevating one into a realm of unbounded and indescribably blissful spiritual elation.

The spiritual and psychological rewards of the five components of Spirituality are intertwined and are mutually amplifying and reinforcing. For example, spiritual elation can strengthen beliefs, enhance feelings and thoughts, bolster attitudes, and promote good and moral conduct, which in turn heightens the positive psychological impact.

Just as stress results in physical effects that accompany a rise in the levels of the stress hormones, the positive psychological feelings of Spirituality result in beneficial physical effects that accompany a rise in the levels of the feel-good hormones, such as dopamine, serotonin, and oxytocin. The presence of positive feelings and the absence of stress and anxiety are reflected in a physical well-being that is manifested in resistance to diseases and in less disabling and slower aging.

Evidently, when Spirituality is embraced by an increasing number of individuals, it will have a very significant salutary influence on interpersonal relations, and hence on society, transforming its very fabric. Just imagine a society in which interpersonal relations are governed by compassion, thoughtfulness, cooperation, and concern for the common good instead of greed, envy, opportunism, ruthless competition, exploitation, selfish interests, and overriding individualism. Unfortunately, this pernicious individualism is often cloaked in the false and misleading banners of individual liberty, and sanctification of personal choices, no matter how bizarre or how destructive they are of family ties and social cohesion.

Am I Developing My Self?

The thesis was presented at the beginning of the chapter that self-development is what provides meaning to life. But what does self-development exactly imply, and how do we gauge it?

What is meant by self-development is advancement of one's self spiritually, psychologically, morally, and intellectually. How one is doing on these four fronts can be assessed in a straightforward manner by a simple yardstick, the question that one should ask oneself every day: "Am I a better person today than I was yesterday?" This calls for an honest appraisal of what one went through in the preceding day and whether or not this has led to one's betterment in these respects. If the answer is in the affirmative, then one has every reason to be content with oneself and to find in this the incentive to do even better. If not, then one has to do some serious thinking and planning for the coming day to avoid pitfalls and ward off malicious leanings that have impeded or thwarted self-development.

Spiritual and Psychological Development

Spirituality is considered to be the foundation for comprehensive self-development. It was discussed at length in the preceding sections in terms of its five components, illustrated in Figure 7.1, and what they mean in actual practice. In terms of beliefs, Spirituality is based on the firm belief in the existence of The Almighty and the Afterlife, and in His Qualities that encompass Omnipotence, Omniscience, Omnipresence, and maximal perfection. Human beings cannot but feel utterly humble in the face of His Greatness, Majesty, and Glory and have no viable, realistic choice for successful self-fulfillment other than submitting to His will. In terms of thoughts, The Almighty should be ever-present in our minds, glorifying Him in His Essence and in what He has created; affirming our gratitude for what He has provided; and supplicating directly and in a personalized manner for His Mercy and forgiveness. In terms of attitudes, one would have absolute reliance on The Almighty and trust in Him; would unconditionally defer to His Will; and would be mindful of the real, unworthiness of material possessions, of the ephemeral nature of life's pleasures and rewards, and of the frivolity of this worldly life. In terms of conduct, one would be dedicated to the Service of The Almighty alone and not to anyone or anything else. This means refraining from unrighteous conduct, doing-good to others, giving to charity, forgiveness and humbleness, restraining anger, avoiding boastfulness and conceit in their various manifestations, good treatment of parents, and love and mercy in marital relations. This Spirituality has a very beneficial psychological impact in conquering negative feelings such as envy and anger, in alleviating anxiety and stress, fostering good feelings and attitudes, and experiencing the joy of living.

Spiritual and psychological development means advancement in the foregoing respects. Evidently this development is reflected in an intensifying inner peace and tranquility that drive towards the ideal of the serene self described earlier. Moral and intellectual self-development are considered in what follows.

Moral Development

Moral development is concerned with fostering moral behavior, or doing what is right, and abstaining from immoral behavior, or not doing what is wrong. But what exactly is moral behavior? This question has been the subject of intense debate over the years. On the one hand, some argue that there is no such thing as objective moral truths, that these are simply instinctive or the result of evolutionary pressures or cultural traditions and social conventions. On the other hand, others argue that there are objective moral truths, which they consider evidence for the existence of The Almighty.[19,20,21] The British writer and theologian C.S. Lewis has compared moral teachings across different cultures since ancient times and has found many commonalities such as injunctions of alms-giving, honesty, and kindness to the weak, the aged, and the young as well as denunciations of murder, oppression, treachery and falsehood.[22] Lewis makes a distinction between feeling a desire to help and feeling that one *ought* to help, whether one wants to or not. He gives the example of encountering a drowning man crying for help, which arouses two opposing, instinctive desires: the desire to help and the desire to avoid danger and preserve oneself. But there is "a third thing which tells you that you ought to follow the impulse to help, and suppress the impulse to run away. Now this thing that judges between two instincts, that decides which should be encouraged, cannot itself be either of them." Lewis ascribes this "thing" to an objective "Moral Law"[23] which includes righteous conduct such as fair play, unselfishness, courage, good faith, honesty and truthfulness.[24]

In the preceding discussion under "Virtuous Conduct" we considered forms of conduct that would fall under "Moral Law" as well as specific forms that are accorded special significance in the Quran as exemplars of Serving The Almighty. Of special interest in connection with "immoral conduct" is *munkar*, translated as "abomination", which is interpreted as "deeds that any person of sound intellect and rational faculties could not fail to recognize as inherently wrong." This premises an innate recognition by a normal person of what is inherently wrong, and by comparison, what is inherently right. So that deep down, every such person recognizes acts that are inherently right or wrong.

Ultimately, the final judgement of one's conduct and its consequences are up to The Almighty on the Day of Judgement. Spirituality, involving submitting to the Will of The Almighty and Serving Him, should provide an indispensable guide for moral development.

Intellectual Development

In Chapter 1, under "Human Development" we referred to the "Cognitive Revolution" that endowed *Homo sapiens* with new thinking and communication abilities that together with manual dexterity allowed humans to become the undisputed masters of planet Earth. The communication abilities centered around language production and understanding, whereas thinking abilities involved the development of the higher mental functions including cognition, as explained in Chapter 1. This ability to acquire knowledge and expand it by various thought processes including reasoning, deduction, abstract thinking, and creative imagination is what is meant by intellect or intellectual capacity. Intellectual development refers therefore to acquisition of knowledge and its expansion through increasingly refined thinking and reasoning. Since these mental functions are most highly developed in humans, intellectual development is a tribute to our humanness and is highly praiseworthy for its own sake. In addition, intellectual development can reinforce and enhance Spirituality. On both counts, therefore, intellectual development is integral to self-development.

That intellectual development enhances Spirituality is indicated by the high esteem that the Quran places on acquisition of knowledge. The first Quranic revelation included the following verses:

> **Recite! Your *Rabb* is most generous. Who taught by the pen. He taught the human being what he knew not.** (96:3-5)

These verses affirm the two main ways of acquiring and disseminating knowledge: spoken and written language. Human manual dexterity was not only meant for making tools and later all kinds of artefacts, but just as importantly, for writing purposes. Writing and its modern extensions of printing, recording, storing, and displaying the written word have been crucial in disseminating knowledge and preserving it for future generations. Cultures and civilizations cannot grow and flourish without this preservation of knowledge and its transmission to future generations.

A commonly invoked supplication that attests to the importance of knowledge is:

> **... and say: "My *Rabb*, increase me in knowledge."** (20:114)

The increase in knowledge is a direct reference to intellectual development, for the intellect is nourished and nurtured by knowledge. Knowledge is increased by acquiring new knowledge or by expanding existing knowledge through research and thought processes such as reasoning and deduction. The knowledge in question encompasses all useful knowledge, which comprises: (i) Knowledge that is beneficial to humans in their worldly affairs, including for example, medical interventions for improving health and combatting disease, and technological innovations that ease the burden of living, and (ii) knowledge that enhances one's Spirituality by having a more profound sense of connectedness to The Almighty. This includes scientific discoveries about the universe and about the workings of our brain and body organs and systems, for such discoveries provide additional signs of His Greatness and Mercy and more reason for His Glorification and for being grateful for His favors. This is attested in the following verse:

> **...Of all His servants, only those endowed with knowledge stand truly in awe of Allāh...** (35:28)

This emphasizes that true appreciation of the Greatness and Glory of The Almighty can only come about through knowledge of His Essence, His Nature, and His Signs.

The major step in intellectual development is therefore the acquisition of useful knowledge and reflecting on it. This can and should be done by everyone and would serve to expand one's horizon, open up new vistas for the mind, and inform about what could be beneficial to the person in many different ways, in such matters as health, vocation, social relations, hobbies, travel, etc. For the pious, an additional and prime objective of acquisition of knowledge and reflecting on it is to enhance one's Spirituality. For some, intellectual development involves, in addition, the dissemination of knowledge, as in teaching, its expansion through study and scientific discovery, and its beneficial application through engineering and technology.

Physical Well-Being

In pursuing self-development, proper care of the body cannot be neglected. If one is in constant pain, or preoccupied with health issues, one can hardly devote the time and effort to Spirituality and self-development. Good advice on physical well-being, through proper diet and exercise, abounds and will not be repeated here; rather, the following serves to emphasize some issues, particularly oncs that arc not commonly appreciated, and to indicate the positive role that Spirituality plays. Three main topics will be considered: excessive fat, muscle weakness, and exercise.

Excessive fat tissue in the form of overweight or obesity is quite harmful, particularly visceral fat, which accumulates around internal organs in the abdomen, lungs, and heart. It is well known that excess fat leads to increased risk for high blood pressure, heart disease, stroke, type 2 diabetes, musculoskeletal disorders such as osteoarthritis and osteoporosis, sleep disorders, liver disease, gallbladder disease, and some cancers – such as those of the esophagus, colon, rectum, kidney, pancreas, gallbladder, liver, breast, ovaries, and lining of the uterus. Fat-soluble environmental toxins such as organochlorine pesticides, and polybrominated diphenyl ethers, are stored in fat tissue. Moreover, excessive fat can lead to psychological problems, such as low self-esteem and depression. In addition, fat tissue is not passive tissue. Its adverse effects and many others are due to it being metabolically active in secreting a relatively large number of hormones and chemical agents, more of which are being discovered all the time, including male hormones and hormones causing inflammation.[25] Like stress, inflammation is beneficial over the short term but highly detrimental to health if chronic.

Spirituality, through its psychological impact, greatly helps in curtailing food cravings and compulsive eating once their dangers are recognized, and moderation and self-control are exercised. One would regard food for what it basically is, a nourishment for the body, so one would naturally focus on nutritious rather than junk food and would savor good food and one's favorite food with small, sampling portions rather than gorging on them.

Age-related sarcopenia is the loss of skeletal muscle mass and function with age. It is estimated that after the age of 30 to 40 years, skeletal muscle mass is lost at the rate of 3% to 5% per decade, the rate increasing after the age of 65-80 years. This is at least partly due to reduced physical activity, loss of nerve cells, reduced levels of some hormones such as testosterone and growth hormone, insufficient calorie and protein intake, stress, and inflammation. In addition to loss of muscle mass, there is also loss of muscle strength and function because of morphological, physiological, biochemical, and metabolic changes that occur in nerve and muscle cells. The result is physical weakness, reduced mobility, increased risks of falls and vulnerability to injury, which can lead to disability and loss of functional independence among the elderly.

Muscle weakness is aggravated by reduced activity with aging, which in turn weakens muscle in a kind of vicious cycle. The muscle weakness affects posture and gait, resulting in attributes or signs of aging such as walking with a shuffle and bent knees, or having a stooping posture, a sagging shoulder, or mild curvature of the spine (scoliosis). *Barring pathological causes, these changes in posture and gait are the consequences of muscle weakness*, particularly if asymmetrical between the two sides of the body or between front and back. They *need not be an unavoidable consequence of normal aging. They can be largely avoided or ameliorated through proper exercise.*

It is imperative, therefore, to counteract age-related sarcopenia through proper exercise, discussed next, and adequate protein intake. In obtaining protein from food, one should be mindful of the Amino Acid Utilization (AAU) of various dietary sources of protein. Different dietary proteins are made up of different proportions of 22 amino acids. When dietary protein is digested, it is broken into its constituent amino acids, which are eventually taken up by cells of the body and used to synthesize the different types of proteins needed. But these body proteins have amino acids in proportions that are different from those in the dietary proteins, which means that not all the amino acids in a given dietary protein source will be used in synthesizing body proteins. The amino acids that are not so utilized will be burned for energy. Not surprisingly, breast milk has the highest AAU of 49%, which means that 49% of the amino acids in the proteins of breast milk are used to synthesize body proteins, the remaining 51% are burnt for energy. Next are whole eggs with an AAU of 47% (egg whites alone, although they are 88% water and 11% protein, have an AAU of only about 17%). Then comes meat, poultry and fish with an AAU of about 32%. Vegetable proteins have an AAU of 17% or less. Hence, the same amounts of proteins from different dietary sources will not yield the same amounts of body proteins.

For most of their history of some 200,000 years *Homo sapiens* were physically-active hunter-gatherers. Even after the Agricultural Revolution physical activity was a necessity of life, until modern times when power from machinery began to substitute for muscle power. Our bodies, therefore, have not had time to adapt to the prevalent sedentary lifestyle, which leads to many chronic health problems. Of all the measures that one can take to maintain and improve good health, no single measure comes anywhere near exercise.

Generally speaking, there are two main types of exercise: aerobic, or endurance, exercise like walking, jogging, or running, and strength, or resistance, exercise like working with weights, elastic bands, or against body weight. Other types of exercise focus on balance or flexibility. Many forms of exercise combine elements of these four types, such as swimming, cycling, stair climbing, yoga, and Pilates.

The well-known benefits of exercise include: counteracting sarcopenia, increasing bone density, boosting the immune system, enhancing memory, combatting cognitive decline, improving mood and sleep, bettering balance and posture and mobility by strengthening muscles and counteracting joint stiffness. Exercise boosts endurance, benefits cardiovascular health – by strengthening the heart, improving circulation and enhancing the elasticity of blood vessels – and reduces the risk of many diseases such as coronary artery disease, stroke, and some cancers. In addition, endurance type exercise has been found to have antiaging effects.[26]

To counteract age-related sarcopenia, strength exercise is essential but aerobic exercise can be very useful as well. The muscles that are particularly important to strengthen are leg muscles and the core muscles of the abdomen and back. Aerobic exercise is also very effective in controlling body weight by having a negative energy balance, that is, increasing calorie burning over calorie intake. But it must be borne in mind that body mass loss under these conditions is not only fat but muscle as well, the ratio being roughly 75% fat and 25% muscle.[27]

With Spirituality, one would have the discipline, self-control, and motivation for pursuing a wholesome lifestyle that accommodates a regimen of regular exercise, a nutritious diet, and adequate, restful sleep while maintaining a healthy weight and avoiding unhealthy habits such as smoking and not sleeping enough.

The Gist of It

The Almighty has created humans for a purpose, which, out of His infinite Mercy and Love, is for them to have eternal bliss in Heaven. In His Omniscience and Wisdom, He created them with a wondrous conscious self having a free will that allows them to choose between the right path that leads to eternal bliss in Heaven and the wrong path that leads to suffering in Hell. The right path is that of submitting to His Will and Serving Him. Progress along this path is through self-development, spiritually, psychologically, morally, and intellectually, reflected in a target state of sublime serenity and self-fulfillment.

The preceding paragraph encapsulates the essence of the human condition. It is a view that is based on Quranic revelations and is clear in its simplicity, is coherent, and makes sense, without recourse to any convoluted philosophical or theological arguments.

The Spirituality advocated in this book provides a solid foundation for spiritual, psychological, and moral development and is conducive to intellectual advancement and physical well-being, thereby enabling self-development over a wide spectrum. The linchpin of this Spirituality is the belief in The Almighty and in His Revelations in the Quran, which is addressed to all humankind, and not only to Muslims. As mentioned in the

Preface, the Quran is to be regarded by non-Muslims as a stand-alone text that should be appraised on its merits without prejudice or bias. Anyone who believes that the Quran is of human origin, faces the insurmountable challenge of explaining the miraculous features of the Quran, including the miraculous verses and numerical relations of letters and words in the Quran, some of which were presented in Chapter 4. Failing to do that, intellectual honesty demands that one should at least admit that the Quran is of Divine origin, which in turn leads to the possibility of the Existence of The Almighty. Having admitted this possibility, one is then faced with a pragmatic choice: to believe in the Existence of The Almighty and reap the immense benefits of Spirituality, as detailed previously, or not to believe and forfeit these benefits. Common sense dictates that one should choose to believe in the Existence of The Almighty, in His Essence and Nature (Chapter 5), in the Afterlife (Chapter 6), and in His Revelations in the Quran, which constitute the basis for the aforementioned human condition and for all the Spirituality and self-development discussed in this chapter. *It cannot be overemphasized in this regard that the advocated Spirituality aims primarily toward the attainment of serenity and self-fulfillment in this life. The requital in the Afterlife is contingent on the Will, Grace, Mercy, and Judgement of The Almighty.*

I really cannot help but feel sorry for men and women of science, learning, and intellect who under the guise of high-minded intellectualism refuse to admit of anything that is not based on science. They argue that if science cannot prove the existence of a divine being, then they cannot believe in Him nor in a Spirituality centered around Him. They seem to have a blind faith in science without full awareness of the nature of present-day science and its limitations, as explained in Chapter 2. They do not appreciate that embracing Spirituality is simply stepping beyond the limitations of present-day science without repudiating science. How can any rational person adamantly refuse to believe in the Existence of The Almighty, based on science, when present-day science, because of its very nature, cannot affirm or refute His Existence? This brings back the allegory mentioned earlier of the blind man who refuses to believe in the existence of something he cannot see.

It is hoped that after reading this book most readers will set out on the path of ever-fulfilling self-development through the advocated Spirituality. Atheists and agnostics will hopefully be sufficiently convinced of the existence of The Almighty to embrace Spirituality and experience its benefits for themselves. Those who do not believe strongly in the existence of The Almighty should have their belief strengthened as they embrace Spirituality. Those whose belief in The Almighty is compartmentalized in some routine and habitual practices, without it infusing their very being, will come to realize what it means to submit to His Will, to Serve Him, and to have Him our sole beacon and guide. Those who believe in The Almighty and are engaged in the practice of a particular religion should be able to incorporate Spirituality in their belief system as a highly personalized way of experiencing a close connection with The Almighty and reaping the benefits of Spirituality.

Spirituality and its attendant, all-encompassing self-development is incredibly rewarding and is in itself a most worthy and humanistic endeavor. It has immense benefits that are reflected in a rational and coherent view of the meaning and purpose of our existence, a deep sense of self-fulfillment, sublime serenity, a highly gratifying relationship with others, and an exhilarating feeling of an intimate, mystical connection with The One and Only.

The human predicament in modern life is starkly and poignantly expressed in the following quotation from an unknown author:

"What surprises me most about Man is that he sacrifices his health in order to make money. Then he sacrifices money to recuperate his health. And then he is so anxious about the future that he does not enjoy the present; the result being that he does not live in the present or the future; he lives as if he is never going to die, and then dies having never really lived."[28]

This is like an animal pointlessly thrashing about within the confines of a cage. Only a wide opening would securely liberate from the cage of worldly concerns to the exhilarating liberty outside the cage and to the sublime heights of serenity and self-fulfillment. That wide opening is ***Spirituality***.

Blessed Spirituality Everyone!

Biographical Note

Nassir Sabah is a neuroscientist and Professor, Electrical and Computer Engineering Department, American University of Beirut, Lebanon. He received his B.Sc. (Hons. Class I) and his M.Sc. in Electrical Engineering from the University of Birmingham, UK, and his PhD in Biophysical Sciences from the State University of New York at Buffalo (SUNY/Buffalo). His PhD advisor was Sir John C. Eccles, Nobel Laureate in Physiology or Medicine. He has served as Chairman of the Electrical Engineering Department, founding Director of the Institute of Computer Studies, and Dean of the Faculty of Engineering and Architecture, all at the American University of Beirut. Professor Sabah has more than 35 years of teaching experience in neuroengineering, biomedical engineering, electronics, and electric circuits. He has over 100 technical publications, mainly in neurophysiology, biophysics, and biomedical instrumentation. He has authored four books on electric circuits, electronics, and neuroscience, published by CRC Press, the most recent being: *Neuromuscular Fundamentals: How Our Musculature is Controlled*, CRC Press, Boca Raton, FL, 2021, 574 pp.

With my background in science and engineering, readers may well wonder how I came to write a book about spirituality. Looking back, it all started when I was an electrical engineering undergraduate at the University of Birmingham, England. The chairman of the department used to meet with first-year students from overseas – about ten of us – for a couple of hours on Wednesday afternoons to talk informally about the sciences in general – particularly modern physics, cosmology, and biology – from an integrated, engineering, and philosophical viewpoint. What made a lasting imprint in my impressionable teenager mind was that: (i) deep down there is an underlying unity to it all; boundaries are artificial (a favorite quote in this regard is one by Swami Vivekananda, "The whole universe is a play of unity in variety, and of variety in unity"), and (ii) therefore, one should not harbor a circumscribed worldview but should venture beyond the confines of particular tenets. That made me seek in earnest to broaden my horizon by reading about psychology (in as much as it sheds light on human nature), religion (in as much as it seeks to provide meaning and purpose to life), and philosophy (in as much as it applies rational thinking and logical reasoning to any thought process). Inevitably, this bred an awareness of what is beyond oneself and which transcends everyday concerns and preoccupations – the stirrings of spirituality.

At a more practical level, I was fascinated by biophysics as a confluence of two basic sciences and by bioengineering as the study of biological systems from an engineering viewpoint. For my PhD I therefore joined the Department of Biophysical Sciences at SUNY/Buffalo, which at the time was one of the top departments in the field, under the chairmanship of Professor Fred Snell. During my first year of coursework I happened to come across the book *The Cerebellum as a Neuronal Machine* by J.C. Eccles, M. Ito, and J. Szentágothai. The title and contents absolutely electrified me. The subject matter held a dream promise of bringing together neuroanatomy, neurophysiology, and electrical engineering. "What a wonderful topic for my PhD thesis that would be," I thought. Then Lo and behold! John C. Eccles himself, the Nobel Laureate, took up an appointment as Professor of Physiology and Biophysical Sciences at SUNY/B.

The years I spent with Sir John, as he was known to those around him, were unforgettable. An imposing presence, Sir John was superbly erudite, particularly in science and philosophy. Not only did I learn so much from him, but I was deeply impressed by his strong views on the spiritual aspects of the mind, some of which are quoted at the end of Chapter 1. By then, and with my expanded reading and thinking about science, religion, and philosophy, my spirituality had evolved and was now inspiringly shaped by Sir John's views on these matters.

Fast forward to my academic career at the American University of Beirut. During this time my spirituality continually developed along the lines presented in Chapter 7. The administrative positions I held at the university allowed me to introduce several academic programs that opened up new career paths for thousands of young men and women. That was highly gratifying but always left the nagging thought that it was not enough, as it did not address the reality of our existence. What is it that one should really strive for? What is the measure of success in life? Is it status, scholarship, fame, influence, happiness, or material possessions? Are these, or should they be, ends in themselves? Once achieved, if ever, then what? Many people have their own answers to such questions, but as a long-time educator, I felt I had to promulgate in simple language the answers that I find most persuasive and satisfying.

Writing this book was the natural consequence of this urge, based on my keen and continuing interest in the subject matter and my experience in practicing the advocated Spirituality. I sincerely hope that readers will find this of benefit in finding meaning and purpose to our existence and to the perpetual struggles of our worldly life.

References

(Short citations consisting of the name of the (first) author, the date of publication, and page number(s) refer to a previous citation by the same author(s) in the same chapter.)

Chapter 1

1. Panksepp, J. (2004) *Affective Neuroscience: The Foundations of Human and Animal Emotions*, New York, Oxford University Press.
2. Schacter, D.L., Gilbert, D.T. and Wegner, D.M. (2011) *Psychology*, 2nd edn, New York, Worth Publishers.
3. Rosenblum, B. and Kuttner, F. (2011) *Quantum Enigma: Physics Encounters Consciousness*, New York, Oxford University Press, pp. 126-127.
4. Schuurmans-Stekhoven, J. (2014) "Measuring spirituality as personal belief in supernatural forces", *Implicit Religion*, vol. 17, no. 2, pp. 211-222 [Online]. DOI: 10.1558/imre.v17i2.211 (Accessed 27 November 2021).
5. Fingelkurts, A.A. and Fingelkurts, A.A. (2009) "Is our brain hardwired to produce God, or is our brain hardwired to perceive God? A systematic review on the role of the brain in mediating religious experience", *Cogn Process*, vol. 10, no. 4, pp. 293-326 [Online]. Available at https://link.springer.com/article/10.1007/s10339-009-0261-3 (Accessed 27 November 2021).
6. Suntsova, M.V. and Buzdin, A.A. (2020) "Differences between human and chimpanzee genomes and their implications in gene expression, protein functions and biochemical properties of the two species", *BMC*

Genomics, vol. 21, suppl. 7, pp. 535-547 [Online]. Available at https://doi.org/10.1186/s12864-020-06962-8 (Accessed 27 November 2021).

7. Jabr, F. (2015) "How humans evolved supersize brains", *Quanta Magazine*, November 10 [Online]. Available at https://www.quantamagazine.org/how-humans-evolved-supersize-brains-20151110/ (Accessed 27 November 2021).
8. Dicke, U. and Roth, G. (2016) "Neuronal factors determining high intelligence", *Philos Trans R Soc Lond B Biol Sci.*, vol. 371, no. 1685, 20150180 [Online]. Available at https://doi.org/10.1098/rstb.2015.0180 (Accessed 27 November 2021).
9. Harari, Y.N. (2015) *Sapiens: A Brief History of Mankind*, London, Vintage, pp. 22-44.
10. Peoples, H.C., Duda, P. and Marlowe, F.W. (2016) "Hunter-gatherers and the origins of religion", *Human Nature*, vol. 27, no. 3, pp. 261-282 [Online]. DOI: https://www.ncbi.nlm.nih.gov/pmc/articles/PMC4958132/ (Accessed 27 November 2021).
11. Pearce, J.M. (2008) *Animal Learning & Cognition: An Introduction*, 3rd edn, Hove (UK), Psychology Press.
12. Ebel, S.J., Schmelz, M., Herrmann, E. and Call, J. (2019) "Innovative problem solving in great apes: the role of visual feedback in the floating peanut task", *Anim Cogn*, vol. 22, pp. 791-805 [Online]. Available at https://doi.org/10.1007/s10071-019-01275-0 (Accessed 27 November 2021).
13. "Red light runners" (2010) BBC Four, 17 May [Online]. Available at https://www.bbc.co.uk/programmes/p007xvww (Accessed 27 November 2021).
14. Kohda, M., Hotta, T., Takeyama, T. et al. (2019) "If a fish can pass the mark test, what are the implications

for consciousness and self-awareness testing in animals?", *PLOS Biol*, vol. 17, no. 2, e3000021 [Online]. Available at https://doi.org/10.1371/journal.pbio.3000021 (Accessed 27 November 2021).

15. Low, P. (2012) "The Cambridge Declaration on Consciousness" [Online]. Available at https://fcmconference.org/img/CambridgeDeclarationOnConsciousness.pdf (Accessed 27 November 2021).
16. Pennartz, C.M.A., Farisco, M. and Evers, K. (2019) "Indicators and criteria of consciousness in animals and intelligent machines: An inside-out approach", *Front Syst Neurosci*, 16 July [Online]. Available at https://www.frontiersin.org/articles/10.3389/fnsys.2019.00025/full (Accessed 27 November 2021).
17. Goodall, J. (2005) "Primate spirituality", in Taylor, B. (ed), *The Encyclopedia of Religion and Nature,* London, Continuum, pp. 1303-1306 [Online]. Available at www.religionandnature.com/ern/sample/Goodall--PrimateSpirituality.pdf (Accessed 27 November 2021).
18. Hauser, M.D., Chomsky, N. and Fitch, W.T. (2002) "The Faculty of Language: What Is It, Who Has It, and How Did It Evolve?", *Science*, vol. 298, no. 5598, pp. 1569-1579.
19. "Definition of Humanism", *American Humanist Association* [Online]. Available at https://americanhumanist.org/what-is-humanism/definition-of-humanism/ (Accessed 27 November 2021).
20. Available at https://whatistranshumanism.org/ (Accessed 27 November 2021).
21. Hoyle, F. (1984) *The Intelligent Universe*, New York, Holt, Rinehart and Winston, pp. 233-235.
22. Eccles, J.C. (1989) *Evolution of the Brain: Creation*

of the Self, London and New York, Routledge, p. 237.
23. Eccles (1989), p. 241.

Chapter 2

1. "Our definition of science", *Science Council* (UK) [Online]. Available at https://sciencecouncil.org/about-science/our-definition-of-science/ (Accessed 27 November 2021).
2. "Glasgow Coma Scale", *Royal College of Physicians and Surgeons of Glasgow* [Online]. Available at https://www.glasgowcomascale.org (Accessed 27 November 2021).
3. Levy, J. (1974) "Psychological implications of bilateral asymmetry", in Dimond, S.J. and Beaumont, J.G. (eds), *Hemisphere Function in the Human Brain*, New York, Wiley, pp. 121-183.
4. Eccles, J.C. (1989) *Evolution of the Brain: Creation of the Self*, London and New York, Routledge, p. 210.
5. Chalmers, D.J. (2000) "What is a neural correlate of consciousness?", in Metzinger, T. (ed), *Neural Correlates of Consciousness: Empirical and Conceptual Questions*, Cambridge MA, MIT Press, pp. 17-39.
6. Chalmers, D.J. (2011) *The Character of Consciousness*, Oxford Scholarship Online, pp. 1-16. Available at https://doi.org/10.1093/acprof:oso/9780195311105.001.0001 (Accessed 27 November 2021).
7. Noë, A. (2009) *Out of Our Heads*, New York, Hill and Wang, p. 64.
8. Noë, A. (2009), p. xi.
9. Hawthorne, J.N. (1960) *Questions of Science and*

Faith, London, Tyndale, p. 4.

10. Wheeler, J. (1984) "The mystery and message of the quantum", Lecture given at the *American Physical Society Symposium of the Texas Section: Frontiers of Physics*, February 1.
11. Galilei, G. (1954 [1638]) *Dialogues Concerning Two New Sciences* (trans. H. Crew and A. de Salvio), New York, Dover Publications Inc., p. 203.
12. Newton, I. (1999 [1726, 3rd edn]) *The Principia* (trans. I.B. Cohen and A. Whitman), Berkeley and Los Angeles, University of California Press.
13. "Newton's Laws of Motion", *Glenn Research Center, National Aeronautics and Space Administration* [Online]. Available at https://www.grc.nasa.gov/www/k-12/BGP/newton.html (Accessed 27 November 2021).
14. Petersen, A. (1963) "The philosophy of Niels Bohr", *Bulletin of the Atomic Scientists*, vol. 19, no. 7, p. 12.
15. "Conversations About Science with Theoretical Physicist Matt Strassler" [Online]. Available at https://profmattstrassler.com/articles-and-posts/particle-physics-basics/virtual-particles-what-are-they/ (Accessed 27 November 2021).
16. Jaeger, G. (2019) "Are Virtual Particles Less Real?", *Entropy*, vol. 21, no. 2, pp. 141-157 [Online]. Available at https://doi.org/10.3390/e21020141 (Accessed 27 November 2021).
17. Cited in Rosenblum, B. and Kuttner, F. (2011) *Quantum Enigma: Physics Encounters Consciousness*, New York, Oxford University Press, p. 155.
18. *Todayinscience* [Online]. Available at https://todayinsci.com/E/Einstein_Albert/EinsteinAlbert-God-Quotations.htm (Accessed 27 November 2021).

19. Misner, C.W., Thorne, K.S. and Wheeler, J.A. (2017) *Gravitation*, Princeton NJ, Princeton University Press, p. 5.
20. Gron, O. (2013) "The twin paradox and the principle of relativity", *Physica Scripta*, vol. 87, no. 3, p. 035004. DOI: 10.1088/0031-8949/87/03/035004 (Accessed 27 November 2021).
21. Trimmer, J.D. (1980) "The present situation in quantum mechanics: a translation of Schrödinger's'cat paradox' paper", *Proceedings of the American Philosophical Society*, vol. 124, no. 5, pp. 323-338.
22. Polkinghorne, J. (1989) *The Quantum World*, Princeton NJ, Princeton University Press, p. 33.
23. Linde, A. (1990) *Particle Physics and Inflationary Cosmology*, Chur (Switzerland), Harwood, p. 242 [Online]. Available at https://arxiv.org/pdf/hep-th/0503203.pdf (Accessed 27 November 2021).
24. Chalmers (2011), pp. 16-31.
25. Silk, J. (2009) *Horizons of Cosmology: Exploring Worlds Seen and Unseen*, Templeton Science and Religion Series, Conshohocken PA, Templeton Press, pp. 16-37.
26. Lashley, K.S. (1950) "In search of the engram", *Society of Experimental Biology Symposium No 4: Physiological mechanisms in animal behavior*, pp. 454-482, Cambridge (UK), Cambridge University Press.
27. Goleman, D. (1979) "Holographic memory", Karl Pribram interviewed by Goleman, D., *Psychology Today*, vol. 12, no. 9, pp. 71-84.
28. Rosenblum, B. and Kuttner, F. (2011) *Quantum Enigma: Physics Encounters Consciousness*, New York, Oxford University Press, p. 137.
29. Morgan, T.H. (1901) *Regeneration*, New York,

Macmillan.

30. Sea Urchin Genome Sequencing Consortium (2006) "The Genome of the Sea Urchin *Strongylocentrotus purpuratus*", *Science*, vol. 314, no. 5801, pp. 941-952.
31. Maher, B. (2008) "The case of missing heritability", *Nature*, vol. 456, no. 7218, pp. 18-21.
32. *Todayinscience* [Online]. Available at https://todayinsci.com/W/Wheeler_John/WheelerJohn-Quotations.htm (Accessed 27 November 2021).
33. Rosenblum and Kuttner (2011), p. 213.

Chapter 3

1. Hamadeh, S. (2000) *Mu'jam 'Aja'ib al-Lughah* (Dictionary of the Wonders of the Language), Beirut (Lebanon), Dār Ṣādir (In Arabic).
2. van Dyck, E.A. (1894) *History of the Arabs and their Literature: Before and After the Rise of Islam*, Bamberg in Laibach (Germany), Ig. V. Kleinmayr & Fed., p. 40.
3. Lane, E.W. (1863) *An Arabic-English Lexicon*, London and Edinburgh, Williams and Northgate, reproduced (1980) Beirut (Lebanon), Librairie du Liban, vol. 8, Supplement, Book I, vol. 4, p. 1485.
4. Lane (1863), vol. 5, p. 2214.
5. Lane (1863), vol. 7, pp. 2618-2619.
6. Khalidi, T. (2008) *The Qur'an*, London, Penguin Classics.
7. Maulana Muhammad Ali (1951) *The Holy Qur'an, Arabic Text, Translation and Commentary*, 4th edn, Lahore (Pakistan), Ahmadiyyah Anjuman Isha'at Islam.
8. Garcia, P. (2020) "On Beauty and Language in Islam and Islamic Tradition", 14 March [Online].

Available at https://insidearabia.com/on-beauty-and-language-in-islam-and-islamic-tradition/ (Accessed 27 November 2021).

9. Al-Salih, S. (1977) *Mabaḥith fi ʿUlum al-Qurʾān*, new edn (Investigations in Quranic Sciences), Beirut (Lebanon), Dar al-ʿIlm lil-Malayīn, pp. 65-100 (In Arabic).
10. Maulana Muhammad Ali (1951), pp. xxxv-lix.
11. Bucaille, M. (1978 [1977, 4th edn]) *The Bible, The Qurʾan and Science* (trans. A.D. Pannell and M. Bucaille), Indianapolis IN, North American Trust Publications, pp. 126-132.
12. Schoeler, G. (2010) "The Codification of the Qurʾan: A Comment on the Hypotheses of Burton and Wansbrough", in Neuwirth, A., Sinai, N. and Marx, M. (eds), *The Qurʾān in Context: Historical and Literary Investigations into the Qurʾānic Milieu*, Leiden and Boston, Brille, pp. 779-794.
13. Hamdan, O. (2010) "The second maṣāḥif project: A step towards the canonization of the Qurʾanic text", in Neuwirth, A., Sinai, N. and Marx, M. (eds), *The Qurʾān in Context: Historical and Literary Investigations into the Qurʾānic Milieu*, Leiden and Boston, Brille, pp. 795-835.
14. Smith, R.B. (1874) *Mohammed and Mohammedanism*, London, Smith, Elder, & Co., p. 21.
15. Lane-Poole, S. (1879) "Introduction", in E.W. Lane, *Selections from the Ḳur-án*, Ludgate Hill London, Trübner & Co., p. c.
16. Muir, W. (1923) *The Life of Moḥammad, from Original Sources*, Edinburgh, John Grant, pp. xxii-xxiii.
17. Nasr, S.H. (editor-in-chief) (2015) *The Study Quran: A New Translation and Commentary*, New York,

HarperOne.
18. Munajjid, S. (1974) *Al-Islam wa'l-ʿakl* (Islam and the Mind), Beirut (Lebanon), Dar al-Kitāb al-Jadid, p. 18 (In Arabic).
19. Kiraz, C. (2015) "The Prophet Abraham, resurrection after death and parable of four birds", *Review of the Faculty of Divinity, University of Süleyman Demirel*, vol. 1, no. 34, pp. 7-31 [Online]. Available at https://dergipark.org.tr/en/download/article-file/794208# (Accessed 27 November 2021).
20. Gwynne, R.W. (2004) *Logic, Rhetoric and Legal Reasoning in the Qur'an: God's Arguments*, London, Routledge, p. 203.
21. Abdul-Raof, H. (2003) *Exploring the Qur'an*, Dundee, Al-Makhtoum Institute Academic Press, p. 64.
22. Draz, M.A. (2000) *Introduction to the Qur'an*, London, I.B. Tauris, p. 90.
23. Cited in Islahi, A.A. (2007) *Pondering Over the Qur'an: Tafsir of Surah al-Fatiha and Surah al-Bakarah*, vol. 1, (trans. M.S. Kayani), Kuala Lumpur (Malaysia), Islamic Book Trust, p. 26.
24. Zammit, M.R. (2002) *A Comparative Lexical Study of Qur'anic Arabic*, Leiden, Brill, p. 37.
25. Arberry, A.J. (1998) *The Koran: Translated with an Introduction by Arthur J. Arberry*, Oxford, Oxford University Press, p. x.
26. Palmer, E.H. (1900) *The Qur'an. Part I*, Oxford, Clarendon Press, p. lv.
27. Al-Suyuṭi, J. (2005) *Al-Itqan fi ʿUlum al-Qur'an* (The Proficiency in the Sciences of the Quran), Madina, Mujamma Malik Fahad, p. 1881 (In Arabic).
28. Tzortzis, H.A. (2019) *The Divine Reality*, newly revised edition, Middletown DE, Lion Rock

Publishing, p. 242.
29. Tzortzis (2019), pp. 215-247.

Chapter 4

1. Bostrom, N. (2002) *Anthropic Bias*, New York, Routledge, pp. 43-56 [Online]. Available at https://www.anthropic-principle.com/q=book/table_of_contents/ (Accessed 27 November 2021).
2. Davis, P. (2007) *Cosmic Jackpot: Why Our Universe Is Just Right for Life*, New York, Orion Publications.
3. *Inspiringquotes.us* [Online]. Available at https://www.inspiringquotes.us/author/9504-fred-hoyle (Accessed 27 November 2021).
4. Carr, B. (ed) (2007) *Universe or Multiverse?*, Cambridge (UK), Cambridge University Press.
5. Collins, R. (2007) "The multiverse hypothesis: a theistic perspective", in Carr, B. (ed), *Universe or Multiverse?*, Cambridge (UK), Cambridge University Press, p. 460.
6. Bucaille, M. (1978 [1977, 4th edn]) *The Bible, The Qur'an and Science* (trans. A.D. Pannell and M. Bucaille), Indianapolis IN, North American Trust Publications.
7. Becker, W. (ed) (2009) *Neutron Stars and Pulsars*, Berlin and Heidelberg, Springer-Verlag.
8. "The Sounds of Pulsars" (2001) [Online]. Available at http://www.jb.man.ac.uk/research/pulsar/Education/Sounds/sounds.html (Accessed 27 November 2021).
9. Lane, E.W. (1863) *An Arabic-English Lexicon*, London and Edinburgh, Williams and Northgate, reproduced (1980) Beirut (Lebanon), Librairie du Liban, vol. 5, p. 1846.
10. Lane (1863), vol. 5, p. 1850.

11. Nasr, S.H. (editor-in-chief) (2015) *The Study Quran: A New Translation and Commentary*, New York, HarperOne.
12. Lane (1863), vol. 1, pp. 341-342.
13. Manchester, R.N. (2009) "Radio Emission Properties of Pulsars", in Becker, W. (ed), *Neutron Stars and Pulsars*, Berlin and Heidelberg, Springer-Verlag, pp. 19-39.
14. Wikipedia (2021) *Cat's Eye Nebula* [Online], 24 July 2020. Available at https://en.wikipedia.org/wiki/Cat%27s_Eye_Nebula (Accessed 27 November 2021).
15. Harrington, J.P. and Borkowski, K.J. (1995) *Cat's Eye Nebula* [Online]. Available at https://hubblesite.org/contents/media/images/1995/01/254-Image.html (Accessed 27 November 2021).
16. Wikipedia (2021) *Rosette Nebula* [Online], 20 November 2021. Available at https://en.wikipedia.org/wiki/Rosette_Nebula (Accessed 27 November 2021).
17. Dean, J. (2019) *The Rosette Nebula in Monoceros* [Online]. Available at https://apod.nasa.gov/apod/ap190412.html (Accessed 27 November 2021).
18. Lane (1863), vol. 4, p. 1576.
19. Lane (1863), vol. 3, p. 926.
20. Ali, J. (1993) *Al-Mufaṣṣal fī Tārīkh al-ʿArab Qabla'l-Islām*, 2nd edn (Detailed Account of the History of the Arabs Before Islam), Baghdad (Iraq), University of Baghdad, v. 4, pp. 610-615, and v. 7, pp. 530-540 (In Arabic).
21. Bahcall, N.A. (2015) "Hubble's Law and the expanding universe", *Proc Natl Acad Sci USA, Commentary*, vol. 112, no. 11, pp. 3173-3175 [Online]. Available at https://www.pnas.org/

content/112/11/3173 (Accessed 27 November 2021).

22. Lineweaver, C.H. and Davis, T.M. (2005) "Misconceptions about the Big Bang", *Scientific American*, vol. 292, no. 3, pp. 36-45.
23. O'Raifeartaigh, C. (2018) "Investigating the legend of Einstein's 'biggest blunder'", *Physics Today, Commentary and Reviews*, 30 October [Online]. Available at https://physicstoday.scitation.org/do/10.1063/PT.6.3.20181030a/full/ (Accessed 27 November 2021).
24. Maulana Muhammad Ali (1951) *The Holy Qur'an, Arabic Text, Translation and Commentary*, 4th edn, Lahore (Pakistan), Ahmadiyyah Anjuman Isha'at Islam.
25. Pickthall, M. (1930) *The Meaning of the Glorious Koran*, New York, A.A. Knopf.
26. Yusuf Ali, A. (1983) *The Holy Qur'ān: Text, Translation and Commentary*, Brentwood MD, Amana Corp.
27. Asad, M. (1980) *The Message of the Quran*, Gibraltar, Dar al-Andalus Ltd.
28. Khattab, M. (2016) *The Clear Quran*, Bolingbrook IL, Book of Signs Foundation & Al-Furqaan Institute of Islamic Education.
29. Bucaille (1978), pp. 166-167.
30. La'li, M. (2007) *A Comprehensive Exploration of the Scientific Miracles in Holy Quran*, Bloomington IN, Trafford Publishing, pp. 31-34.
31. Wikipedia (2021) *Big Bang* [Online], 24 November 2021. Available at https://en.wikipedia.org/wiki/Big_Bang (Accessed 27 November 2021).
32. Lane (1863), vol. 3, p. 1027.
33. Lane (1863), vol. 6, p. 2331.
34. Nasser, U. (2019) "Big Bang cosmology in the

Quran: A response to atheist objections", *Rational Religion*, 24 August [Blog]. Available at https://rationalreligion.co.uk/how-the-quran-really-does-predict-the-big-bang-the-expansion-of-the-universe (Accessed 27 November 2021).

35. Ibn Manẓur al-ʾAnṣari (1970 [1290]) *Lisān al-ʿarab al-muḥit* (The Encompassing Tongue of the Arabs), rearranged by Y. Khayyat and N. Miraʿshli, Beirut (Lebanon), Dar Lisān al-ʿArab, p. 1119 (In Arabic).
36. Wikipedia (2021) *Chronology of the universe* [Online], 20 November 2021. Available at https://en.wikipedia.org/wiki/Chronology_of_the_universe (Accessed 27 November 2021).
37. Hamden, E. (2019) "Observing the cosmic web", *Science*, vol. 3669, no. 6461, pp. 31-32.
38. Bucaille (1978), pp. 149-150.
39. Seidenberg, A. (1959) "The Separation of Sky and Earth at Creation", *Folklore*, vol. 70, no. 3, pp. 477-482.
40. Mark, J.J. (2018) "Enuma Elish - The Babylonian Epic of Creation - Full Text", *World History Encyclopedia* [Online]. Available at https://www.ancient.eu/article/225/enuma-elish---the-babylonian-epic-of-creation---fu/ (Accessed 27 November 2021).
41. Lane (1863), vol. 5, pp. 1880.
42. Lane (1863), vol. 7, pp. 2596.
43. Lane (1863), vol. 7, pp. 2637.
44. Weissman, P.R. (2014) "The Solar System and Its Place in the Galaxy", in Spohn, T., Breuer, D. and Johnson, T.V. (eds), *Encyclopedia of the Solar System*, 3rd edn, Amsterdam, Elsevier, p. 26.
45. Springel, V. et al. (2005) *Pictures of the galaxy distribution* [Online]. Available at https://wwwmpa.mpa-garching.mpg.de/galform/virgo/millennium/

seqD_063.jpg (Accessed 27 November 2021).
46. Umehata, H., Fumagalli, M., Smail, I. et al. (2019) "Gas filaments of the cosmic web located around active galaxies in a protocluster", *Science*, vol. 3669, no. 6461, pp. 97-100 [Online]. Available at https://www.science.org/doi/10.1126/science.aaw5949 (Accessed 27 November 2021).
47. Lane (1863), vol. 2, p. 503.
48. Khalidi, T. (2008) *The Qur'an*, London, Penguin Classics.
49. Wikipedia (2021) *Ultimate fate of the universe* [Online], 6 November 2021. Available at https://en.wikipedia.org/wiki/Ultimate_fate_of_the_universe (Accessed 27 November 2021).
50. "Positive and negative effects of UV" (2015), *Science Learning Hub* [Online]. Available at https://www.sciencelearn.org.nz/resources/1304-positive-and-negative-effects-of-uv (Accessed 27 November 2021).
51. Wikipedia (2021) *Ozone-oxygen cycle* [Online], 19 November 2021. Available at https://en.wikipedia.org/wiki/Ozone-oxygen_cycle (Accessed 27 November 2021).
52. Lane (1863), vol. 3, p. 1040.
53. Wikipedia (2021) *Greenhouse effect* [Online], 21 November 2021. Available at https://en.wikipedia.org/wiki/Greenhouse_effect (Accessed 27 November 2021).
54. Nasr, S.H. (2015), p. 627.
55. Wikipedia (2021) *Plate tectonics* [Online], 21 November 2021. Available at https://en.wikipedia.org/wiki/Plate_tectonics (Accessed 27 November 2021).
56. Nasser, T. (2019) "Is the earth really flat according to

the Quran? Wiki-Islam refuted", *Rational Religion*, 4 July [Blog]. Available at https://rationalreligion.co.uk/is-the-earth-really-flat-according-to-the-quran-wiki-islam-refuted/ (Accessed 27 November 2021).

57. Lane (1863), vol. 7, p. 2695.
58. Wikipedia (2021) *Seamount* [Online], 17 September 2021. Available at https://en.wikipedia.org/wiki/Seamount (Accessed 27 November 2021).
59. Lane (1863), vol. 3, p. 1086.
60. Nasser, U. (2017) "New scientific research proves true 1400 year-old Qur'anic claim on mountains & earthquakes", 4 November [Blog]. Available at https://rationalreligion.co.uk/1400-year-old-quranic-claim-on-mountains-earthquakes-proven-true-by-new-scientific-research/ (Accessed 27 November 2021).
61. "Seamounts", *Woods Hole Oceanographic Institution* [Online]. Available at https://www.whoi.edu/know-your-ocean/ocean-topics/seafloor-below/seamounts/ (Accessed 27 November 2021).
62. Lane (1863), vol. 4, p. 1308.
63. Lane (1863), vol. 7, p. 2746.
64. Wang, K. and Bilek, S.L. (2011) "Do subducting seamounts generate or stop large earthquakes?", *Geology*, vol. 39, no. 9, pp. 819-822 [Online]. Available at https://doi.org/10.1130/G31856.1 (Accessed 27 November 2021).
65. "Sinking sea mountains make and muffle earthquakes", *University of Texas at Austin* (2020), 2 March [Online]. Available at https://www.sciencedaily.com/releases/2020/03/200302113353.htm (Accessed 27 November 2021).
66. Singh, S.C., Hananto, N., Mukti, M. et al. (2011)

"Aseismic zone and earthquake segmentation associated with a deep subducted seamount in Sumatra", *Nature Geoscience*, vol. 4, no. 5, pp. 308-311.

67. Gutenberg, B. (1943) "Seismological evidence for roots of mountains", *Bulletin of the Geological Society of America*, vol. 54, no. 4, pp. 473-498.
68. Wikipedia (2021) *Internal wave* [Online], 12 January 2021. Available at https://en.wikipedia.org/wiki/Internal_wave# (Accessed 27 November 2021).
69. Cushman-Roisin, B. and Beckers, J-M (2011) *Introduction to Geophysical Fluid Dynamics: Physical and Numerical Aspects*, 2nd edn, Waltham MA, Academic Press.
70. Sissons, C. (2020) "What is the average percentage of water in the human body?", *Medical News Today*, 27 May [Online]. Available at https://www.medicalnewstoday.com/articles/what-percentage-of-the-human-body-is-water# (Accessed 27 November 2021).
71. Lane (1863), vol. 1, p. 220.
72. Ibn Manẓur al-ʾAnṣari (1970 [1290]), p. 1056.
73. Bucaille (1978), pp. 195-197.
74. "Miracles of Quran: From Arithmetics to Astrophysics", *Miracles of Quran* [Online]. Available at https://miracles-of-quran.com/ (Accessed 27 November 2021).
75. Miller, G. (1992) *The Amazing Quran*, Jeddah (Saudi Arabia), Abul-Qasim Publishing House.
76. Al-Kaheel, A.D., *Kaheel Encyclopedia for Quran Miracles/Numeric Miracle* [Online]. Available at https://kaheel7.net/?cat=43&lang=en (Accessed 27 November 2021).
77. Jarrar, B., "Numeric Miracles of the Holy Qur'an

- Chosen Examples", *Noon Center for Qur'anic Studies & Research* [Online]. Available at http://www.islamnoon.com/language/chosen%20examples.pdf (Accessed 27 November 2021).

78. Al-Kaheel, A.D., *The Marvels of the Number Seven in the Noble Qur'an* (trans. M.R. Al-Salah) [Online]. Available at http://kaheel7.com/book/marvels_bookseven.pdf (Accessed 27 November 2021).
79. Bucaille (1978), p. 135, p. 140
80. Al-Kaheel, *The Marvels of the Number Seven in the Noble Qur'an*, pp. 37-42.
81. Al-Kaheel, *The Marvels of the Number Seven in the Noble Qur'an*, p. 65.
82. Al-Kaheel, *The Marvels of the Number Seven in the Noble Qur'an*, p. 77.
83. Al-Kaheel, *The Marvels of the Number Seven in the Noble Qur'an*, p. 87.
84. Al-Kaheel, *The Marvels of the Number Seven in the Noble Qur'an*, p. 12.
85. Al-Kaheel, *The Marvels of the Number Seven in the Noble Qur'an*, p. 72.
86. Al-Kaheel, *The Marvels of the Number Seven in the Noble Qur'an*, p. 81.
87. Al-Kaheel, *The Marvels of the Number Seven in the Noble Qur'an*, p. 82.
88. Al-Kaheel, *The Marvels of the Number Seven in the Noble Qur'an*, p, 57.
89. Al-Kaheel, "Magnificence of the number 19 in the Holy Quran", *Kaheel Encyclopedia – For Quran Miracles* (In Arabic), [Online]. Available at https://kaheel7.net/?p=180 (In Arabic), (Accessed 27 November 2021).
90. Al-Kaheel, *The Marvels of the Number Seven in the Noble Qur'an*, p. 16.

91. Al-Kaheel, *The Marvels of the Number Seven in the Noble Qur'an*, p. 2.
92. Al-Kaheel, *The Marvels of the Number Seven in the Noble Qur'an*, pp. 100-101.
93. Al-Kaheel, A.D., *Kaheel Encyclopedia for Quran Miracles/Numeric Miracle/Quran Statistics Program* (In Arabic), [Online]. Available at https://kaheel7.net/?p=132 (In Arabic), (Accessed 27 November 2021).
94. "Quranic Search Tool", *The Page of the Holy Quran* [Online]. Available at holyquran.net/search/sindex.php (In Arabic), (Accessed 27 November 2021).
95. Al-Kaheel, A.D., *The Marvels of the Number Seven in the Noble Qur'an*, pp. 26-33.
96. Lawrence, B. (2000) *The Qur'an: A Biography*, London, Atlantic Books, p. 8.

Chapter 5

1. Wikimedia Commons (2021) *Michelangelo – Creation of Adam (cropped).jpg* [Online], 20 October 2021. Available at https://commons.wikimedia.org/wiki/File:Michelangelo_-_Creation_of_Adam_(cropped).jpg (Accessed 27 November 2021).
2. "Saint Thomas Aquinas" (2014) *Stanford Encyclopedia of Philosophy* [Online]. Available at https://plato.stanford.edu/entries/aquinas/ (Accessed 27 November 2021).
3. Kreeft, P. (1990) *Summa of the Summa*, San Francisco, Ignatius Press, pp. 74-77.
4. Craig, W.L. (1999) "The Ultimate Question of Origins: God and the Beginning of the Universe", *Astrophysics and Space Science*, vol. 269, no. 270, pp. 723-740.
5. Lane, E.W. (1863) *An Arabic-English Lexicon*,

London and Edinburgh, Williams and Northgate, reproduced (1980) Beirut (Lebanon), Librairie du Liban, Book I, vol. 3, p. 1003.

6. Maulana Muhammad Ali (1951) *The Holy Qur'an, Arabic Text, Translation and Commentary*, 4th edn, Lahore (Pakistan), Ahmadiyyah Anjuman Isha'at Islam, p. 3.
7. Nasr, S.H. (editor-in-chief) (2015) *The Study Quran: A New Translation and Commentary*, New York, HarperOne.
8. Maulana Muhammad Ali (1951), p. 16, note 45.
9. Bucaille, M. (1978 [1977, 4th edn]) *The Bible, The Qur'an and Science* (trans. A.D. Pannell and M. Bucaille), Indianapolis IN, North American Trust Publications, p. 137.
10. Yusuf Ali, A. (1983) *The Holy Qur'ān: Text, Translation and Commentary*, Brentwood MD, Amana Corp.
11. Nasr, S.H. (2015), p. 1267, commentary on (50:16).
12. Nasr, S.H. (2015), p. 1310, commentary on (55:1).
13. Rahman, F. (1989) *Major Themes of the Qur'ān*, 2nd edn, Chicago & London, the University of Chicago Press, pp. 1-16.
14. Tzortzis, H.A. (2019) *The Divine Reality*, newly revised edition, Middletown DE, Lion Rock Publishing, pp. 80-139.
15. Collins, F. (2006) *The Language of God*, New York, London, Toronto and Sydney, Free Press, pp. 22-29.
16. Al-Ghazzālī (2007 [early 12th century CE]) *Kimiya'al-Sa'adah* (The Alchemy of Happiness), (trans. C. Field), Kuala Lumpur (Malaysia), Islamic Book Trust, p. 22.

Chapter 6

1. Abusch, T. (2001) "The development and meaning of the Epic of Gilgamesh: An interpretive essay", *Journal of the American Oriental Society*, vol. 121, no. 4, pp. 614-622.
2. Ziolkowski, T. (2011) *Gilgamesh among Us*, Ithaca and London, Cornell University Press.
3. George, A. (trans.) (2000) *The Epic of Gilgamesh: The Babylonian Epic Poem and Other Texts in Akkadian and Sumerian*, London, Penguin Books, pp. 77-78.
4. Batchelor, S. (1998) *Buddhism Without Beliefs: A Contemporary Guide to Awakening*, London, Bloomsbury Publishing PLC, p. 32.
5. *goodreads* [Online]. Available at https://www.goodreads.com/quotes/1367508 (In Arabic), (Accessed 27 November 2021).
6. Al-Ṭabarī, M. (1988 [10th century CE]) *Tarīkh al-Umam wal-Mulūk (History of Nations and Kings)*, Beirut (Lebanon), Dār al-Kutub al-ʿIlmiyyah, vol. 2, p. 321 (In Arabic).
7. *International Association for Near-Death Studies, Inc.* (2015) [Online]. Available at https://iands.org/ndes/nde-stories/iands-nde-accounts/1067-three-beings-of-light.html (Accessed 27 November 2021).
8. Mauro, J. (1992) "Bright Lights, Big Mystery", *Psychology Today*, vol. 25, no. 4, pp. 54-57 and pp. 80-82.
9. Greyson, B. (1983) "The Near-Death Experience Scale: Construction, Reliability, and Validity", *Journal of Nervous and Mental Disease*, vol. 171, no. 6, pp. 369-75.
10. Greyson, B. (2021) *After*, New York, St. Martin's Essentials, pp. 108-109.

11. Palmieri, A., Calvo, V., Kleinbub, J.R. et al. (2014) "'Reality' of near-death experience memories: evidence from a psychodynamic and electrophysiological integrated study", *Front Hum Neurosci*, vol. 8, pp. 429-455 [Online]. Available at https://doi.org/10.3389/fnhum.2014.00429 (Accessed 27 November 2021).
12. Martial, C., Charland-Verville, V., Cassol, H. et al. (2017) "Intensity and memory characteristics of near-death experiences", *Consciousness and Cognition*, vol. 56, pp. 120-127 [Online]. Available at https://doi.org/10.1016/j.concog.2017.06.018 (Accessed 27 November 2021).
13. *International Association for Near-Death Studies, Inc.* (2021) [Online]. Available at https://iands.org/ndes/about-ndes/key-nde-facts21.html (Accessed 27 November 2021).
14. Greyson (2021), pp. 82-86.
15. Timmermann, C., Roseman, L., Williams, L. et al. (2018) "DMT Models the Near-Death Experience", *Front Psychol*, vol. 9, p. 1424 [Online]. Available at https://doi.org/10.3389/fpsyg.2018.01424 (Accessed 27 November 2021).
16. Parnia, S. (2017) "Understanding the cognitive experience of death and the near-death experience", *QJM: An International Journal of Medicine*, vol. 110, no. 2, pp. 67-69 [Online]. Available at https://doi.org/10.1093/qjmed/hcw185 (Accessed 27 November 2021).
17. Greyson, B. (2015) "Western Scientific Approaches to Near-Death Experiences", *Humanities*, vol. 4, no. 4, pp. 775-796 [Online]. Available at https://doi.org/10.3390/h4040775 (Accessed 27 November 2021).

18. Greyson (2021), pp. 98-107.
19. Greyson (2021), pp. 110-111.
20. Greyson (2021), p. 109.
21. Greyson (2021), p. 80.
22. Greyson (2021), p. 81.
23. Greyson (2021), pp. 171-173.
24. van Lommel, P., van Wees, R., Meyers, V. and Elfferich, I. (2001) "Near-death experience in survivors of cardiac arrest: a prospective study in the Netherlands", *Lancet*, vol. 358, no. 9298, pp. 2039-2045 [Online]. Available at https://doi.org/10.1016/S0140-6736(01)07100-8 (Accessed 27 November 2021). Also commentary by C. French, pp. 2010-2011.
25. Greyson (2021), pp. 194-200.
26. Greyson (2021), pp. 142-143.
27. Rubenstein, A., Cohen, E. and Jackson, E. (2006) "The Definition of Death and the Ethics of Organ Procurement from the Deceased", *President's Council on Bioethics* [Online]. Available at https://bioethicsarchive.georgetown.edu/pcbe/background/rubenstein.html (Accessed 27 November 2021).
28. French, C.C. (2005) "Near-death experiences in cardiac arrest survivors", *Progress in Brain Research*, vol. 150, pp. 351-367 [Online]. Available at https://doi.org/10.1016/S0079-6123(05)50025-6 (Accessed 27 November 2021).
29. Greyson (2021), pp. 64-68.
30. Ring, K. (2001) "Mindsight: Eyeless vision in the blind", in Lorimer, D. (ed), *Thinking Beyond the Brain: A Wider Science of Consciousness*, Edinburgh, Floris, pp. 59-70.
31. Kosslyn, S.M., Koenig, O.M. (1992) *Wet Mind*, New York, Free Press/Macmillan, p. 4.

32. Greyson (2021), p. 118.
33. Greyson (2021), pp. 124-129.
34. Carhart-Harris, R.L., Leech, R., Hellyer, P.J. et al. (2014) "The entropic brain: a theory of conscious states informed by neuroimaging research with psychedelic drugs", *Front Hum Neurosci*, vol. 8, article 20 [Online]. Available at https://doi.org/10.3389/fnhum.2014.00020 (Accessed 27 November 2021).
35. Dossey, L. (2009) *The Power of Premonitions*, New York, Dutton, p. 191.
36. Greyson (2021), p. 40.
37. Sheldrake, R. (2012) *The Presence of the Past*, revised and expanded edition, Rochester VT, Park Street Press, p. 441.
38. Sheldrake (2012), p. 106.
39. Sheldrake (2012), p. 134.
40. Sheldrake (2012), p. 174.
41. Sheldrake (2012), pp. 199-200.
42. Bohm, D. (1983) *Wholeness and the Implicate Order*, London and New York, Ark Paperbacks, pp. 77-80.
43. Bohm, D.J. (1990) "A new theory of the relationship of mind and matter", *Philosophical Psychology*, vol. 3, no. 2-3, pp. 271-286 [Online]. Available at https://doi.org/10.1080/09515089008573004 (Accessed 27 November 2021).
44. Sheldrake, R. and Bohm, D. (1982) "Morphogenetic fields and the implicate order", *ReVision*, vol. 5, no. 2, pp. 41-48.
45. Bohm (1983), p. 196.
46. Bohm, D. and Weber, R. (1982) "Nature as Creativity", *ReVision*, vol. 5, no. 2, pp. 35-40.
47. Myrvold, W.C. (2003) "On some early objections

to Bohm's theory", *International Studies in the Philosophy of Science*, vol. 17, no. 1, pp. 7-24 [Online]. Available at https://www.tandfonline.com/doi/abs/10.1080/02698590305233 (Accessed 27 November 2021).

48. "soul" [Online]. Available at https://dictionary.cambridge.org/dictionary/english/soul (Accessed 27 November 2021).
49. Al-Kaheel, A.D., "What is the difference between self and spirit", *Encyclopedia for Quran Miracles* (In Arabic), [Online]. Available at http://kaheel7.com/pdetails.php?id=774 (In Arabic), (Accessed 27 November 2021).
50. Al-Rāzī, F. (1207) *al-Tafsīr al-Kabīr* (The Extensive Interpretation), also known as *Mafātīḥ al-ghayb* (Keys of the Unseen), [Online]. Available at https://www.altafsir.com/ (In Arabic), (Accessed 27 November 2021).
51. Lane, E.W. (1863) *An Arabic-English Lexicon*, London and Edinburgh, Williams and Northgate, reproduced (1980) Beirut (Lebanon), Librairie du Liban, vol. 8, Supplement, p. 3057.
52. Nasr, S.H. (editor-in-chief) (2015) *The Study Quran: A New Translation and Commentary*, New York, HarperOne.
53. Greyson, B. (1983) "The Near-Death Experience Scale: Construction, Reliability, and Validity", *Journal of Nervous and Mental Disease*, vol. 171, no. 6, pp. 369-75.
54. Lane (1863), vol. 1, p. 187.
55. Lane (1863), vol. 3, p. 1239.
56. Lane (1863), vol. 4, p. 1552.
57. Nasr, S.H. (2015), pp. 1849-1850.
58. Maulana Muhammad Ali (1951) *The Holy Qur'an,*

Arabic Text, Translation and Commentary, 4th edn, Lahore (Pakistan), Ahmadiyyah Anjuman Isha'at Islam, p. xxxi.

Chapter 7

1. Lane, E.W. (1863) *An Arabic-English Lexicon*, London and Edinburgh, Williams and Northgate, reproduced (1980) Beirut (Lebanon), Librairie du Liban, Book I, vol. 8, Supplement, p. 3059.
2. Nasr, S.H. (editor-in-chief) (2015) *The Study Quran: A New Translation and Commentary*, New York, HarperOne, pp. 1305-1307 and p. 1773.
3. Nasr, S.H. (2015), p. 1267.
4. Yusuf Ali, A. (1983) *The Holy Qur'ān: Text, Translation and Commentary*, Brentwood MD, Amana Corp.
5. Batchelor, S. (1997) *Buddhism Without Beliefs*, New York, The Berkley Publishing Group.
6. Ibn 'Arabī M. (d. 1240 CE) *Risālatu'ladhi la ū'awwalū 'alayh* (Treatise on What Cannot Be Counted On) [Online]. Available at: https://takweenkw.com/book/15090/single (In Arabic), (Accessed 27 November 2021).
7. Nasr, S.H. (2015), p. 1427.
8. Maulana Muhammad Ali (1951) *The Holy Qur'an, Arabic Text, Translation and Commentary*, 4th edn, Lahore (Pakistan), Ahmadiyyah Anjuman Isha'at Islam.
9. Lane (1863), Book I, vol. 5, p. 1935.
10. Tzortzis, H.A. (2019) *The Divine Reality*, newly revised edition, Lion Rock Publishing, p. 293.
11. Asad, M. (1980) *The Message of the Quran*, Gibraltar, Dar al-Andalus Ltd., Note 38 for the verse (51:56).

12. Rahman, F. (1989) *Major Themes of the Qur'ān*, 2nd edn, Chicago & London, the University of Chicago Press, p. 8.
13. Lane (1863), Book I, vol. 5, p. 1973.
14. Lane (1863), Book I, vol. 1, p. 231.
15. Nasr, S.H. (2015), p. 40, commentary on verse (2:83).
16. Al-Rāzī, F. (1207) *al-Tafsīr al-Kabīr* (The Extensive Interpretation), also known as *Mafātīḥ al-ghayb* (Keys of the Unseen) [Online]. Available at https://www.altafsir.com/ (In Arabic), (Accessed 27 November 2021).
17. Asad, M. (1980), Note 145 for verse (2:177).
18. Hamid, T. (2019) *fa la iqtahama 'l-aqaba* (He did not storm the Steep), 6 December [Online]. Available at https://www.alhurra.com/ (In Arabic), (Accessed 27 November 2021).
19. Tzortzis (2019), pp. 160-168.
20. Collins, F.S. (2006) *The Language of God*, New York, Free Press, pp. 22-25.
21. Lewis, C.S. (1980) *Mere Christianity*, a revised and amplified edition, HarperCollins e-books, pp. 3-32.
22. Lewis, C.S. (1996) *The Abolition of Man*, New York, Simon & Schuster, pp. 89-109 (Appendix).
23. Lewis (1980), pp. 9-10.
24. Lewis (1980), p. 30.
25. Madhusoodanan, J. (2021) *Chemical and Engineering News* [Online]. Available at https://cen.acs.org/biological-chemistry/biochemistry/Hormones-reveal-secret-life-fat/96/i40 (Accessed 27 November 2021).
26. Werner, C.M., Hecksteden, A., Morsch, A. et al. (2019) "Differential effects of endurance, interval, and resistance training on telomerase activity and

telomere length in a randomized, controlled study", *European Heart Journal*, vol. 40, no. 1, pp. 34-46.

27. Carbone, J.W., McClung, J.P., and Pasiakos, S.M. (2012) "Skeletal muscle responses to negative energy balance: effects of dietary protein", *Adv Nutr*, vol. 3, no. 2, pp. 119-126.
28. Cited in A. Nour (2021) "Letter from beyond the grave", *The Saker*, 24 October [Blog]. Available at https://thesaker.is/letter-from-beyond-the-grave/ (Accessed 27 November 2021).

Select Index

(Italicized page numbers refer to figures)

O-BOOKS

SPIRITUALITY

O is a symbol of the world, of oneness and unity; this eye represents knowledge and insight. We publish titles on general spirituality and living a spiritual life. We aim to inform and help you on your own journey in this life.
If you have enjoyed this book, why not tell other readers by posting a review on your preferred book site?

Recent bestsellers from O-Books are:

Heart of Tantric Sex

Diana Richardson

Revealing Eastern secrets of deep love and intimacy to Western couples.

Paperback: 978-1-90381-637-0 ebook: 978-1-84694-637-0

Crystal Prescriptions

The A-Z guide to over 1,200 symptoms and their healing crystals

Judy Hall

The first in the popular series of eight books, this handy little guide is packed as tight as a pill-bottle with crystal remedies for ailments.

Paperback: 978-1-90504-740-6 ebook: 978-1-84694-629-5

Take Me To Truth

Undoing the Ego

Nouk Sanchez, Tomas Vieira

The best-selling step-by-step book on shedding the Ego, using the teachings of *A Course In Miracles*.

Paperback: 978-1-84694-050-7 ebook: 978-1-84694-654-7

The 7 Myths about Love...Actually!

The Journey from your HEAD to the HEART of your SOUL

Mike George

Smashes all the myths about LOVE.

Paperback: 978-1-84694-288-4 ebook: 978-1-84694-682-0

The Holy Spirit's Interpretation of the New Testament

A Course in Understanding and Acceptance

Regina Dawn Akers

Following on from the strength of *A Course In Miracles*, NTI teaches us how to experience the love and oneness of God.

Paperback: 978-1-84694-085-9 ebook: 978-1-78099-083-5

The Message of A Course In Miracles

A translation of the Text in plain language

Elizabeth A. Cronkhite

A translation of *A Course in Miracles* into plain, everyday language for anyone seeking inner peace. The companion volume, *Practicing A Course In Miracles*, offers practical lessons and mentoring.

Paperback: 978-1-84694-319-5 ebook: 978-1-84694-642-4

Your Simple Path

Find Happiness in every step

Ian Tucker

A guide to helping us reconnect with what is really important in our lives.

Paperback: 978-1-78279-349-6 ebook: 978-1-78279-348-9

365 Days of Wisdom

Daily Messages To Inspire You Through The Year

Dadi Janki

Daily messages which cool the mind, warm the heart and guide you along your journey.

Paperback: 978-1-84694-863-3 ebook: 978-1-84694-864-0

Body of Wisdom

Women's Spiritual Power and How it Serves

Hilary Hart

Bringing together the dreams and experiences of women across the world with today's most visionary spiritual teachers.

Paperback: 978-1-78099-696-7 ebook: 978-1-78099-695-0

Dying to Be Free

From Enforced Secrecy to Near Death to True Transformation

Hannah Robinson

After an unexpected accident and near-death experience, Hannah Robinson found herself radically transforming her life, while a remarkable new insight altered her relationship with her father, a practising Catholic priest.

Paperback: 978-1-78535-254-6 ebook: 978-1-78535-255-3

The Ecology of the Soul
A Manual of Peace, Power and Personal Growth for Real People in the Real World
Aidan Walker
Balance your own inner Ecology of the Soul to regain your natural state of peace, power and wellbeing.
Paperback: 978-1-78279-850-7 ebook: 978-1-78279-849-1

Not I, Not other than I
The Life and Teachings of Russel Williams
Steve Taylor, Russel Williams
The miraculous life and inspiring teachings of one of the World's greatest living Sages.
Paperback: 978-1-78279-729-6 ebook: 978-1-78279-728-9

On the Other Side of Love
A woman's unconventional journey towards wisdom
Muriel Maufroy
When life has lost all meaning, what do you do?
Paperback: 978-1-78535-281-2 ebook: 978-1-78535-282-9

Practicing A Course In Miracles
A translation of the Workbook in plain language, with mentor's notes
Elizabeth A. Cronkhite
The practical second and third volumes of The Plain-Language *A Course In Miracles*.
Paperback: 978-1-84694-403-1 ebook: 978-1-78099-072-9

Quantum Bliss

The Quantum Mechanics of Happiness, Abundance, and Health

George S. Mentz

Quantum Bliss is the breakthrough summary of success and spirituality secrets that customers have been waiting for.

Paperback: 978-1-78535-203-4 ebook: 978-1-78535-204-1

The Upside Down Mountain

Mags MacKean

A must-read for anyone weary of chasing success and happiness – one woman's inspirational journey swapping the uphill slog for the downhill slope.

Paperback: 978-1-78535-171-6 ebook: 978-1-78535-172-3

Your Personal Tuning Fork

The Endocrine System

Deborah Bates

Discover your body's health secret, the endocrine system, and 'twang' your way to sustainable health!

Paperback: 978-1-84694-503-8 ebook: 978-1-78099-697-4